# Best Plants

## For Your Garden

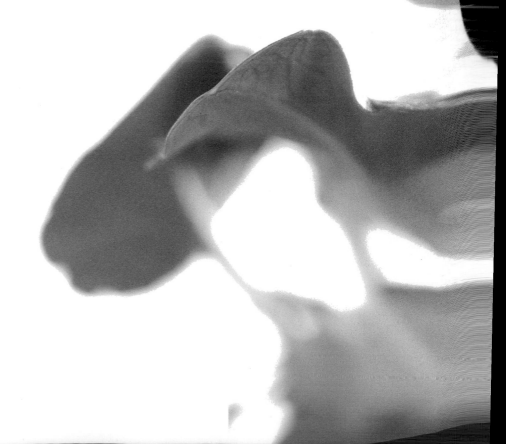

# Best Plants

## For Your Garden

Peter McHoy

Foreword by
Stefan Buczacki

THUNDER BAY
P·R·E·S·S

Publishing Director  Laura Bamford
Executive Editor  Julian Brown
Assistant Editor  Karen O'Grady
Art Director  Keith Martin
Executive Art Editor  Mark Winwood
Designers  Ginny Zeal, Peggy Sadler and Peter Burt
Picture Researchers  Jenny Faithfull and Sally Claxton
Production Controller  Dawn Mitchell
Illustrators  Pond and Giles

First published in the United States in 1998 by
Thunder Bay Press
5880 Oberlin Drive, Suite 400
San Diego, CA 92121-9653
1-800-284-3580

Library of Congress Cataloging-in-Publication Data
McHoy, Peter.
    Best plants for your garden / Peter McHoy : foreword by Stefan
Buczacki.
        p.   cm.
    Includes index.
    ISBN 1-57145-137-4
    1. Plants, Ornamental. 2. Plants, Ornamental--Pictorial works.
I. Title.
SB407 .M48    1998
635.9--dc21                                        98-5058
                                                        CIP

1 2 3 4 5 98 99 00 01 02


Printed in China

# Contents

# Foreword

Gardeners today are fortunate in so many respects. The range of tools and equipment to help them in their various tasks has never been greater and the range of plants with which they can fill their gardens has now become almost bewildering. Around seventy thousand varieties of hardy garden ornamental plants are available in Britain alone. It's small wonder that a visit to a nursery or garden center can be daunting as well as pleasurable.

But if choosing your plants from the numbers offered is one problem, planting and using them in the best and most appropriate way when you arrive home is quite another. How do you mix and match; which plants can be used together to good effect and which combinations will never look right? Because hard as the retailers try, there's a serious limit to the planting guidance that can be crammed onto one label. And of course, no summary of advice can possibly take account of the different characteristics and requirements of each and every garden.

That is where this book will be your salvation. It explains in a clear and concise way the merits of the main group of plants, and, most importantly, describes the various ways in which they can be used together to create garden features that not only work well but give you the maximum enjoyment.

No books or gardening experts should expect you to follow their advice to the letter, and while you will find masses of interesting and exciting ideas here, I'm delighted to see that the text encourages you to think for yourself. And of course to experiment. But armed with the knowledge and information contained here, you can now experiment without feeling that horticulturally, you are simply groping in the dark.

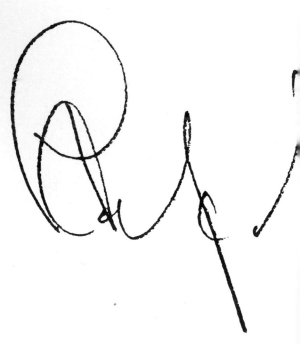

Whether your garden is a small collection of containers or a rolling spread of herbaceous borders, shrubberies, and lawn, you will find help at hand. And because the text neither goes "over your head" nor patronizes, the information will be valuable whatever the level of your gardening knowledge. It is packed with sound advice, beautifully and clearly presented. This is a book that I have no hesitation in saying should be in everyone's hands before making that important first planting.

Stefan Buczacki

# How to use this book

*A visit to a good garden center or even a cursory glance through a comprehensive catalog will make it clear that there are more plants to discover than any of us could ever possibly try to grow.*

It may come as a surprise to learn that there are over 3,000 different rhododendrons and azaleas and more than 2,000 roses that can be bought, while a single nursery offers more than 150 different hostas – and that's just in the UK! A good alpine specialist might offer many hundreds of plants suitable for the rock garden, and herbaceous and shrub nurseries offer just as much choice.

Most of us only have space for a mere handful of plants in comparison, but our gardens need not be inferior because of it. A small number of carefully positioned reliable performers is all it takes to create a breath-takingly beautiful garden.

Even in a book of this size, only a very tiny portion of the readily available plants can be included, but huge lists can bewilder rather than assist; most of us need help and advice to narrow the choices, not expand them. This book sets out to do just that; to reflect the diversity of wonderful plants that we can grow in our gardens, but to shortlist some of the best.

It has been written for the vast majority of ordinary gardeners who love to discover plants and simply want guidance on what to grow where, and how to display them in an attractive way.

## Finding your way around

To help you get the most out of this invaluable book, the following explanations show how it is arranged and how to interpret the advice on aspects like hardiness and heights, nomenclature and soil requirements.

Chapter One explains how to plan and plant, and the principles of colour planning. The other chapters deal with specific kinds of plants, to make it easier to choose the most appropriate ones for a particular purpose.

Each one is packed with special features that explore the possibilities for the creative use of particular groups of plants, such as ferns or fuchsias.

Also, running throughout the book are in-depth profiles of a cross-section of the plants covered by each chapter. To get the most from these, see the typical entry below and read the following explanations.

## Leucojum aestivum
*Summer snowflake*

A cool-looking plant for the border or perhaps by the water's edge, with white bell flowers that are surprisingly conspicuous. Height: 45cm (1½ft).

*Varieties to look for*
'Gravetye Giant' is an improved form.

*Soil and site*
Well-drained but moisture-retentive soil, in full sun. Zone 4.

*Propagation*
Divide an established clump in early autumn.

## Key to Plant Profiles

### Latin name

This is used internationally and will help to identify the plant when you go shopping for it. Commonly used synonyms or new name changes are indicated where appropriate.

### Common name

Only the most widely used common names have been included. Bear in mind that these can sometimes be confusing because they vary from country to country, even from one region to another, and may apply to more than one plant.

### Soil and site

The majority of plants will grow in most soils, and it is only relatively few (but important) groups, such as rhododendrons and camellias, that are especially demanding. If no special needs are indicated it can be assumed that they are undemanding plants.

Well-drained means any soil that will not become waterlogged easily. Well-drained but moisture-retentive means the soil should contain sufficient humus or organic matter to retain moisture to prevent the soil from drying out quickly, but be free-draining enough not to become waterlogged.

If a fertile soil is indicated, the plant makes more than the normal demands on nutrients and should be enriched with manure, garden compost, or fertilizers.

If a plant requires (or will not tolerate) an acid or alkaline (chalky) soil, this has been indicated. Otherwise the plant tolerates a wide pH range (see Glossary for an explanation of pH).

### Description

The main features of the plant are described and possible uses suggested.

### Height

These are typical heights in normal conditions – but bear in mind they can vary considerably according to soil, site, and where you live. The measurements are the final height for quick-maturing plants like annuals, bulbs, and herbaceous plants; the likely height after 10 years for shrubs; and 15 years for trees. Both the trees and shrubs may eventually grow larger.

### Varieties to look for

Recommended varieties and other species to look for will help identify other useful plants.

### Soil and site

These are the preferred situations. The plants may tolerate other soils and positions but not thrive. (See Box for information on how to interpret the soils.)

### Hardiness

Study the maps on pages 220–221, to determine the hardiness zone for your area. But use it only as a guide – in some areas a garden could be plus or minus one zone depending on altitude and whether it is sheltered or exposed, in town or country.

Where practical, it is worth looking for plants one zone lower than indicated unless you are prepared to risk winter losses or protect the plants if necessary.

Zones have not been indicated for annuals that are lifted and discarded at the end of the season anyway, and summer bulbs that are lifted to be stored for winter in a frost-free place can usually be grown in areas with a lower number than indicated.

### Hardiness zone

Use this as a guide to whether a plant can be left outside all year without protection. (See Box below for information on hardiness.)

### Propagation

Only the most practical methods, and usually the quickest, have been described. Other techniques may be used commercially to provide a larger number of plants.

### Nomenclature

Botanists sometimes reclassify plants in the light of research … a practice scientifically justified but which is often disconcerting to the gardener.

We have tried to strike a balance between being up to date yet helpful for anyone trying to purchase plants. It often takes a number of years before nurseries and garden centers adopt new names. Wherever a new name is likely to be used by some nurseries and garden centers, the plants have been listed under that name, but with the old one given as a synonym. But bear in mind that the old name may still be the one most often encountered.

Where at the time of writing the new name is seldom used commercially, there is simply an acknowledgment that it now has a new name. As both old and new names are given in each case, you should always be able to identify the plant.

The word "variety" has been used in its loose sense, though technically some of them are cultivars (varieties raised in cultivation). However, the correct typographical presentation has been used in each case.

# Creative Planting

Anyone who has waited at the garden center check-out behind a long line of enthusiastic gardeners with carts loaded with enough plants to pack the car to capacity, can be forgiven for wondering why there are not more stunning gardens to be seen. Regrettably, once that cart-load has been planted, the impact is seldom as wonderful as hoped for.

Usually it's because plants are bought on impulse and planted without an overall strategy and clear planting plan. A successful bed or border, or even a rock garden, usually works because it is more than a collection of individual plants: it has a cohesion that comes from planning. The plants look right together because they have been grouped for pleasing associations.

The most successful gardens are also planted for year-round interest. Placing too much emphasis on say a spring display or summer bedding can leave the garden with many bleak and uninspiring months. By planting creatively and with imagination, all the seasonal delights can be enjoyed without months of disillusionment.

The following pages contain many planting ideas, but avoid slavishly following a planting scheme in this or any other book. In your own garden the aspect or soil may be unsuitable for some of the plants, and the size and dimensions of beds and borders should always suit the individual garden. Use other people's ideas, whether in books or in real gardens, as a source of inspiration ... but modify and adapt them to suit your own garden and your own taste.

11

# Painting with plants

*Colors are central to a successful garden, and how they are used sets the tone of the planting. Even foliage areas that lack colorful flowers, perhaps in a shade bed or a fern garden, look better if attention is paid to the role of the many different leaf colors and textures.*

The art of successful planting lies in the ability to paint a picture with flowers and foliage, always with an eye to the overall picture rather than the individual plant.

A color wheel, like the one illustrated below, can help to visualize which plants may work together successfully. But it should be an aid to resolving doubts, rather than the starting point of a planting plan. Begin with the plants that appeal, then use the wheel to decide which combinations work best, always bearing in mind the importance of neutral colors like grays and silvers.

The way colors interrelate visually can be seen by using the color wheel. The red, blue, and yellow are primary colors, the orange, green and violet a 50:50 mix of their neighboring primaries. Those colors with shared pigments (violet, blue, and green, for example) are regarded as harmonious. Those without shared pigments (red and green, for example) are said to be in contrast.

Flowers come in a multitude of colors, however, and a whole range may be present within a single bloom. While this makes artificial devices like color wheels difficult to relate to, there is usually a dominant color with which to work.

Marvellous borders can be created without any conscious regard to color scheming, but most people who are gardeners rather than artists or designers appreciate aids that will give their planting schemes a strong visual theme. If you are planting with color in mind, rather than texture and shape, one of the four "themes" described below will almost certainly help you create some eye-catching planting schemes.

### Monochromatic planting

Single-color planting, using shades and tints of one basic color are the most dramatic and obvious examples of color scheming. A white bed might use masses of white roses, irises, lilies, and argyranthemums, for example, together with silver or gray foliage plants. A yellow theme could include roses in many shades of yellow, with yellow achilleas, hemerocallis, lilies, and argyranthemums, perhaps with yellow hostas and golden sedges and grasses.

Left: Use this color wheel to help decide which colors will harmonize or contrast, and which are likely to clash or look discordant. See above for an explanation of how the color wheel works.

Monochromatic borders are most often seen in large gardens where there is space to indulge in such themes without missing out on all the other colors elsewhere in the garden! In a small garden, it's better to create small groups of plants with a single color theme, such as a yellow *Berberis thunbergii* "Aurea" or *Lonicera nitida* "Baggesen's Gold" at the back with yellow argyranthemums such as "Jamaica Primrose" boosted by *Anthemis tinctoria* for summer-long flowers in front, with foliage color from a golden hosta and perhaps an edging of golden marjoram (*Origanum vulgare* "Aureum") in front.

This kind of small grouping shows a strong element of planning and design without sacrificing opportunities to use valuable space for other colors.

## Complementary planting

Using complementary (also termed contrasting) colors on the color wheel can produce vivid and even aggressive-looking combinations. Using orange with blue, red with green, or violet with yellow will really shout for attention. Such combinations work well for spring and summer bedding schemes, but can also make a statement in the herbaceous or mixed border — though discrete contrasting groups within the border are likely to be more pleasing than a whole border of contrasting colors.

## Analogous planting

This type of color combination uses neighbors on the color wheel. Orange, yellowish-orange, and yellow flowers look pleasing together and are an example of analogous planting. Blue, violet-blue, purple, and pink form another analogous group.

These are much "softer" combinations, easy on the eye, and are generally more pleasing for an informal style of gardening.

## Polychromatic planting

This is a technical name for mixed colors where the planting deliberately uses plants from all around the color wheel. It produces an almost random appearance, often found in the cottage garden style. This type of planting works well if adopted for the whole bed or border; it only jars visually if there is a patch of uncoordinated color in an otherwise carefully color-orchestrated garden.

A polychromatic or multi-colored bed or border will benefit enormously from the lavish use of silver and gray foliage plants and white flowers to separate the stronger colors and provide a sense of unity throughout.

## Synchronize as well as co-ordinate

The most marvelous color scheme, full of promise on paper, will be a disaster if the plants flower at different times. Even those that flower in the same month may not bloom together; one may flower in the first half and be dying as another that blooms in the second half is coming into bloom. The best way to avoid this dilemma is to try and observe good combinations that flower at the same time in your area, and to use plenty of foliage within your color coordinated plantings.

# Herbaceous and mixed borders

*Important though color scheming is, coordinated flower colors are a feature in any border for a couple of months at most.*

This may not matter in a large garden where there are many other year-round features, but in a small or medium-sized garden it's best to plant for a long period of interest. The illustrations opposite show how important structural and foliage plants are in creating a border that looks attractive for most of the year. The focus of the color scheme has been to create pockets of interest at different times, with a succession of interest provided by plants that reach their peak at different times.

The drawback of planting for succession is the risk of bare areas as plants pass their peak. This can be overcome partly by using later-flowering plants in front of early-bloomers. Penstemons are smaller than Oriental poppies or lupins, but reach their peak later and will continue into early autumn, and the poppy or lupin can be cut back when the blooms have finished, leaving the penstemons to spread and flourish. The early cutting back may even stimulate a second flush of flowers in late summer or autumn. Border irises, at their peak in early summer, can be masked by phlox that flower later in the summer.

## Bulbs and bedding

Bulbs and summer bedding plants are ideal for sustaining interest and avoiding "blank spots." Wherever possible, use bulbs hardy enough to be left in the ground, where they will make larger and bolder clumps with time (but don't be tempted to cut the leaves off before they start to die back naturally, otherwise future flowering will be jeopardized).

It's usually possible to plant summer bedding plants over the area where the bulbs were. Using bushy plants slightly to one side will cover the area without damaging the bulbs while planting. Alternatively, sow hardy annuals, such as pot marigolds (calendulas) or California poppies (eschscholzias). The seeds only need to be scratched into the surface, so the bulbs won't be damaged.

## Foliage and form

Use foliage plants lavishly in the year-round border. They will clothe the ground and remain attractive for many months and, provided the soil is well covered, the area won't look neglected or unplanned.

Greens can be very pleasing in a bright border, but use lots of plants with silver and gray foliage. Some of these, such as *Artemisia* "Powis Castle" or *Perovskia atriplicifolia,* are superb plants in their own right and will act as a "bridge" between colors and plants with different flowering times.

## Stature and structure

Borders need height, and in a mixed border this can be provided by suitable shrubs. In a non-shrubby border a similar function can be achieved with some of the taller grasses such as *Stipa gigantea* or *Miscanthus sinensis.* Grasses like this will remain attractive well into autumn and some look very pleasing covered with a thick frost.

Cordylines and phormiums, with their spiky and usually colored or variegated leaves, make excellent year-round border plants where the climate is suitable. Both are frost-hardy, but they will succumb in cold areas so check whether they are suitable where you live.

## Foliage contrasts

Purple foliage can look dull on its own, but partner it with light-colored leaves to bring out the best in both. The purple *Heuchera* "Palace Purple" will look much more pleasing partnered with a golden hosta. The almost black *Ophiopogon planiscapus* "Nigrescens" will go almost unnoticed on its own, but becomes a real feature planted in front a golden acorus such as *A. gramineus* "Ogon" – they go well together as they both have grass-like leaves.

## Long-life leaves

Whether edging a shrub border or a mixed or herbaceous border, evergreen non-woody edging plants are particularly useful. Two that are remarkably tolerant of varying types of soil and will grow in sun or shade are bugle (*Ajuga reptans*), best grown in one of its purple or variegated varieties as a ground-covering carpet, and bergenias. The large, leathery foliage of some bergenias colors particularly well in winter, assuming shades or red or purple.

Foliage plants that die back for winter are still worth including if they look bright all summer. *Houttuynia cordata* "Chameleon" will sustain its bright foliage right into autumn.

## Planting for year-round interest

Plant for year-round interest as well as for clever color combinations. This is especially important if you have only a small border that has to work hard to produce interest over a long period. The planting plan below is illustrated as the border might look through the seasons on the following four pages. The illustrations show the advantages a mixed border that incorporated many different kinds of plant: bulbs and bedding plants as well as shrubs and border perennials.

The planting plan should be used for ideas and inspiration, however, rather than as a blueprint for your particular garden. There is no point including plants that do not appeal to you, and perhaps sacrificing personal favorites just because they do not happen to form part of someone else's design. It will also be necessary adjust the number of plants to suit the size of your border.

This plan is designed for a border about 23 ft. (7m) long and 8 ft. (2.4m) deep, and more than one specimen will be required for smaller plants best grown in a drift, such as the lavender (*Lavandula stoechas*) and heathers (*Erica carnea*),

or for ground cover, like the bugle (*Ajuga reptans*) and *Euonymus fortunei*.

Always choose plants that suit the soil. The rhododendron and camellia prefer an acid soil, and are unsuitable for chalky or alkaline soils. If you garden on an alkaline soil, simply replace them with shrubs that thrive on this kind of soil, such as aucubas or mahonias if you want evergreens, or lilacs (syringas) or hypericums if flowers are more important than year-round foliage.

## Key to Planting

**1** *Erica carnea* "Vivellii," underplanted with chionodoxa
**2** Hosta and daffodils
**3** *Alchemilla mollis* and *Galanthus nivalis*
**4** *Vinca minor* "Argenteovariegata"
**5** *Euonymus fortunei* "Emerald 'n' Gold"
**6** *Ajuga reptans* "Atropurpurea,"

underplanted with *Anemone blanda* and *Cyclamen coum*
**7** *Bergenia cordifolia*
**8** *Skimmia japonica* (female form)
**9** *Arum italicum* "Marmoratum"
**10** *Lavandula stoechas*
**11** *Berberis thungbergii* "Atropurpurea Nana"
**12** *Phormium* "Bronze Baby"
**13** *Helleborus niger*
**14** *Santolina chamaecyparissus*
**15** *Sarcococca hookeriana digyna*
**16** *Nerine bowdenii*
**17** *Viburnum davidii*
**18** *Artemisia* "Powis Castle"
**19** *Iris foetidissima*
**20** *Euphorbia*

*amygaloides* "Purpurea"
**21** *Viburnum tinus*
**22** *Rhododendron* "Vintage Rose"
**23** *Kniphofia* "Samuel's Sensation"
**24** *Skimmia japonica* "Rubella"
**25** *Camellia* "Donation"
**26** *Rosa* "Scabrosa" (syn. *R. rugosa* "Scabrosa")
**27** *Ribes sanguineum* "Brocklebankii"
**28** *Lavatera* "Rosea"
**29** *Elaeagnus pungens* "Maculata"

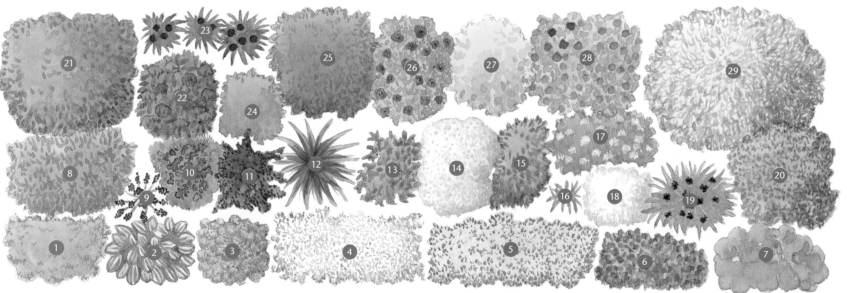

# Bedding schemes

*Spring and summer bedding plants ensure the garden looks bright and colorful over a long period.*

All kinds of plants can be used for bedding: hardy and tender perennials as well as the more usual hardy biennials and half-hardy annuals. It is how they are used that makes them bedding plants. Any plants used for a single season then discarded or lifted and replanted can be considered a bedding plant. Each year there is the opportunity to use fresh plants, and different varieties, in a new way.

The appeal of bedding plants lies partly in the colorful planting schemes that can be devised, but also in the ability to make a fresh start every year!

## Variations on a traditional theme

The traditional beds so popular with parks and large private gardens of the past, with carpets of plants like geraniums (pelargoniums) and antirrhinums punctuated with taller "dot" or "spot" plants like abutilons, argyranthemums, or burning bushes (kochias), are still popular, though many of the plants have changed. The pelargoniums are nearly all seed-raised now, and short-season plants like antirrhinums are more likely to have been replaced by summer-long flowers such as fibrous-rooted begonias and Busy Lizzies (impatiens). However, the principles still work and the blocks of color and symmetry of design make them appealing.

Although the permutations are endless, there are still basic design "rules" that will ensure a summer spectacular:

● In a border with a hedge or wall at the back, place taller plants towards the back but use a few even taller "spot" plant further forward to serve as punctuation points.

● Use the tallest plants in the center of an island bed, but again include a few focal point plants further forward so the bed does not look too tiered and predictable.

● Plant in blocks and drifts of color, unless a very formal and regimented appearance is required. Simple rows can look rather "municipal" for a small private garden.

● Avoid a uniform height across the whole bed unless it is a single-subject planting. Use "spot" or "dot" plants to add extra height and interest. Exotic-looking plants like cannas can be spectacular, but standard fuchsias and argyranthemums (marguerites) are widely available and very pleasing.

● Do not overlook foliage plants. Use gray-leaved plants like *Helichrysum petiolare* where you need the color to spread through the other plants and *Cineraria maritima* where you need a visual divider between bright colors. Silvers and grays look pleasing with pink flowers, such as pink pelargoniums.

The golden *Tanacetum parthenium* (formerly *Chrysanthemum parthenium*, *Matricaria eximia*) "Aureum" can be used to break up the brighter colors, and is easily raised from seed. To confuse matters further, this is sometimes sold in seed catalogs under the name *Pyrethrum* "Golden Moss" or "Golden Ball."

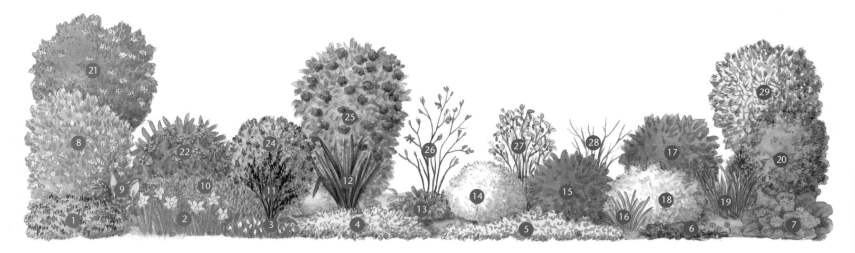

## Spring

Spring is a season of transformation. Plants that are dormant in early spring may be in full flower by late spring. Some early spring-flowering bulbs have been included here to fill in gaps left where herbaceous plants die down. New growth on the summer herbaceous plants soon hide the dying leaves of spring bulbs.

## Carpets of color

Carpet bedding is associated with public parks and large ornamental gardens, but you can emulate the style in a small garden. It's appropriate for a formal style of gardening.

Carpet bedding depends on large numbers of mainly foliage plants being planted to form a pattern: either a geometric design or an emblem, crest or other "picture." Traditionally, most of the plants used were tender perennials propagated from cuttings, and included succulents such as echeverias. The pattern was maintained by regular clipping to restrain the plants and preserve the crisp outline of the pattern.

Such designs are only for the most dedicated private gardener, but it's possible to adapt this style of bedding using widely-available compact plants that are easily raised from seed and undemanding to grow.

Stunning effects can be achieved using fibrous-rooted begonias (with white, red, or pink flowers and green or bronze leaves, there is a good choice of combinations), with silver foliage cinerarias (*Senecio cineraria*) or *Tanacetum ptarmiciflorum* and golden *Tanacetum parthenium* "Aureum" to form geometric or freestyle patterns to give the illusion of traditional carpet bedding.

## Informal adventures

If the color of summer bedding appeals but the formality of it doesn't, then plant in a random way. Choose a mixture of plants such as pink pelargoniums, white argyranthemums, yellow African marigold, and yellow coreopsis and plant them so that they appear to grow randomly. But include a few taller annual grasses that will grow through them and provide high points without formality.

## Sub-tropical spectacular

Provided the climate is not too cold in summer, plant a bed with a sub-tropical look. Choose some tall and bold plants like *Ricinus communis*, dwarf bananas, and cordylines. Incorporate plenty of tender but readily available plants like cannas and brugmansias (daturas), then fill in the gaps with colorful flowers such as lantanas and vivid foliage plants like coleus. Choose a sunny but sheltered bed, pack them in closely so the growth looks lush and dense and they offer each other mutual protection, then water and feed well.

## Spring bedding

Two broad groups of plants are used for spring bedding: bulbs and hardy biennials. Spring bedding usually works best when both types of plants are used together. Beds of a single type of bulb, such as tulips, look fine on a large scale but the show will be too transient for a small garden. If using only bulbs, interplant different types: hyacinths with grape hyacinths or scillas, or dwarf yellow daffodils with a carpet of blue *Anemone blanda*, for example. This spreads the period of interest and makes the ground between the bulbs look more clothed.

Use biennials such as double daisies, wallflowers, forget-me-nots, and winter pansies lavishly. They are cheap space-fillers, and will make the more expensive bulbs go further. Avoid late-flowering biennials such as sweet williams as the beds should be cleared for summer plants before they flower.

Wallflowers are striking planted alone but dwarf varieties can be interplanted with tulips very effectively. Forget-me-nots and winter pansies are ideal for interplanting with most spring-flowering bulbs.

Be prepared to experiment with perennials – whether foliage or flowering – to add that special touch. The blues and purples of aubrieta and the yellow *Alyssum saxatile* (now more correctly *Aurinia saxatilis*) can add that extra sparkle if interplanted with forget-me-nots and dwarf yellow wallflowers or pink tulips.

In summer the evergreens become a backdrop against which to view the more colorful flowers. But foliage has an important role to play in summer too: many colorful evergreens, like the phormium and euphorbia in this border, look bright and colorful at this time of the year when new growth is fresh and vigorous.

# Summer

# Using shrubs

*Shrubs require much more careful selection and placing than herbaceous plants and annuals. They usually remain in their positions for decades and, as they mature, have a profound influence on the overall structure of the garden.*

Few gardens are large enough for long, dedicated shrub borders of the kind associated with park landscaping or large estates. But there is usually space for a modest border where shrubs dominate, and where there may also be space to accommodate a tree or two.

The plants included are less important than the basic design strategy. A big *Yucca gloriosa* or a cordyline may look incongruous among the less angular shrubs typical of a dedicated border, but if this kind of focal point plant suits individual whim then indulge your instinct. Generally, however, shrub borders should give the appearance of a well integrated group of plants with few gaps and lots of interesting flowers or foliage.

## Design considerations

Few shrubs flower for more than a couple of weeks, so the border is best designed to make the most of different textures, shapes, and foliage color.

Include plenty of evergreens, but not so many that you miss the beauty of flowers and autumn foliage color. If at least a quarter of the shrubs are evergreen, but not more than half, the border will retain winter interest without looking boring, especially if a few deciduous shrubs with attractive winter stems, such as *Cornus alba* and *C. stolonifera*, are included.

Group some of the evergreens together, rather than stringing them out, to make attractive scenes even when other parts look bleak. A typical group could include a dark green laurustinus (*Viburnum tinus*) with its white winter-long flowers, with a gold-splashed *Elaeagnus pungens* "Maculata" alongside, and a carpet of gray-leaved *Hebe pinguifolia* "Pagei" in front.

Make the most of flowering evergreens such as camellias and rhododendrons where

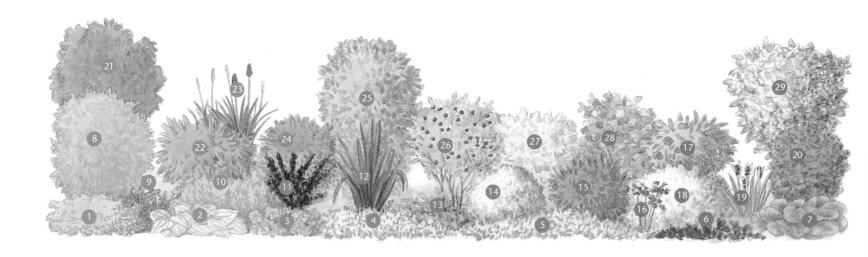

Autumn  Any border will benefit if you include a few flowers that are at their best in autumn. Although the choice is limited, many autumn-interest plants pack plenty of punch. Flowers like nerines look stunning, and shrubs with bright fruits, berries, or seeds, like the rose and iris in this border, can be as bright as many flowers.

conditions suit (these demand an acid soil as well as some shade). Less demanding are escallonias, *Choisya ternata*, mahonias, osmanthus, and some of the viburnums, such as *Viburnum tinus*.

Evergreen berrying shrubs are important too, with hollies and skimmias high on any wish-list. Bear in mind that to produce a good display of berries, you need a female plant, and possibly a pollinator too.

## Foliage color and texture

Leaf color is usually far longer-lasting than flowers, and golds and grays can be particularly pleasing, especially where they break up an area of dark green shrubs.

*Sambucus racemosa* "Plumosa Aurea" needs to go towards the back of the border, but if pruned drastically each spring will remain compact enough for most borders. Its large feathery leaves are bright yellow and always stand out from across the garden. The evergreen *Choisya ternata* "Sundance" is another popular choice, but it is not as tough and will be damaged by a severe winter. The golden privet (*Ligustrum ovalifolium* "Aureum") is another reliable golden evergreen (semi-evergreen in cold regions).

Although its leaves turn green by the end of the season, *Philadelphus coronarius* "Aureus" can be a ray of sunlight in a dull border in early summer with its soft yellow foliage.

Gray-leaved shrubs like *Senecio* (now *Brachyglottis*) "Sunshine" and cotton lavender (*Santolina chamaecyparissus*) also reduce the risk of a shrub border becoming boring. Their woolly texture and golden flowers in summer also add that vital sense of vibrance and variation.

## Continuity of flower

If the shrubs suggested above are included, the border will have all the qualities of a good garden feature . . . and then there are all the flowering shrubs to be incorporated!

Aim for continuity of flower. No matter how attractive shrub roses may be in bloom, the border will look boring for many months if these are planted to the exclusion of other, possibly less spectacular, flowering shrubs. It is perfectly possible to have shrubs in flower every month of the year: choose flowering shrubs with this in mind.

**Key to Planting**

**1** *Erica carnea* "Vivellii," underplanted with chionodoxa
**2** Hosta and daffodils
**3** *Alchemilla mollis* and *Galanthus nivalis*
**4** *Vinca minor* "Argenteovariegata"
**5** *Euonymus fortunei* "Emerald 'n' Gold"
**6** *Ajuga reptans* "Atropurpurea," underplanted with *Anemone blanda* and *Cyclamen coum*
**7** *Bergenia cordifolia*
**8** *Skimmia japonica* (female form)
**9** *Arum italicum* "Marmoratum"
**10** *Lavandula stoechas*
**11** *Berberis thungbergii* "Atropurpurea Nana"
**12** *Phormium* "Bronze Baby"
**13** *Helleborus niger*
**14** *Santolina chamaecyparissus*
**15** *Sarcococca hookeriana digyna*
**16** *Nerine bowdenii*
**17** *Vibumum davidii*
**18** *Artemisia* "Powis Castle"
**19** *Iris foetidissima*
**20** *Euphorbia amygaloides* "Purpurea"
**21** *Viburnum tinus*
**22** *Rhododendron* "Vintage Rose"
**23** *Kniphofia* "Samuel's Sensation"
**24** *Skimmia japonica* "Rubella"
**25** *Camellia* "Donation"
**26** *Rosa* "Scabrosa" (syn. *R. rugosa* "Scabrosa")
**27** *Ribes sanguineum* "Brocklebankii"
**28** *Lavatera* "Rosea"
**29** *Elaeagnus pungens* "Maculata"

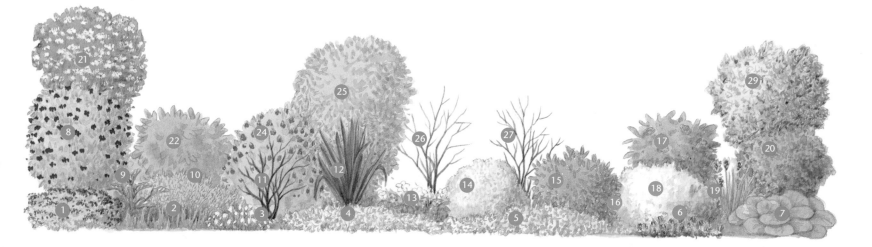

Evergreens are essential for a year-round border, but a few winter flowers can prevent it from becoming predictable. Berries also play an important role, like the skimmia above. But remember that some fruiting shrubs require a male pollinator for a display like this, which is why *Skimmia japonica* "Rubella" has been included.

# Winter

# Annuals and Biennials

These provide the budget way to a bright and ever-changing garden, where each year you can change the appearance of your garden so that it never becomes dull or predictable. Although cheap and cheerful, there's nothing second-rate about these plants, and they are at the heart of some of the best and brightest gardens.

The plants in this chapter are those usually offered in seed catalogs as annuals and biennials. But don't become too hung up on exact technical definitions; it's how you use plants that matters. Many plants that we treat as annuals (like Busy Lizzies and fibrous-rooted begonias) are tender perennials, though most gardeners treat them as annuals. Even fairly hardy plants, such as antirrhinums, are better treated as annuals and discarded at the end of the season.

Annuals are sown, flower, and die within a season – though in mild areas some can be sown in autumn to flower earlier the following spring or early summer. Biennials are sown in late spring or early summer to flower the following year.

# Features

ANNUALS AND BIENNIALS

## Alyssum maritimum

*see Lobularia maritima*

## Antirrhinum majus

*Snapdragon*

A classic bedding plant, with stiff spikes of lipped flowers that can be induced to open their "mouths" by gentle pressure on the sides. Colors include reds, yellows, oranges, pinks, and white. If rust disease has been a problem, buy rust-resistant varieties.

Height: 6–36 in. (15-90cm).

### Varieties to look for

There are tall varieties and doubles, but the ordinary single intermediate height varieties which grow to about 1–1½ ft. (30–45cm) are the best for

● TIP TO TRY

Cut out the dead flowering stems when the first flush of flowers is over – you may be rewarded with a second flush in late summer.

bedding. There are good F1 hybrids, such as "Coronette," which has plenty of secondary flower spikes forming even before the first flush is over. For containers, consider some of the many dwarf varieties. "Bells" is only about 8 in. (20cm) tall, and has open-faced flowers that look like upward-pointing bells.

### Soil and site

Undemanding regarding soil, but best in full sun. Though strictly perennials, sometimes able to winter in Zone 8, they are best discarded and treated as half-hardy annuals.

### Propagation

Sow mid winter to early spring in warmth under glass, and plant outdoors in late spring.

## Aster

*see Callistephus*

## Begonia semperflorens

*Fibrous-rooted begonia, wax begonia*

Neat, compact plants ideal for an edging, containers, and formal bedding. Flowers come in various shades of white, pink, and red, in various permutations with green, bronze, and very dark foliage. A tender perennial, but flowers continuously until first frost.

Height: 10–20cm (4–8in).

### Varieties to look for

The Olympia series in separate colors is among the best of the taller varieties at about 8 in. (20cm). "Cocktail" is a pleasing compact mixture with bronze foliage at about 4–6 in. (10–15cm).

### Soil and site

Undemanding regarding soil, but best in partial shade. Will also tolerate full sun.

### Propagation

Sow seed in warmth under glass in mid or late winter.

● TIP TO TRY

Before the first frost, pot a few plants to take indoors. If necessary, trim off some of the longest shoots to make a compact plant. They should continue to bloom through the winter as houseplants if given a sunny position.

## Bellis perennis

*Double daisy*

Although a form of the same daisy that sometimes infests lawns as a weed, these highly bred varieties have double flowers, sometimes like small pompons. Colors are white, pink, and red. They are usually used for spring edgings or interplanting with spring bulbs.

Although they can be grown for another year, it is best to treat them as biennials and sow fresh each year.

Height: 4–6 in. (10–15cm).

### Varieties to look for

"Pomponette Mixed" is one of the best small varieties, growing to 4–6 in. (10–15cm). "Rosina" is an outstanding large-flowered variety with salmon-pink flowers about 2 in. (5cm) across.

### Soil and site

Undemanding and easy to grow in full sun or partial shade. Suitable for growing in Zone 4 or above.

### Propagation

Sow outdoors in late spring or early summer.

## Calendula
*Pot marigold, English marigold*

Hardy annual with bright orange or yellow double flowers, ideal as an easy cottage-garden plant. Keep an eye open for mildew and treat promptly if the disease appears.

Height: 1–2½ ft. (30–75cm).

### Varieties to look for

Typical of the best taller varieties is "Pacific Beauty Mixed," which grows 2–2½ ft. (60–75cm) with large flowers

in shades of orange and yellow. "Bons Bon" and "Fiesta Gitana" are dwarf varieties about 1 ft. (30cm) tall.

### Soil and site

Undemanding regarding soil, but best in full sun.

### Propagation

Sow seed in early spring, where they are to flower, for a summer display. They can also be sown in autumn and kept through winter to flower in spring or early summer, but may the protection of a covering below Zone 8.

## Callistephus
*China aster, bedding aster*

Late-flowering, half-hardy annuals, blooming in late summer. These highly bred flowers vary enormously in height, flower size, petal formation, and color.

The singles are still popular for cutting, the dwarf doubles more favored for bedding. Good

catalogs offer a wide range of varieties.

If wilt disease has been a problem, plant in a different part of the garden each season.

Height: 6–30 in. (15–75cm).

### Varieties to look for

"Milady Mixed" is a reliable bedding variety with fully double flowers on plants about 10 in. (25cm) tall. "Thousand Wonders Mixed" is worth considering for a very dwarf plant about 6 in. (15cm) tall. "Duchess Mixed" is an old variety but still reliable, with incurved flowers on plants 1½–2 ft. (45–60cm) tall.

### Soil and site

Moisture-retentive soil, in full sun.

### Propagation

Sow seed in warmth under glass between late winter and mid spring to flower between mid summer and mid autumn.

### ● TIP TO TRY

Grow a few plants of a tall variety for cutting. Asters will last up to a week in water if you cut when the flowers are just opening.

ANNUALS AND BIENNIALS

23

# Mix and match

*Avoid thinking of annuals and biennials in isolation – they often work most effectively when combined with other plants. This often extends the period of interest and color, and gives beds and borders a more "designed" look.*

### Spring delights

Biennial spring bedding plants, such as forget-me-nots (myosotis) and double daisies (*Bellis perennis*), are ideal for filling in around the base of bulbs such as tulips and hyacinths, which can look depressingly bare at the base. You can overcome this to some extent by planting bulbs very close together, but it's less expensive to use plants that you can raise from seed ... and often visually more attractive too.

It's difficult to synchronize the flowering of bulbs and spring bedding plants, as many bulbs have a short flowering period and when they flower depends, to some extent, on the variety. The best way to decide what to plant together is to note what blooms at the same time in local parks and gardens, then

Left: A very effective and beautiful mixed planting, with muscari planted in a huge drift alongside red tulips in a woodland setting.

pick and choose combinations that flower at the same time and that appeal to you.

Don't be deterred from interplanting bulbs with spring bedding plants just because you can't get them to flower together. If one flowers before the other, it extends the flowering season, and plants like forget-me-nots are great as ground cover even before they flower (much better than bare soil beneath tall tulips).

Heights are easier to check, so make sure the bulbs are taller than the biennials.

If you want to create a stunning effect that will stand out in the garden, try strong and contrasting colors like bright red tulips underplanted with white pansies. Pansies have a long flowering season so you are fairly sure of synchronized flowering. Other strong combinations are yellow polyanthus or dwarf yellow wallflowers with tall red tulips.

More subtle combinations can be particularly pleasing too, like dwarf brick-red wallflowers with blue forget-me-nots and fuchsia-pink tulips. For bulbs like hyacinths and muscaris, you will need to use very compact biennials such as pansies or double daisies (*Bellis perennis*). Try white hyacinths and white *Muscari botryoides* "Album" with pink double daisies for a pale and subtle effect.

You don't have to mix your biennials with bulbs; group them with each other. Combine blue forget-me-nots with pink double daisies, for instance, or with dwarf perennials like the bright yellow *Alyssum saxatile* (now *Aurinia saxatilis*). Try blue forget-me-nots with pink double daisies and the yellow alyssum, all interplanted to create a carpet of pink, blue, and yellow.

## Summer companions

Use appropriate annuals lavishly among the border perennials. Plants like annual verbenas, the taller ornamental tobacco plants (nicotianas), and biennial foxgloves (*Digitalis purpurea*), all look perfectly at home among herbaceous perennials … and the annuals will continue to flower for months longer than most border plants.

If you wish to emphasize the mixed effect of your summer borders, then grow shrubs, herbaceous perennials, and annuals together. In a mixed border, formal and rather stiff-looking annuals like French marigolds and celosias can work well. But if your intention is to fill out an herbaceous border with color and have "flower power" over a long period in summer, with plants that blend in with the perennials, then choose looser and more informal-looking plants. Try the spider flower (cleome), annual larkspur, scarlet flax (*Linum grandiflorum*), annual lupins, and rudbeckias, nasturtiums, and lavateras.

Annual grasses, like the squirrel-tail grass (*Hordeum jubatum*) and quaking grass (*Briza maxima*), look perfectly at home among herbaceous plants. They have a summer-long period of interest so they will sustain the border when more transient herbaceous flowers have finished.

Don't forget those quick-flowering perennials that can be induced to flower in their first year if treated like a half-hardy annual and sown early in warmth. You can leave them to grow or discard them at the end of the season. One of the best is *Coreopsis* "Early Sunrise" – from an early sowing you can have it in flower continuously from early summer to the first frost … and expect a repeat performance the next year! Deadhead regularly to keep those flowers coming.

The herbaceous border is an ideal place to plant sunflowers. Not only the giants that tower tall above the other plants, but also the smaller and bushier types that grow perhaps 6–8 ft. (1.8–2.4m) tall and produce a succession of flowers for months.

All the plants mentioned above will look as though they belong in an herbaceous or mixed border. If you have space, there are many more to experiment with.

Above: A good combination is planting compact biennials like double daisies (*Bellis perennis*) among myosotis.

Left: Compact spring-flowering biennials like the forget-me-not *Myosotis* "Dwarf Indigo" make pleasing companions for early bulbs such as the *Narcissus triandrus* hybrid "Howera."

# Centaurea cyanus
*Cornflower*

A traditional cottage-garden hardy annual, popular for its bright blue color. Modern varieties also include pinks and white. The display is short-lived but they are quick-growing. Tall varieties are best for cutting.
Height: 1–3 ft. (30–90cm).

### Varieties to look for
"Blue Diadem" is a good choice for a traditional blue cornflower, but grows to 2–2½ ft. (60–75cm). "Florence Pink," "Florence White," and "Florence Mixed" are splendid dwarf plants about 1 ft. (30cm) tall.

### Soil and site
Well-drained, fertile soil, in full sun or partial shade.

### Propagation
Sow in spring where the plants are to flower. In mild areas (Zone 8 or higher) they can be sown in early autumn for an earlier display the following year.

# Cheiranthus cheiri
*see Erysimum cheiri*

# Convolvulus tricolor (syn. C. minor)
*Bush morning glory*

This low-growing plants is treated as a hardy annual. Except in frost-free areas the plant will die at the end of the season and no roots will remain, so it is not invasive despite being a convolvulus. The normal color is a blue trumpet with white and yellow throat, but there are also pinks.
Height: 8–12 in. (20–30cm).

### Varieties to look for
"Royal Ensign" is the best blue.

### Soil and site
Undemanding and will grow in poor soil, in a sunny position.

### Propagation
Sow in spring where the plants are to flower.

# Coreopsis "Early Sunrise"

An outstanding hardy perennial with double yellow flowers, which can be treated as an annual if sown early. The semi-double yellow flowers are produced all summer long if deadheaded.

Also very useful for cutting.
Height: 1¼ft. (38cm).

### Varieties to look for
Choose this variety. It has won gold medals for performance as an annual in the U.S. and Europe.

### Soil and site
Undemanding regarding soil, in sun or shade.

### Propagation
Sow in warmth under glass in late winter or early spring for blooming from early summer; in late spring where the plants are to flower for later flowering.

### ● TIP TO TRY
Cosmos makes an excellent cut flower, with its big blooms and ferny foliage. Cut when the petals have opened but are not yet lying flat, and keep away from heat and direct sunshine. They should then last for about five days.

Bottom: *Cosmos bipinatus "Sonata Mixed."*
Right: *Dianthus "Princess Mixed."*

## Cosmos bipinnatus
### Cosmea

An outstanding half-hardy annual with large single flowers and ferny foliage, invaluable for late summer and early autumn flowering. The tall varieties, which benefit from unobtrusive support, are ideal for gap-filling in a border. Colors are shades of pink, red, and white.

Height: 2–3 ft. (60–90cm).

### Varieties to look for

"Sonata" (available in separate colors or as a mixture) has an abundance of bloom on compact plants about 2 ft. (60cm) tall. "Sensation" is an old favorite among the taller varieties at 2½ ft. (75cm). "Sea Shells" is a mixture with distinctive fluted petals, growing to about 3 ft. (90cm).

### Soil and site

Undemanding regarding soil, but best in full sun. Will tolerate partial shade.

### Propagation

Sow in warmth under glass in late winter or early spring, or outdoors in late spring for later flowering.

## Dianthus, annual
### Annual pinks

The dianthus used for summer bedding are treated as half-hardy annuals. They make a cheerful show in sunny beds and borders, most having single, upward-facing flowers in shades of scarlet, crimson, rose, salmon, and pink, together with white, and often with a contrasting center.

Height: 6–18 in. (15–45cm).

### Varieties to look for

"Snow Fire" has particularly bright flowers, white with a scarlet center. "Princess Mixed" has a good range of colors. Some varieties of Sweet William, like "Indian Carpet," can be grown as annuals if sown early

### Soil and site

Well-drained alkaline soil produces the best plants, but they will grow in most soils. Best in full sun.

### Propagation

Sow in warmth under glass between mid winter and early spring.

## Dianthus barbatus

Popularly known as Sweet Williams, these very fragrant and colorful plants bloom in late spring and early summer and look best toward the front of an herbaceous border. These traditional cottage-garden plants are probably less popular than spring-flowering biennials because they bloom later and are not appropriate for spring bedding, but deserve to be more widely planted.

Tall varieties about 1½ ft. (45cm) tall are ideal for a bold border display; dwarfs of 6–8 in. (15–20cm) more suitable for an edging or even the rock garden.

Sow Sweet Williams outdoors in late spring or early summer.

# Cut Flowers

*Enjoy your annuals in the home as well as in the garden. Many of them make excellent cut flowers (some of the "everlastings" will last for years) and, if you have space, it's worth reserving an area just to provide a supply of flowers for the home.*

If you are planting or sowing with cut flowers in mind, be sure to include some that will flower early, like autumn-sown calendulas, and late, such as annual asters, callistephus. Also find space for a few everlasting flowers to dry for winter decoration. If you don't have space for a dedicated cut-flower area, don't hesitate to cut a few stems from those used for garden decoration. Provided you cut just one or two stems from each plant the harvesting will go almost unnoticed. To get the best from your cut flowers, "harvest" them at the best time (see advice for individual plants below) and use a cut-flower food and preservative in the water.

These help to keep the water clear and provide nutrients to keep the flowers looking fresh for longer. If the flowers last more than a few days, it's worth changing the water before it becomes smelly and affects the flowers (bacterial growth may block the water uptake in the cut stems).

Always remove any leaves that would be below water level.

**Above:** Sweet Williams (*Dianthus barbatus*) are traditional cottage-garden flowers that are grown as biennials to flower in early summer. They are also great as cut flowers, and have a heady fragrance as a wonderful bonus.

**Far right:** Love-in-a-mist (*Nigella damascena*) is really easy to grow and can be cut as a fresh flower or dried for its decorative seed heads that can be appreciated long after the flowers in the garden have died.

Left: Sunflowers (*Helianthus annuus*) are cut flowers you simply can't ignore! Their huge flowers demand attention. This variety is "Starburst."

## Bright and early

Grow these for spring and early summer flowers:

**Forget-me-not (myosotis)**
Cut when half the flowers are open. The flowers may discolor as they age, but should last for about 10 days.

**Stocks, Brompton**
See summer stocks for treatment.

**Sweet William (*Dianthus barbatus*)**
Should last 7–10 days.

**Wallflowers**
Cut when two or three flowers are open on the stem. They should last for between 7 and 10 days.

## Summer sparklers

Grow these for summer flowers:

**Antirrhinum**
Cut when the lowest flowers are open. They should last 8–10 days.

**Carnation, annual**
Should last 10–14 days.

**Cornflower (*Centaurea cyanus*)**
Should last 5–7 days.

**Chrysanthemum, annual**
May only last for about 4 days.

**Coreopsis, annual**
Cut when the flowers are at least half open. They should last for about 10 days.

***Cosmos bipinnatus* (cosmea)**
Should last for about 7 days.

**Gaillardia hybrids**
Cut when two or three flowers are open on the stem. They should last 7–14 days.

**Gypsophila**
Cut when most of the flowers are open. They should last for about 14 days if the water is kept clean.

**Larkspur (*Delphinium consolida*)**
Cut when the bottom 6–8 flowers are open. They should last 8–12 days.

**Love-in-a-mist (*Nigella damascena*)**
Cut when the flowers are fully open. They should last for about 7 days.

**Pot marigold (calendula)**
Cut when fully open. They should last for about 7 days.

**Stock (*Matthiola incana*)**
Make sure the first flowers on the stem are fully open. They should last 7–14 days.

**Sunflower (*Helianthus annuus*)**
Make sure the flower is well open before cutting. Be sure to use a cut-flower food, in which case they should last for about 7 days.

**Sweet pea (*Lathyrus odoratus*)**
Cut when the bottom flower is open. They should last 6–10 days.

**Sweet sultan (*Centaurea moschata*)**
They should last 5–7 days.

***Zinnia elegans***
To reinforce a hollow stem neck, try sticking a match though the center of the flower. They should last for about 7 days.

## Late delights

Grow these for autumn flowers:

**Annual aster (callistephus)**
They should last for about 10 days.

**Rudbeckia**
Cut when petals have fully formed, and be sure to use a cut flower food. They should last for about 14 days.

## Winter and beyond

Grow some of these everlasting flowers for winter and long-term decoration:

***Ammobium alatum* (everlasting sand flower)**
Cut and hang upside down when most of the flowers are open.

***Helichrysum bracteatum* (straw flower)**
These are best picked when the outer two rows of petals are fully out but the center is still closed, though it is still worth harvesting them if they are more open. Cut and hang upside down by their stem, or just remove the heads and wire them.

**Limonium (statice)**
Cut and dry when the flowers are fully out, hanging upside down or propping upright in a vase.

***Lonas annua***
Cut and dry when the flower head is fully open.

***Lunaria annua* (honesty)**
Cut and dry at the green pod stage, or when fully mature. When the seed case opens the silvery center is exposed. Prop upright or hang upside down.

***Moluccella laevis* (bells of Ireland)**
Cut and dry when the flower stems are just maturing, when the small white "bell" in the center is out. Pick off the leaves and any unformed bells before hanging upside down to dry.

***Nigella damascena* (love-in-a-mist)**
Cut and dry the inflated seed heads as soon as they have reached full size.

***Xeranthemum annuum* (paper flower)**
Cut and dry when in full flower, but avoid those that have been open for a week or so, as they tend to look dull when dried.

# Throwing light on shade

*Most of the annuals that we grow as garden plants originate in sunny climates, and few thrive in shade. Yet most small gardens have gloomy areas whether the shade is cast by buildings, fences, or hedges.*

The plants suggested here will put in a respectable performance in shade, though they may grow taller and flower less prolifically than those in a sunny position. Shady areas are often dry areas, because the obstruction that blocks the sun may just as easily cause a rain shadow. Avoid handicapping your plants further by incorporating plenty of moisture-retaining material such as garden compost and well-rotted manure into the soil, and be prepared to water thoroughly when the soil becomes very dry.

Don't dismiss foliage plants for shade — they often look more appropriate, and plants like the bright and exotic-looking coleus can look more colorful than many flowers. This is usually regarded as an indoor plant, but it can be used for seasonal bedding if acclimatized carefully first and planted in a

sheltered position. It will do surprisingly well in the shade beneath trees and large shrubs if kept watered.

## Flowers to try

*Anchusa capensis* (summer forget-me-not)
Hardy annual. Blue forget-me-not-like flowers. Height: 1½ft. (45cm). Tolerates partial shade.

*Asperula azurea* (syn. *A. orientalis*) (woodruff)
Hardy annual. Lavender-blue flowers. Fragrant. Height: 1 ft. (30cm). Tolerates full shade.

*Begonia semperflorens* (fibrous-rooted begonia)
Half-hardy annual. Masses of small red, pink, or white flowers. Green or bronze foliage. Height: 6–9 in. (15–23cm). Tolerates full shade but better in partial shade.

*Bellis perennis* (double daisy)
Biennial. Double daisy-type flowers in shades of red, pink, and white in spring. Height: 4–6in (10–15cm). Tolerates partial shade.

*Digitalis purpurea* (foxglove)
Biennial. Spikes of purple, pink, or white flowers. Height: 4–6 ft (1.2–1.8m). Best in partial shade but tolerates full shade.

*Hesperis matronalis* (sweet rocket)
Biennial. Large spikes of single lilac or purple flowers, fragrant in the evening. Height: 2–3 ft. (60–90cm). Tolerates full shade but better in partial shade.

*Impatiens* hybrids (Busy Lizzie)
Half-hardy annual. Popular flowers in many colors. Height: 6–12 in. (15–30cm). Tolerates full shade but better in partial shade.

*Impatiens balsamina* (balsam)
Half-hardy annual. Spikes of double flowers, and not at all like the more popular Busy Lizzies. Height: 1–2 ft. (30–60cm). Tolerates full shade but better in partial shade.

*Lobelia erinus*
Half-hardy annual. The popular blue lobelia used for bedding and in containers. Height: 4–6 in. (10–15cm). Tolerates partial shade.

**Above: This border contains just a few of the many delightful shade-tolerant plants. Among the plants are ivies, lilies, and the yellow spikes of *Ligularia przewalskii*.**

**Below: The ornamental tobacco (*Nicotiana alata* hybrids) do well in sun or shade, and some are fragrant. The China asters also tolerate some shade.**

Right: The foxglove (*Digitalis purpurea*) is a biennial woodland plant at home in shade. Here a magnificent clump is framed by arching sprays of rose "Zéphirine Drouhin" on the sunny side of the wall.

*Lunaria annua* (honesty)
Biennial. Purple or white flowers in late spring, followed by decorative seed heads. Height: 2½ ft. (75 cm). Tolerates full shade but better in partial shade.

*Myosotis* (forget-me-not)
Biennial. Popular plant with blue flowers (sometimes pink) in spring. Height: 6–12 in. (15–30 cm). Tolerates partial shade.

*Nemophila menziesii* (baby blue eyes)
Hardy annual. Small blue flowers with white centers. Height: 6 in. (15 cm). Partial shade.

*Nicotiana* (ornamental tobacco)
Half-hardy annual. There are many varieties, ranging from compact plants with flowers that open during the day to taller ones with evening-opening flowers. Height: 1–3 ft. (30–90 cm). Tolerates partial shade.

*Petunia*
Half-hardy annual. One of the most popular bedding plants, available in a wide range of colors. Height: 1 ft. (30 cm), or trailing. Tolerates partial shade.

*Viola* (viola and pansy)
Hardy annual or biennial. Very popular plants grown everywhere, with many varieties and colors. Height: 4–6 in. (10–15 cm). Tolerates partial shade.

## Foliage plants to try

*Coleus* (flame nettle)
Annual. Multi-colored and prettily patterned leaves, mainly in shades of red, yellow, pink, and green. Tolerates full shade if kept moist enough, but better in partial shade.

*Lunaria annua* "Variegata" (honesty)
Biennial. Purple flowers in late spring, leaves variegated creamy-white. 2½ ft. (75 cm). Tolerates full shade; better in partial shade.

Below left: *Erysimum cheiri* (syn. *Cheiranthus cheiri*) with tulips.
Bottom: *Eschscholzia californica*.

## Erysimum cheiri
*Wallflower*

Strictly a perennial in zone 7 and above, but it is almost always grown as a biennial. The very fragrant late spring flowers are mainly yellows, reds, and oranges, but there are also creams and purples. In mild climates flowering may be early or later, and in warm climates they may flower in summer as well as spring. Pinch out the growing tips when the plants are a few inches high to make them bushier and bloom more prolifically.

Height: 8–18 in. (20–45cm).

### Varieties to look for
For containers, look for dwarfs like "Tom Thumb" and the "Princess" range of varieties, which grow to about 8 in. (20cm). For general bedding, larger varieties such as scarlet "Fire King" and "Orange Bedder" are still hard to beat.

### Soil and site
Undemanding regarding soil (in the wild they often grow in crevices in walls!), but best in full sun. Tolerates partial shade.

### Propagation
Sow seed outdoors in early or mid summer for flowering the following spring. It is not usually convenient to sow them where they are to flower, so use a spare piece of ground and move to their flowering positions in autumn.

### NOW YOU KNOW!
Although you will usually find wall-flowers listed in seed catalogs under their common name, until comparatively recently their Latin name was *Cheiranthus cheiri*, a name you will still see mentioned in catalogs and books. But botanists now say we should call them *Erysimum cheiri*.

Whatever the name, they are some of our sweetest-smelling spring flowers.

## Eschscholzia californica
*California poppy*

California's state flower comes in shade of yellow, cream, gold, red, pink, and scarlet. There are singles and doubles. This is one of the brightest hardy annuals, is easy to grow and self-seeds freely. It will flower for a long period through the summer. Although it can be a short-lived perennial from Zone 6 upward, it is best treated as an annual.

Height: 9–15 in. (23–38cm).

### Varieties to look for
Mostly sold as mixtures, but separate colors are available. "Dali" is a compact variety at about 9 in. (23cm), with a succession of bright red ruffled flowers.

### Soil and site
Undemanding regarding soil, but grow in full sun.

### Propagation
Sow where the plants are to flower in spring. In mild regions (Zone 8 or higher), sowing in early autumn will achieve earlier flowers. They do not transplant well.

## Gazania
*Treasure flower*

The plants widely grown as summer bedding plants are hybrids from a number of South African species, and the bright daisy-type flowers over often silvery foliage give the impression of a flower from a warm climate. They are

perennial in climates without frosts, but they are usually grown as annuals – the only practical option in colder climates. The flowers close on dark days, so performance depends on the site and the season – they are ideal for a dry, sunny position where their yellow, orange, red, pink, or cream flowers can be stunning.

Height: 6–12 in. (15–30cm).

### Varieties to look for
"Mini Star Mixed" is low, neat, and compact.

### Soil and site
Well-drained, fertile soil, in full sun.

### Propagation
Sow seed in warmth under glass in late winter and early spring. It is possible to take cuttings for winter, but seed is easier and more convenient.

## Helianthus annuus
*Sunflower*

This giant among the hardy annuals needs no introduction; its huge yellow flowers on tall stems 6 ft. (1.8m) or more tall are known to most children. But there are smaller varieties with more delicate-looking flowers, and colors include reds. Some grow to only 4–5 ft. (1.2–1.5m) and there are really dwarf varieties suitable for containers. Tall varieties will require staking. Height: 2–8 ft. (60–240cm).

### Varieties to look for
Most seed companies offer giant sunflowers, but for cutting try "Oranges and Lemons," which has big, bright flowers 10 in. (25cm) across on 2–3 ft. (60–90cm) plants. "Teddy Bear" is a saucer-sized fully double variety that looks more like a huge African marigold than a sunflower, and it stands at about 2 ft. (60cm). "Red Sun" is one of the red-flowered varieties, and grows to about 6 ft. (1.8m).

### Soil and site
Undemanding regarding soil for an ordinary display, but for big plants and huge flowers, rich and fertile ground is required. Grow in full sun.

### Propagation
Sow in mid or late spring where the plants are to flower, or start off in warmth under glass in early or mid spring.

## Helichrysum bracteatum
*Straw flower*

A hardy annual Australian "everlasting" flower, with double flowers that have papery flowers ideal for drying. Colors include shades of yellow, orange, red, and white.

Height: 1–3 ft. (30–90cm).

### ● TIP TO TRY
For really huge sunflowers, choose a variety sold for its size, germinate the seeds in individual pots under glass in early or mid spring, and plant outdoors in late spring. Stake early and keep tied to a support without constraining the stem. Water freely (daily if necessary), and feed often with liquid fertilizer.

### Varieties to look for
For long-lasting bedding flowers choose a variety like "Bright Bikini Mix" or "Hot Bikini," bright scarlet and gold, which grow to about 1 ft. (30cm). For cutting and drying, taller varieties may be preferable, although the heads are usually separated and wired anyway.

### Soil and site
Well-drained, fertile soil, in full sun. Best in a warm and sheltered position.

### Propagation
Sow in spring where the plants are to grow.

### DID YOU KNOW?
The colored "petals" on the straw flower are not petals at all, but bracts. The true flowers make up the center of the flower.

Although everlasting when dry, they do not make very good cut flowers. The heads usually droop in a matter of days.

To dry, cut when the flowers are half open, tie in bunches, and hang head-down in a cool, well ventilated place until dry. Remove any leaves.

# Filling a need

*Gaps in herbaceous or shrub borders are often a problem, whether they arise because a plant has died or simply because the bed is newly made and the plants have yet to reach a mature size.*

Don't leave the ground bare for weeds to colonize . . . fill the space with quick and colorful annuals. Bright and cheerful flowers look better than bare soil, so fill those gaps with annuals. If you don't want the sometimes brash flowering annuals to detract from the more subdued effects of a color-schemed border, use foliage annuals instead. Ideally, gap fillers should be bushy and tall enough not to look insignificant among tall border plants or shrubs. There are plenty to choose from, and the ones suggested here are only a selection.

### Big and bold

The spider flower (*Cleome spinosa*) grows to about 4 ft. (1.2m) with great mounds of seven-lobed leaves that soon fill in even a large gap! But it's the pink, white, or lavender flower heads with their whiskery

appearance that make this an eye-catching plant, and it looks as though it should be a perennial border plant. It's not hardy, so you will have to raise plants under glass.

*Cosmos bipinnatus* is at its best in late summer and early autumn, when tall varieties compete with herbaceous plants for impact. Most grow to about 3 ft. (90cm), and the big daisy-like flowers (usually in shades of pink or red, but also white) shout for attention.

For a gap toward the back of an herbaceous border, try one of the medium-height sunflowers such as "Vanilla Ice," which is bushy and branching and grows to about 5 ft. (1.5m). For something a little smaller but still with big impact for a mid-border position, try the annual mallow (*Lavatera trimestris*), which comes mainly in pink or white varieties. These cup-shaped flowers are about 3 in. (7.5cm) across and produced in profusion. They grow to about 4 ft. (1.2m) with a spread of at least 2 ft. (60cm). Sunflowers and lavateras can be sown where they are to flower, though the lavatera is sometimes started under glass for earlier flowering.

Left: The spidery flower heads of *Cleome spinosa* will compete with any border plant.

Right: The burning bush (*Kochia scoparia trichophylla*) is green in summer . . . but turns fiery red in autumn.

Left: Large annual poppies are ideal border fillers and "Danish Flag" is a stunner. But don't let them shed seeds.

Right: *Cosmos bipinnatus* grows to about 3 ft. (90cm) and gives a boost to borders in late summer.

Marvel of Peru (*Mirabilis jalapa*) is a curious plant, but not to everyone's taste. The fragrant flowers, mainly in shades of pink and yellow, open in late afternoon and usually look in a state of collapse by the next morning. It's a bushy that grows to about 3 ft. (90cm), and looks at home in a mixed border. It's not hardy, however, so raise it under glass.

Poppies of various kinds are naturals for a herbaceous border, and the popular annual types can all be sown where they are to flower. But be prepared to deadhead them after flowering if you don't want them to become weeds in future years. "Danish Flag" is a red variety with a white cross in the center followed by large, decorative seedheads, so you may prefer to delay deadheading as long as you do it before the seeds are shed.

Toward the front of a border, bright daisy-type flowers usually look good. African daisies (arctotis) are big and bold…when they are open. They tend to close in gloomy weather or late afternoon, but are well worth considering because they are so eye-catching when they are open, and there's a constant supply of flowers all summer.

### Foliage fillers

Don't overlook foliage plants as fillers for the herbaceous border. The castor oil plant (*Ricinus communis*) has large, hand-like leaves, often in reddish and bronzy colors. This exotic-looking plant will grow 4–6 ft. (1.2–1.8m) high, with a spread to match, so don't use it for a small border, as it will look totally out of proportion.

The summer cypress or burning bush (*Kochia scoparia trichophylla*) is compact enough for any border at about 2 ft. (60cm), and it makes a mound of feathery green leaves reminiscent of a dwarf conifer from a distance. Turns deep red in autumn. Not all varieties change color, so check first.

Below left: *Impatiens* (Busy Lizzies).
Right: *Lavatera trimestris* "Silver Cup."
Bottom: *Lobelia erinus* "Midnight Blue."

## Impatiens
*Busy Lizzie*

Tender perennials, these can be flowered throughout the year indoors or in frost-free climates, but usually they are raised from seed each year as half-hardy annuals for summer bedding.

There is a huge choice of varieties, in many colors, from ground-huggers of 6 in. (15cm) or less, to tall ones of about 1½ ft. (45cm). Most have single flowers but there are also doubles. They will flower until the first frost.

Height: 6–18 in. (15–45cm).

### Varieties to look for
Choosing Busy Lizzies is always difficult, there are so many. The "Super Elfin" series is tried and tested and one of the best garden varieties. There are separate colors, mixtures, and picotees in the range.

### Soil and site
Moisture-retentive, fertile soil achieves the best results, but they seem to survive almost anywhere. Best in full sun or partial shade; they will grow in shade but tend to be taller and flower less freely.

### Propagation
Sow seed in warmth under glass in late winter or spring. Can be propagated from cuttings and kept through winter in warmth, but this is rarely done for varieties that can be raised from seed.

### DID YOU KNOW?
Busy Lizzies from the garden can be used as indoor plants at the end of the season if you lift them before the first frost. However, it's better to take cuttings to start with a compact plant.

New Guinea hybrid Busy Lizzies have larger flowers and usually bronze or variegated leaves, and they also grow taller. Most have to be raised from cuttings. They are better for growing in pots or containers than for massed bedding.

## Lavatera trimestris
*Mallow*

These Mediterranean hardy annuals resemble hibiscus in flower shape. Their bushy growth makes them useful as a gap filler in a border. Colors are mainly shades of pink, and white. Height: 2–3 ft. (60–90cm).

### Varieties to look for
"Silver Cup" is an outstanding pink, "Mont Blanc" a reliable white.

### Soil and site
Well-drained soil, in full sun.

### Propagation
Sow seed in spring where the plants are to flower. Can also be started off earlier in warmth under glass, in individual pots.

## Lobelia erinus

One of the classic bedding plants: trailing varieties are widely used in hanging baskets and window boxes, compact varieties as edging plants. Blue is the basic color, but there are lilacs, pinks, carmines, and white. Do not allow the plants to dry out if you want them to keep flowering.

Height: 6 in. (15cm), or trailing.

Below: *Lobularia maritima* (syn. *Alyssum maritimum*).
Right: *Matthiola incana* in its traditional form as the biennial Brompton stock – summer stocks are usually hybrids between this and *M. sinuata*.
Bottom: *Mesembryanthemum criniflorum*.

### • TIP TO TRY

Choose a "selectable" variety of stock to sow. It is possible to identify the doubles as seedlings because they have paler leaves, provided the temperature is low enough. Discard the dark seedlings. Follow the instructions that come with the seeds.

growing plant needs to be planted in a large block for this to be a feature. White is the basic color, but there are now pinks and purples.

Height: 3–8 in. (7.5–20cm).

### Varieties to look for

"Crystal Palace" is still one of the best blues. Mixed trailing varieties are popular for hanging baskets.

### Soil and site

Moisture-retentive soil, in full sun or partial shade.

### Propagation

Sow seed in warmth under glass between mid winter and early spring.

## Lobularia maritima (formerly Alyssum maritimum)

*Sweet alyssum*

The popular white alyssum is a hardy annual usually treated as a half-hardy annual and raised in seed trays so that they can be planted with other summer bedding plants at a similar stage of development.

Although fragrant, the scent is not strong and the low-

### Varieties to look for

"Snow Crystals" is one of the best whites, "Oriental Night" a good purple. "Wonderland Red" is one of the most convincing reds.

### Soil and site

Undemanding regarding soil. Best in sun or partial shade.

### Propagation

Sow under glass in early spring, or outdoors in mid or late spring where the plants are to flower.

### NOW YOU KNOW!

Although usually listed as an alyssum in seed catalogs and on seed packets in stores, it is now considered by botanists to be a lobularia. You may find it listed under this name in some catalogs and books.

## Matthiola incana

*Stock*

One of the most fragrant summer bedding plants. Unfortunately the single flowered types are unattractive, so try to grow a "selectable" type (see above) that enables doubles to be selected.

Height: 1–1½ ft. (30–45cm).

### Varieties to look for

If raising your own seedlings, choose a "selectable" variety such as "Park Mixed."

### Soil and site

Deeply dug, fertile soil enriched with fertilizer, ideally in full sun though they will grow in partial shade. They prefer an alkaline soil.

### Propagation

Sow seed in warmth under glass in spring.

## Mesembryanthemum criniflorum

*Livingstone daisy*

Ground-hugging half-hardy annual succulent plants with bright daisy flowers in many colors. Super in the sun, but the flowers close in bad weather.

Height: 3 in. (7.5cm).

### Varieties to look for

Usually sold as mixtures.

### Soil and site

Well-drained soil, in full sun.

### Propagation

Sow in warmth under glass in spring.

# On edge

*Be smart with your edgings for formal beds and borders. Choose plants with a long flowering season that remain looking neat and compact.*

Some traditional edging plants are still the best. Ageratums look good if you choose a neat, compact variety such as "Blue Danube." If you don't want blue, there are pinks and even white. Alternating white *Lobularia maritima* (formerly *Alyssum maritimum*) and blue lobelia is perhaps less popular as a combination edging than it used to be, but still looks good if you can balance the height and vigor of the two plants. Lobularia varies considerably in compactness and even height, and you don't want one plant dominating the other. You may be better off with an edging of either plant alone.

French marigolds (*Tagetes patula*) have all the qualities for a neat and long-flowering edging, but some gardeners consider them too stiff-looking for this purpose. The smaller-flowered *Tagetes pumila* makes a more "rounded" plant that forms a more continuous ribbon of flowers, ideal as an edging. The dominant colors are yellow and orange.

Busy Lizzies (impatiens) are sometimes used for an edging, but choose the variety

**Above: French marigolds (*Tagetes patula*) and compact lobelias are traditional edging plants for summer bedding schemes. They remain neat and compact, and continue to flower right through the summer months.**

carefully. They vary enormously in height and spread as well as color. "Elfin" and "Super Elfin" varieties are usually reliable (they are available as separate colors as well as mixtures). Fibrous-rooted begonias (*Begonia semperflorens*) are better if you want a more formal effect, and there are plenty of color combinations to work with. They have red, pink, or white flowers, against green or bronze leaves.

## Nicotiana
*Ornamental tobacco*

Half-hardy annuals flowering over a long period. Some are very fragrant, but the most highly scented ones are usually over 2 ft. (60cm) with flowers that close during the day. There are many compact varieties about 1–1½ ft. (30–45cm) tall with upward-facing flowers that remain open during the day.
  Height: 1–3 ft. (30–90cm).

### Varieties to look for
"Sensation Mixed" has fragrant flowers that remain open during the day, but it grows over 2 ft. (60cm). "Domino Mixed" is a good choice for a compact plant at about 1 ft. (30cm).

### Soil and site
Well-drained soil, in sun or partial shade.

### Propagation
Sow in warmth under glass in late winter or early spring, and plant out after the last frost.

## Petunia

One of the most frequently grown bedding plants, the petunia needs little introduction. Almost all those used for summer bedding and for containers used to be seed-raised as half-hardy annuals, but the outstanding trailing "Surfinia" petunias, propagated from cuttings in vast numbers commercially, has expanded the possibilities for petunias.
  There are still many excellent varieties that are raised from seed, however, and for many this is preferable to buying in plants from the nursery each year (it is difficult to keep them in winter without a heated greenhouse). Deadheading

will keep the flowers coming.
  Height: 6–12 in. (15–30cm), or trailing.

### Varieties to look for
Many new varieties are introduced annually, so it is best to check catalogs for specific varieties, but it is important to

Try cutting rudbeckias for indoor decoration. Cut them when the flowers start to open; then they should last for 6–8 days in water.

Keep them out of direct sunlight or excessive heat. If they look limp, re-cut the stems and place in water in a cool place until they revive.

Below: *Rudbeckia hirta.*
Right: *Salvia splendens.*

understand the different types of petunia.

Multiflora types have masses of medium-sized flowers, and are ideal for outdoor bedding and containers.

Grandiflora varieties have bigger flowers but there are usually fewer of them. They are a good choice where a showy plant is required in a hanging basket or container. There are single and double forms of both types. Doubles are best used as potted plants or in containers.

Trailing petunias can be used as a floral ground cover but are better in hanging baskets and window boxes.

## Soil and site
Well-drained soil containing plenty of organic material such as garden compost or rotted manure. Best in full sun, but they will still do well in partial shade.

## Propagation
Sow in warmth under glass between mid winter and early spring.

Opposite left: *Nicotiana "Domino Salmon Pink."*
Opposite right: Petunias make excellent container plants.

# Rudbeckia hirta
*Black-eyed Susan, gloriosa daisy*

Short-lived hardy perennials and biennials (Zone 4 and higher), usually raised as half-hardy annuals. The large daisy-type orange, brown, or yellow flowers 4 in. (10cm) or more across are excellent for late color. They make good cut flowers too.

Height: 8–24 in. (20–60cm).

### Varieties to look for
"Goldilocks" has large flowers with yellow petals and a black central cone, and branches freely. "Toto" grows to 10 in. (25cm); it is compact enough for containers and bedding.

### Soil and site
Well-drained soil, in full sun or partial shade.

### Propagation
Sow in warmth under glass in late winter or early spring. Can also be sown outdoors in mid or late spring.

# Salvia splendens

These popular bedding plants are traditionally red, but now there are pinks, purples, and white. The red ones are still among the brightest bedding plants, especially effective when planted *en masse*. Pinch out the growing tips while the seedlings are small, to encourage bushy growth.

Height: 9–18 in. (23–45cm).

### Varieties to look for
"Blaze of Fire" is an old variety that's still among the most popular.

### Soil and site
Well-drained soil, in full sun or partial shade.

### Propagation
Sow seed in warmth under glass between mid winter and early spring.

# Now for something different

*Most gardeners go for the tried and tested popular plants, but your garden will be more exciting and show more imagination if you try a few different annuals each year.*

They may not always live up to expectations, but it's fun searching them out and you'll probably discover some super plants that you'll want to grow again.

Never totally abandon the well-proven in your quest for something different. Many of the lesser-known annuals and biennials will remain that way because they have serious shortcomings as garden plants, so grow just two or three new or unfamiliar plants each season unless you have lots of space in which to experiment. A few failures are a small price to pay for the excitement of discovering a really superb plant that will become part of your regular seed order in the future.

### The search

Popular seed companies usually concentrate on the well-proven favorites, and most of the new catalog entries will be for new varieties of these. New varieties of traditional bedding plants are usually, but not always, improvements and well worth trying; but, if you are searching for new species or genera of plants to grow, send for the catalogs of companies specializing in a wide range or seeds, or uncommon types.

The catalogs with the greatest choice, unfortunately, pose the greatest dilemma. There will be more unfamiliar names from which you will have to choose a handful, and you may have to read between the lines in making that decision. Don't go by the flower picture alone – look for a long flowering period, a compact plant, one that will get around to flowering before the cold weather sets in, and one that flowers freely. Be especially cautious of plants that have a description such as "if sown early can be treated as an annual" … it probably means that it won't make it before the first frost unless you live in a mild region.

There are fashions in plants. Obscure genera might suddenly become popular, and are absorbed into the mainstream. If you want to grow a few annuals that friends will ask you the name of, search deeper. The ones suggested here are just a few that are pleasing or interesting. There are scores of others.

**Above:** *Carpanthea* "Golden Carpet."
**Right:** *Anagalis monellii linifolia.*

Left: The spider flower (Cleome spinosa) seldom fails to attract attention, yet it's easy to grow and readily available from a number of seed companies. It grows tall, however, and needs space to show itself off.

stunning together), but it makes a sunny carpet of flowers planted *en masse*.

*Carpanthea* "Golden Carpet" demands attention with its spiked bright yellow flowers that seem almost too large for the 8 in. (20cm) height of this plant. They open in the sun but don't die gracefully so require deadheading. The plant will flower itself out long before the end of summer, so give it a position where it won't leave a conspicuous gap.

*Silene pendula* is a pretty plant about 6 in. (15cm) tall with a spread of about 1 ft. (30cm), and it looks stunning in flower in a hanging basket. Unfortunately it lacks staying power so may be better as a carpeting plant where it won't matter if a gap is left toward the end of the season. "Peach Blossom" is a particularly attractive form that goes through various shades of pink.

## Some to try

There are some readily available annuals that still seem surprisingly unfamiliar to many. The spider flower (*Cleome spinosa*) falls into this category. The spiky-looking pink, lilac, purple, or white flowers are difficult to describe … and perhaps for that reason seem to arrest the attention of anyone who sees the plant for the first time. At about 4 ft. (1.2m), they also have sufficient stature to become a focal point.

The other plants described here are less commonly available, and generally much more modest in stature.

*Anagalis monellii* is a kind of pimpernel that tends to peter out as the season progresses but can't fail to be noticed because of the intensity of its deep blue flowers.

You'll need to start the cleome and anagalis off under glass, but those that follow can be sown where they are to flower (though starting them off under glass will bring them into flower earlier).

*Camissonia* "Sunflakes" comes into flower very early, and will flower for months, though its bright yellow flowers tend to become sparse as the season progresses. Its rather sprawling growth makes it difficult to find suitable neighbors (try it with the anagalis just described – the blue and yellow look

Right: *Silene pendula* "Peach Blossom" does not have as long a flowering period as most summer annuals, but it makes an interesting and impressive display where it can tumble over the edge of a basket or window box.

# Annual perennials

*A perennial that can be treated like an annual sounds a contradiction in terms, but many tender perennials are treated as annuals.*

**Above:** *Coreopsis* "Early Sunrise" is easy to flower, and can be treated as an annual. If deadheaded often, it will flower from early summer to the first frost, from a late winter sowing. That's performance for a perennial.

More uncommon are hardy perennials that will flower in the first year if sown early enough under glass. You can have the best of both worlds with these plants.

Hardy perennials that will flower in the first year if started early enough are usually grown in the herbaceous border, but some can also be used in annual beds.

Plants to try include the following, but note that the variety can be important: some varieties have been especially bred to flower quickly from seed. Those particularly useful for summer bedding schemes include achillea, coreopsis, lobelia, and osteospermum. The others are best used as gap fillers.

*Achillea* "Summer Pastels"
*Coreopsis* "Early Sunrise"
*Delphinium* "Dwarf Magic Fountains Mixture," "Pacific Giants Mixed"
*Eccremocarpus* "Tresco Hybrids"
*Leucanthemum x superbum* (formerly *Chrysanthermum maximum*) "Snow Lady"
*Eriophyllum* "Sunkiss"
*Lobelia* "Cinnabar Rose," "Compliment Mixed," "Fan Scarlet," "Orchid Rose"
*Michaelmas daisy* "Composition Mixed"
*Osteospermum hyoseroides*
*Platycodon grandiflorum* "Blue Pygmy"
*Polemonium caeruleum* "Blue Pearl"

## Salvia farinacea

Unlike the popular red salvia, with blue flower spikes, this forms a useful contrast to other plants. Good in containers or in a mixed bedding scheme.

Height: 1–1½ ft. (30–45cm).

**Varieties to look for**
"Victoria" has dark blue flowers. "Strata" has blue flowers on grayish spikes.

**Soil and site**
Well-drained soil, in sun or partial shade.

**Propagation**
Sow seed in warmth under glass between mid winter and early spring.

## Tagetes erecta
*African marigold, American marigold*

The colors and flower size are bold and brassy: large double blooms in shades of orange and yellow (occasionally white). The foliage has a pungent smell, but only when handled or crushed. Older varieties were often tall, but there are dwarf varieties shorter than 1 ft. (30cm) and compact enough for containers. Deadhead regularly to improve the appearance and prolong flowering.

Height: 1–3 ft. (30–90cm).

**Varieties to look for**
The Inca series (available as separate colors or as a

mixture) is still among the best, with blooms over 4 in. (10cm) across on sturdy plants about 1 ft. (30cm) tall. Perhaps the best white is "French Vanilla."

### Soil and site
Undemanding regarding soil, but grow in full sun.

### Propagation
Sow seed in warmth under glass in late winter.

## Tagetes patula
*French marigold*

One of the most dependable of all half-hardy bedding plants, it is often in flower while still in the pot or seed tray, and continues until the first frost if deadheaded. Apart from singles and doubles, there are carna-tion-flowered varieties (with more petals than a single but not fully double) and crested (with a ring of flat outer petals, and a central boss of tightly crimped individual small flowers). Deadhead to keep them flowering prolifically.

Height: 6–24 in. (15–60cm).

### Varieties to look for
Many new varieties are introduced each year, so check catalogs for outstanding new introductions, but the Boy series (available in separate color or mixed) produces impressive double flowers, "Favorite Mixed" is one of the best single mixtures, and "Tiger Eyes" is fascinating crested variety.

### Soil and site
Undemanding regarding soil. Will perform well in sun or partial shade.

### Propagation
Sow in warmth under glass in late winter or early spring for early flowering, or outdoors in mid or late spring where they are to flower.

# Sun worshippers

*Some of the brightest plants open their flowers only in sun or on a very warm day.*

If you live in a sunny area or want to plant some spectacular annuals for a sunny position, try some of these beauties. Don't be deterred from trying these plants just because you live where summer sun can't be relied upon. Even cool summers have lots of hot, bright days when these plants come into their own. Just make sure you plant them where they will receive as much sunshine as possible, avoiding shady spots.

Many of these plants have bright daisy-shaped flowers which look particularly beautiful when they open, and it is well worth putting up with the closed flowers in very gray weather.

**Right:** *Gazania* **hybrid.**

*Arctotis* (African daisy)
*Arctotis fastuosa,* formerly *Venidium fastuosum* (monarch of the Veldt)
*Bartonia aurea* (blazing star)
*Dimorphotheca sinuata* (star of the Veldt)
*Eschscholzia californica* (California poppy)
*Felicia bergeriana* (kingfisher daisy)
*Gazania*
*Mesembryanthemum criniflorum* (Livingstone daisy)
*Osteospermum hyoseroides*
*Portulaca grandiflora* (sun plant)
*Ursinia anethoides*

# Know your sweet peas

*Sweet peas have an enthusiastic following, and there are societies devoted to the flower. They have come a long way since the first sweet peas were cultivated about 300 years ago ... and they're still being improved.*

The first sweet peas to be cultivated would have had small flowers, little larger than those of the culinary pea, with perhaps two or three blooms on a short stem. It was probably the strong fragrance that made them desirable plants to grow.

After about 100 years of cultivation there were white, black, red, and a pink and white bicolor, as well as the original purple. But these would still have been uninspiring plants, with little to suggest what the modern sweet pea represents.

The modern varieties owe much to Henry Eckford, who spent years carefully cross-fertilizing and selecting sweet peas. Gradually weak points were eliminated and

**Left:** This is a Spencer variety of *Lathyrus odoratus,* the commonly grown annual species.

**Left:** *Lathyrus grandiflorus* is a perennial species, which grows to about 4-6 ft. (1.2-1.8m).

free-flowering and larger blooms on longer stems developed. And of course that superb scent was retained as far as possible.

## Which type?

### Spencer sweet peas
These have large flowers with a waved or frilly standard, typical of most sweet pea varieties grown at the moment. Varieties recommended for exhibition belong to this group.

### Grandiflora
These have smaller flowers in comparison to Spencers, and a plain standard. Although the flower spikes are less impressive than Spencers, they bloom prolifically and the scent is superb.

### Old-fashioned sweet peas
The color range is not so good, and the flowers are smaller than those of modern varieties, but the scent is often stronger.

### Dwarf types
These are grown mainly for garden display, though they can be used for cutting if you

don't mind short and possibly less than straight stems.

Among the varieties that grow to about 3–4 ft. (90–120cm) and suitable for a floral hedge or groups in a large border, are "Continental Mixed" and "Jet Set Mixed."

There are very dwarf varieties suitable for window boxes and other containers. These include "Cupid," "Fantasia Mixed," and "Bijou Mixed."

"Snoopea" is a famous variety, which received numerous awards when it was introduced. This breakthrough in breeding produced a dwarf plant about 2–2½ft. (60–75cm) tall with no tendrils. It has a prostrate growth habit and makes bushy plants covered with flowers … with no worries about staking.

## How to grow?

If you want sweet peas with long straight stems and lots of large blooms, whether for

Left: Another popular variety of sweet peas are the dwarf types, like this *Lathyrus* "Snoopea."

Left: The sweet peas that most of us grow are annuals, but there are also perennial kinds such as *Lathyrus latifolius*, though the color range is very limited.

exhibition or for cutting, use the cordon system of growing single main stems up canes, removing the tendrils and tying in by hand.

If you want long, straight stems for cutting but do not want the work that cordons require, grow up net or mesh columns supported with tall canes.

For a pretty garden display in a border, grow up tents of canes or stake with tall twiggy sticks inserted while the seedlings are still young.

Pinch out plants at 6in. (15cm) high to encourage side shoots. Keep picking the flowers regularly to allow new blooms to come through.

### JARGON BUSTER

*Sweet pea enthusiasts use few jargon words, but it's worth understanding the following, which you will often see mentioned in catalogs:*

**Cordon** *A method of growing the plant up canes, with the tendrils removed – the stem being supported with ties or rings.*

**Haulm** *Another name for the climbing stem of the sweet pea plant.*

**Keel** *Two joined, sheath-like petals, boat-shaped in appearance, at the front of the flower.*

**Standard** *The broad and relatively flat back petal.*

**Tendril** *Wispy thread-like growth at the ends of some leaves, which curl around a support to help the plant climb.*

**Wings** *Two petals spread out between the standard and the keel.*

Above: The lovely modern varieties of sweet peas are descended from *Lathyrus odoratus*. This picture shows the wild form of this highly-bred plant.

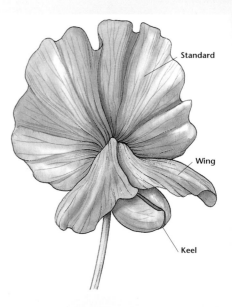

Standard

Wing

Keel

# How to raise half-hardy annuals

*Most summer bedding plants are treated as half-hardy annuals. Even some that are hardy and can be sown where they are to flower, such as sweet alyssum (lobularia), and pansies are treated as half-hardy seedlings to ensure that they are as advanced as other bedding plants by planting time.*

A greenhouse is a distinct advantage, but you can raise a small number of plants on a window sill if necessary. Bear in mind that you will need much more space once they have been spaced out in their final seed trays or individual pots, so don't be over ambitious with the number you try to raise indoors.

**1** Fill a seed tray with a special seed or multipurpose soil. Remove excess potting soil, then level it with a board or stiff card. Firm gently to leave a level surface for sowing.

**2** Large seeds can be scattered directly from the packet. Scatter thinly, first along the length of the seed trays, then across. Mix very fine seeds with fine sand first, then scatter.

**3** Most seeds should be covered with a thin layer of sifted soil (cover with about the depth of the seed), but check the packet as some of them are best left uncovered.

**4** Use a sprinkling-type watering can if the seeds are large enough not to be washed around. For fine seeds, stand in a shallow bowl of water and let it seep through.

**5** Unless you have a propagator, cover the seed tray or pot with glass or enclose in a plastic bag, then top with paper until the seedlings emerge – but check the packet, as some need light. Keep warm.

**6** When the seedlings are large enough to handle, prick them out into individual pots or space them out into seed trays. Loosen the potting soil before lifting the seedlings.

**7** Use a small dibber or a pencil to make holes deep enough to take the roots, and always hold the plant by its seed leaves (the first ones to open). Keep in good light.

**8** Always harden (acclimatize) the young plants over a week or two before planting outdoors when there is no risk of frost. A cold-frame is ideal for this.

## How to sow hardy annuals

Hardy annuals can be sown where they are to flower, and for many this is the best way to treat them as they receive the least setback to growth. Mid and late spring is a suitable time for most kinds to be sown, but check the packet first.

The sequence shown here assumes you are sowing a bed of hardy annuals, but if you just want to sow a few plants to fill in gaps in a border among the perennials, sow a pinch of seed at the final spacing and thin to one plant in each position if more germinate.

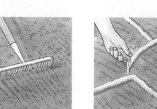   

**1** Dig over the area and clear it of weeds, especially difficult perennial weeds. Break down the large clumps of soil, then rake level ready for sowing.

**2** A bed of hardy annuals looks best if the plants appear to be growing in bold drifts. Mark out the areas to be sown with the different types, using sand as a guide.

**3** Use the end of a stick or cane to mark out shallow drills where the seeds are to be sown. Consult the packet for the spacing between rows.

**4** Sow the seeds as evenly as possible, sprinkling them along the rows between fingers and thumb. If the seeds are very fine, mix them with fine silver sand first.

**5** Alternate the direction of the rows in each section to avoid a regimented appearance. Make sure you label, then rake the soil to cover the seeds.

**6** Although it makes identification of weed seedlings more difficult when they are not sown in rows, the seeds can be scattered broadcast instead.

**7** Cover broadcast seeds by raking first in one direction and then the other. This helps to distribute them evenly as well as covering them.

**8** Water thoroughly after sowing, and whenever the soil begins to dry out. Thin out the seedlings to the spacing recommended on the packet in stages.

Above: All these flowers – nicotianas, French and African marigolds, and celosias – are raised as half-hardy annuals. This is what you can expect from a few packets of seeds!

ANNUALS AND BIENNIALS

## Tropaeolum majus
*Nasturtium*

There are climbing varieties of this hardy annual, but for a bright display in beds and borders choose one of the many bushy varieties that do not climb. They are useful for filling gaps in borders. Blackfly and some caterpillars are attracted to nasturtiums, so be vigilant and control at the first sign.
   Height: 9–12 in. (23–30cm).

### Varieties to look for
"Alaska" is one of the most distinctive varieties because the leaves are marbled and striped cream. "Whirlybird Mixed" flowers early and has upward-facing flowers that stand clear of the leaves.

### Soil and site
Undemanding regarding soil, and will flower more prolifically if the soil is not too fertile (when the leaves tend to hide the flowers). Best in full sun, but tolerates partial shade.

### Propagation
Sow in mid or late spring where the plants are to flower.

## Verbena

Both seed-raised and vegetatively propagated verbenas are used for bedding and containers. The seed-raised varieties, treated as half-hardy annuals, are discussed here. There is a wide color range, with the emphasis on blues and purples, but there are attractive reds, pinks, white, and peach.
   Height: 6–12 in. (15–30cm).

### Varieties to look for
"Peaches and Cream" is an unusual color combination of light salmon, apricot, orange,

**Above left:** *Tropaeolum major.*
**Above:** *Viola x wittrockiana.*
**Below:** *Verbena "Peaches and Cream."*

and cream, blending together in the one flower. "Imagination" has masses of small deep violet-blue flowers and a spreading habit that makes it useful for hanging baskets.

### Soil and site
Undemanding, but best in full sun.

### Propagation
Sow in warmth under glass in late winter or early spring.

## Viola x wittrockiana
*Pansy*

Pansies are invaluable container plants, but the winter-flowering varieties are also widely used for bedding and interplanting with bulbs and other spring flowers. Although small plants, some have flowers over 2 in. (5cm) across.
   There are self colors, but most have blotched "faces." Deadhead regularly to prolong flowering, and feed to sustain the performance.
   Height: 6–9 in. (15–23cm).

## Varieties to look for

The Universal series (separate colors or mixed) is outstanding, flowering through winter whenever the weather is not too severe, and into spring, from an early summer sowing. For flower size "Majestic Giant" is difficult to beat, with blooms often over 3 in. (7.5cm) across.

## Soil and site

Well-drained but moisture-retentive, fertile soil, in full sun or partial shade. In very hot climates they will do better in shade.

## Propagation

Summer varieties are usually treated as half-hardy annuals and sown in warmth under glass in late winter or early spring. Winter varieties can be sown outdoors in late spring or early summer and treated as hardy biennials.

## Xeranthemum annuum
*Paperflower*

This pretty hardy annual is usually grown for winter decoration, but it's a useful filler for gaps toward the front of an herbaceous border. It is easily grown and thrives on poor soil.

Height: 1 1/2–2 ft. (45–60cm).

## Varieties to look for

Usually only available as the species, but "Superbissima" is an improved form.

## Soil and site

Undemanding regarding soil, but best in full sun.

## Propagation

Sow in mid or late spring where the plants are to flower.

## Zinnia

Zinnias are more popular in warm climates than in cold ones, where they are slower to flower and less prolific in bloom. Those with long stems make good cut flowers.

Height: 6–36 in. (15–90cm).

## Varieties to look for

For big flowers on long stems, look for a variety such as "Giant Double," and for a more compact plant, "Dwarf Double."

## Soil and site

Well-drained soil, in full sun.

## Propagation

Sow in warmth under glass in early or mid spring, or outdoors in late spring where they are to flower.

## DID YOU KNOW?

The difference between plants sold as violas and pansies is partly size, partly breeding. The plants sold simply as violas usually have smaller flowers than pansies and the flowers are often less rounded and symmetrical in shape, with a spur at the back of the bloom.

# Patio and Container Plants

Many different kinds of plants may be described as "patio plants" – even some vegetables are described as "patio varieties." The term is used loosely to describe plants that grow well in containers, but of course they do equally well in raised beds and other small beds on the patio or largely paved area.

Many of the plants are widely used in normal summer bedding, of course, but in addition there are excellent tender perennials that can be kept through the winter in a warm area as cuttings wherever there are winter frosts. These are not easy to winter at home unless you have a green-house, but they are widely sold in garden centers and by mail order in spring.

They can be used just as successfully around the garden, whether in containers like tubs or hanging baskets or in flower beds. What they have in common is the ability to produce a good display with lots of impact in a limited space, and a tolerance of being grown in a container if they have to be.

# Features

PATIO AND CONTAINER PLANTS

51

# Arctotis (syn. x Venidioarctotis)

*African daisy, Zulu daisy*

Bright, daisy-like flowers up to 3 in. (7.5 cm) across in shades of red, orange, yellow, and pink, from early summer to the first frost. deadhead regularly to keep the flowers coming (cut the long stems at the base rather than pulling the flower heads off – it will look better). Gray foliage.

Height: 1½ ft. (45cm).

### Varieties to look for

Mixtures can be bought, but for specific colors choose the vegetatively propagated varieties that used to be called x *Venidioarctotis.* There are named varieties such as "Flame" with orange-red flowers; "African Sunrise," yellow; and "Red Blaze," blood red.

### Soil and site

Fertile and well-drained soil in full sun. Hardy in zone 11.

### Propagation

Named hybrids are best wintered as cuttings: take 3–4 in. (7.5–10cm) cuttings of sideshoots in late summer or early autumn, and store them for winter at a minimum of about 39° F (4°C). If you can't store them, discard and buy new plants the following year. The hybrids offered by nurseries are

raised fresh each spring. Sow in warmth under glass in mid or late winter.

### NOW YOU KNOW!

You may find these plants listed as either *X Venidioarctotis* or *X Venidio-arctotis,* because some varieties raised vegetatively were hybrids between species of arctotis and *Vendium fastulosum.* But botanists have reclassified *Venidium fastulosum* as *Arctotis fastulosum,* so now the hybrids are correctly classified simply as varieties of arctotis!

# Argyranthemum

*Marguerite*

Typically the flowers are single and daisy-like, and white is the color normally associated with marguerites. Modern hybrids now come in shades of yellow, pink, and peach too, and there are even double varieties. The green or gray foliage is light and feathery in appearance.

These are superb in the border, useful as "dot" plants to provide height and texture among summer bedding plants, and attractive in containers too. Take in before the first

frost if the plants are to be kept through the winter.

Height: 1½–3 ft. (45–90cm).

### Varieties to look for

There are many new varieties, but reliable tried and tested ones include "Jamaica Primrose" with yellow flowers; "Royal Haze," white flowers with silvery-blue foliage; "Vancouver," pink, double flowers; and the species *A. maderense,* with yellow flowers and silvery foliage. Most grow 1½–2 ft. (45–60cm) tall and bloom from early summer until the first frost.

### Soil and site

Well-drained soil, in full sun or partial shade. Best in full sun. Zone 10.

### Propagation

Old plants can be lifted and wintered in pots in the greenhouse, but it is better to take cuttings in late summer or early autumn and keep them under glass.

Below: *Begonia "Prima Donna Red."*
Bottom: *Bidens ferulifolia.*

## NOW YOU KNOW!

If you're still unfamiliar with the name argyranthemum, you simply have to catch up with the botanists. You will be more familiar with the old name for marguerite, *Chrysanthemum frutescens*. The argyranthemums described here, however, are hybrids, and sometime arise from other species.

## Bacopa "Snowflake"

*see Sutera cordata "Snowflake"*

## Begonia, tuberous-rooted

Tuberous-rooted begonias are ideal container plants: the bushy ones for tubs and pots; the trailing ones for baskets and window boxes. There are many kinds, and tubers are available from bulb merchants and seed companies (the Non-Stop series can be raised from seed or tubers).

Giant begonias may be found under a variety of names, but they will produce flowers 8 in. (20cm) across. Trumpet begonias have the central petals forming a tight spiral around the center of each bloom, the outer petals being flat or reflexed. Fimbriated varieties have attractively fringed petals. Non-Stop have masses of medium-sized blooms over a long period, and a dwarf habit that make them more tolerant

of wind and rain. They are ideal for window boxes and pots.

Basket, Sensation, or Pendula varieties flower on cascading stems, and are the best choice for hanging baskets.

"Crispa Marginata" has large single flowers with a cerise-red picotee edge. It is attractive for bedding or for containers on patios.

Lift and store the tubers at the end of the season (before they are damaged by frost). Keep cool, dry and frost-free until ready for planting. The tubers are best started in pots or trays under glass to get them off to an earlier start.

Height: 1–1½ ft. (30–45cm), or trailing.

### Varieties to look for

They are usually sold simply as colors within the types described above. Specialists

supply named varieties of giant double begonias, but these are usually grown by enthusiasts as greenhouse or conservatory potted plants.

### Soil and site

Well-drained but moisture-retentive, fertile soil. Zone 11.

### Propagation

Tubers can be divided with care, but it is better to make cuttings of the emerging shoots in spring. Non-Stop can be raised from seed sown in warmth under glass in winter, and will flower the first year.

## Bidens ferulifolia

*Tickseed*

Grown as a half-hardy annual, it quickly produces feathery, fennel-like foliage, and a profusion of bright yellow flowers that continue until the end of the season.

Height: 2 ft. (60cm).

### Varieties to look for

"Golden Goddess" is the cultivated form usually sold by seed companies.

### Soil and site

Undemanding regarding soil, but best in full sun. Zone 8.

### Propagation

Sow in late winter or early spring in warmth under glass.

PATIO AND CONTAINER PLANTS

53

# Beautiful baskets

*Hanging baskets make use of space that would otherwise lack color and beauty, and they are particularly appropriate for patios. Half baskets can be just as effective as full baskets if well planted, and these are ideal for enhancing an otherwise dull or boring wall.*

There are so many excellent basket plants that you could plant hundreds of baskets and not run out of ideas for different plant combinations … the choice can be bewildering. There's lots of scope for individual creativity and expression, whether you want to show off your knowledge of unusual plants, go for a color coordinated effect, or simply make a stunning traditional basket using many of the old favorites. The baskets illustrated here are just examples of *types* of plantings that you can use. You may not be able to obtain the exact combination of plants to re-create them, and will probably want to use your own ideas anyway, but use them as the basis for your own planting scheme if you need ideas to start with.

### Traditional mixed baskets

There's nothing wrong with the traditional basket planted with pelargoniums, trailing lobelia, impatiens, petunias, and possibly a fuchsia, but mixed baskets are among the most difficult to plant well unless you have a reasonable knowledge of plants. So many plants with such different growth habits can be difficult to position without some of them swamping their neighbors. Achieving a rounded ball of color demands skill.

**To make success more certain:**
Choose a large basket – at least 14 in. (35cm) diameter, and the bigger the better. Keep to about half a dozen different plants as a maximum. Use several plants of the same kind rather than have every plant different.

Plant the sides as well as the top – don't depend on trailers to hide the basket and make it look well-clothed, though you may have to accept this if you choose a hanging pot rather than a wire basket.

Avoid planting very vigorous trailers, such as "Surfinia" petunias, above compact or less robust plants.

Try to include some foliage plants, such as *Glechoma hederacea* "Variegata" or the silver-leaved *Helichrysum petiolare*. The flowers will look all the better for some foliage to break up the mass of bloom.

## Single-subject baskets

These are the easiest to plant as the vigor and growth habit of all the plants will be the same. Make sure you plant close enough for them to knit together into a ball of color, as there will be no looser-growing plants to hide any gaps.

Busy Lizzies (impatiens) are among the most reliable plants to choose, and you can go for a single color effect or plant a mixture. These are particularly good because they come into flower so quickly and bloom until the first frost.

Fibrous-rooted begonias are also readily available and free-flowering, but they take a little longer to grow themselves into a ball of flower. Again, you can choose single colors or a mixture, but why not show a little more design skill by alternating plants of two varieties: perhaps a red-flowered variety with green leaves together with a white-flowered variety with dark bronze leaves.

Other flowers to use for single-subject baskets include fuchsias, lobelia (try a mixed trailing variety), pansies, pelargoniums, petunias, and verbenas.

## Color coordinated

Themed baskets can be very striking. Ideas for a "cool" and a "hot" basket are described below, but you can make up baskets to suit different moods or personal color preferences.

A golden basket will look light and refreshing in partial shade or a corner that needs a lift. Try the golden foliage of *Helichrysum petiolare* "Aureum," a gold-variegated ivy, with *Lysimachia nummularia* "Aurea" (gold flowers and foliage) or *Lysimachia* "Sunset" (yellow flowers and yellowish-green variegated foliage), coupled with yellow pansies or *Asteriscus maritimus* "Gold Coin."

Try a basket filled with hot colors for a patio area where you want to be bold and daring with your color scheme. Use long-lasting red flowers like red pelargoniums and verbenas and maybe a red impatiens or two. But use silver foliage to form a pleasing backdrop to the red flowers and to soften the effect a little.

*Helichrysum petiolare* and *Lotus berthelotii* are ideal because they have the cascading habit that helps to give a basket a well-clothed look, but try a few more upright silver-foliage plants too, like *Pyrethrum ptarmiciflorum* (now more correctly *Tanacetum ptarmiciflorum*) or *Cineraria maritima* (now *Senecio cineraria*).

## Something unusual

Try a foliage-only basket. Coleus can be stunning, but choose a dwarf and branching variety such as "Wizard." Or use two or three young plants of Abutilon megapotamicum "Variegatum" to fill the basket: the green and yellow foliage will be peppered with unusual red and yellow flowers (pinch back any shoots that grow too long).

To create an all-white basket, use white petunias or white impatiens or alyssum, but a ball of *Sutera cordata* formerly *Bacopa* "Snowflake" would be unusual and attractive.

# Brachycome iberidifolia

*Swan river daisy*

A compact, bushy annual with feathery foliage and a profusion of flowers like small blue Michaelmas daisies. There are also pink, purple, and white forms. Attractive in containers, it flowers into autumn until cut down by frost. Pinch out the tips of the shoots while the plant is still young, to encourage bushier growth.

Height: 9 in. (23cm).

### Varieties to look for
"Purple Splendor" and "White Splendor" are both reliable varieties. "Tinkerbell" is a pleasing variety for baskets.

### Soil and site
Well-drained, fertile soil, in full sun, and if possible, a sheltered position.

### Propagation
Sow seed in warmth under glass in late winter or early spring. Can also be sown outdoors in late spring where the plants are to flower.

# Brugmansia x candida

*Angels' trumpets*

This large semi-evergreen shrub can be used on the patio only during the summer, but it is often the centerpiece of the summer show when the huge creamy-white pendulous trumpet flowers fill the air with scent on a warm summer's day. They are especially fragrant in the evening.

Feed freely throughout the summer, and don't let the soil dry out. It must be taken indoors before the first frost, and if it can be moved without pruning it may continue to flower in the house in winter – a single flower can fill a room with scent in the evening. It may be more convenient, however, to cut it down to about 2 ft. (60cm) to bring indoors or into a greenhouse. New shoots will soon be produced and the plant will be bushier the following year.

Height: 6–8 ft. (1.8–2.4m) in a tub.

### Varieties to look for
"Grand Marnier" is one of the best whites, "Knightii" (syn. "Plena") is semi-double. The flowers of *B. sanguinea* are red.

### Soil and site
Moist, fertile soil, in full sun or partial shade. A loam-based potting soil is best because of its weight and stability, as the plant grows large. Zone 10.

### Propagation
Take cuttings from spring to autumn. They root easily, and cuttings may be more convenient to store through winter than a very large plant. They are likely to flower in in their first summer.

# Chrysanthemum

*see Dendranthema*

# Datura

*see Brugmansia*

### NOW YOU KNOW!
Brugmansias are still widely sold under their older name of datura. You may find them sold in garden centers in spring often as small plants just coming into growth. They can also be bought by mail order. Although probably small when received, they grow rapidly and should flower in the first summer. The best displays can be expected from older plants, however, which often have dozens of flowers open at once.

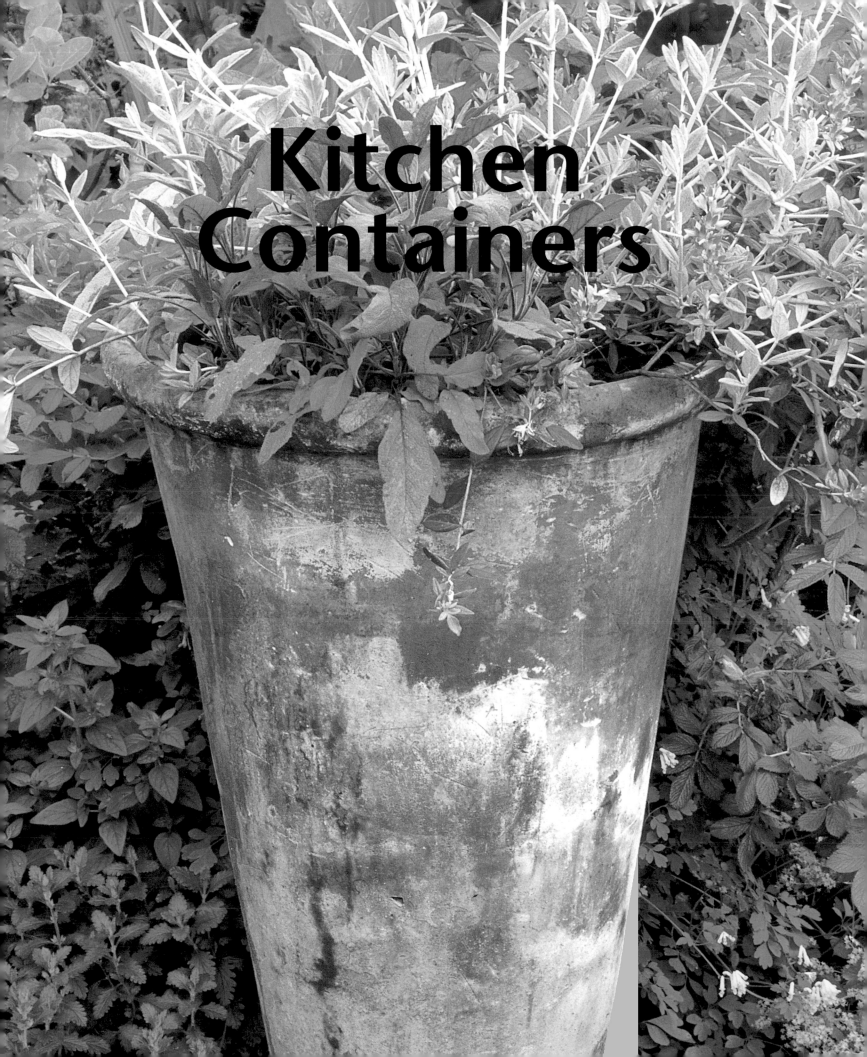

# Kitchen
# Containers

# Kitchen Containers

Looks good, tastes good. There are worthwhile edible crops that you can grow in containers if you don't have space for a kitchen garden. You won't feed a family this way, but it's fun to grow a few edible crops and there's no comparison between the flavor of something you've freshly harvested from your own garden and produce bought from the market.

With imagination and suitable choice of varieties, you can grow herbs, vegetables, and even fruit, in tubs and pots, and even in window boxes and baskets. Many vegetables are quite ornamental, and many fruits – such as apples and red currants – are visually attractive as well as tasty. Don't expect heavy harvests: just plant imaginatively and have fun!

**Above:** Tomatoes do well in containers of all kinds if fed and watered well.
**Below:** Pears and apples can be grown very successfully in a small space if a dwarfing root stock is used, and they can be trained into attractive shapes.
**Previous page:** Purple and golden forms of sage (*Salvia officinalis*) are attractive foliage plants for a container. Here a purple-leaved form is being grown with the gray-leaved ornamental *Teucrium fruticans*, in an old rhubarb-forcing pot.

**Right:** The purple-leaved sages (*Salvia officinalis* "Purpurascens") make super foliage plants, yet can still be used in the kitchen.

**Overleaf:** Here the herb, golden marjoram (*Origanum vulgare* "Aureum"), has been grown in a container and artfully combined within the design of a vegetable garden, among rows of lettuce and tomato plants.

# How to plant a hanging basket

*Planting a basket is easy, especially if you follow these simple tips. But how good it will look afterwards will depend on how well you care for it. All containers need regular watering and feeding, but hanging baskets are particularly demanding.*

### Tips for success

Give the plants time to root into the potting soil and to start growing again before hanging up the basket. Always harden (acclimatize) the planted basket for at least a few days before hanging. Add slow-release or controlled-release fertilizer pellets or granules if not already incorporated into the potting soil. Superabsorbent polymers (moisture-holding granules) will not eliminate the need to water frequently, but will act as a buffer against disaster through temporary neglect. Spray your plants with an insecticide before hanging. Consider using a systemic insecticide. Deadhead flowers regularly if possible.

**1** Most wire baskets have a rounded bottom, so they are difficult to secure in an upright position for planting. If you stand it in a bucket you should be able to work on it easily.

**2** Line the basket with moss or proprietary liner. You can even use black plastic, as shown here, if you plant the sides well to mask it. Partially fill with a light-weight potting soil.

**3** Introduce plants around the sides. If using moss, just add enough moss and potting soil to the appropriate level, plant, then add more moss. With plastic you will have to make planting slits.

**4** Add more potting soil (preferably incorporating a slow-release fertilizer and water-absorbing granules), then place a large plant in the central position.

**5** Fill in the spaces around the edge at the top, angling the plants slightly to encourage them to grow over the edge. Add more potting soil, tamp lightly, then water thoroughly.

**6** Don't place it outside yet. Hang it in a cool green-house, or stand it in a cold-frame or porch, to become established for a week or two. Hang it outside only after hardening.

## Dahlia

Only dwarf, compact varieties
are suitable for growing in a pot
or tubs on the patio. They do
not flower well until late summer, but by early autumn they
are among the brightest flowers
on the patio.

Lilliput varieties, with small
single flowers, can be used to
edge borders and can even be
used in a window box (don't
mix with other summer plants,
as they flower late). There are
dwarf cactus and decorative
dahlias with flowers equal to
those of their taller-growing
counterparts, ideally suited for
tubs and large pots.

### Varieties to look for

There are over 20,000 recognized dahlia varieties, and new
ones are introduced continu-
ally, so consult a nursery or a
catalog that offers summer-
flowering bulbs.

Plant the tubers in mid
spring, but do not set plants out
until late spring or early summer – shoots will be killed by
frost. Lift and dry the tubers
once the tops have been black-
ened by frost, then store in a
frost-free place.

Plants raised from cuttings
are available from specialty
nurseries and from some garden centers.

Look for Lilliput varieties; the
plants are about 1 ft. (30cm)
tall, and bedding dahlias up to
about 1½ ft. (45cm) tall.

### Soil and site

Moisture-retentive, fertile soil,
in full sun or partial shade.
Feed as long as the plants are
flowering. Zone 10 if left in the
ground.

### Propagation

Divide tubers (each tuber must
be attached to a piece of old
stem; otherwise no shoots will
grow), or take cuttings in spring
when the new shoots are produced. Start the tubers off early
in boxes to produce shoots for
cuttings.

Seed companies offer bed-
ding dahlias, but these are
usually more suitable for general summer bedding than for
growing in containers.

## Dendranthema

*Chrysanthemum*

Although dendranthema is now
the correct name for these
plants, they are likely to be sold
in garden centers and from catalogs as chrysanthemums – the
name most gardeners continue
to apply to these autumn-
flowering plants.

There are many types, but
only early-flowering, dwarf, and
compact varieties are suitable
for containers. These form a
mound of flowers without the
necessity to keep removing the
tips of growing shoots.

Most of them make mounds
of small double flowers in all
the usual chrysanthemum colors. They flower for weeks and
are sometimes colorful for a
month, in early and mid

autumn, just when the patio
needs a shot of color.

Feed during the summer to
sustain plenty of vigorous
growth. Although it is beneficial
to pinch out the growing tip
when the plant is a few inches
high, regular pinching to
induce branching is unneces-
sary with this type of
chrysanthemum.

If bought as young plants,
grow on under cover until late
spring, then plant outside. They
can be grown entirely in pots,
gradually moving into larger
pots, but care and watering can
be tedious throughout the summer. Alternatively they can be

planted in the soil in a spare piece of ground for the summer and potted as they come into flower. Provided they are lifted with a good ball of soil around the roots, they should flower without setback.

In mild areas, old plants can be left in the ground for the winter, but the roots are best lifted and stored in a cold-frame or cool or unheated greenhouse. They are frost-hardy but a combination of cold and damp can be fatal.

Height: 1–2 ft. (30–60cm).

## Varieties to look for
There are thousands of chrysanthemum varieties, and new ones are introduced every year. Send for specialty catalogs or keep an eye open in garden centers (they may be described as patio chrysanthemums or "mums"). Started plants are available in spring; larger plants already coming into bloom may be available from garden centers in late summer.

## Soil and site,
Well-drained, fertile soil, in full sun. Zone 4.

## Propagation
Take cuttings when the old roots produce new shoots in late winter or spring. Alternatively, divide the old clump.

## Diascia

Mainly hybrids are grown, of which there are many, but all produce a succession of small pink, red, or purple flowers on wiry-stemmed, compact plants in summer and autumn. Although individual flowers are small, they are produced so prolifically that the effect is very colorful. They can be used in beds and borders, but make good container plants, and those with a spreading or trailing habit are pleasing in hanging pots.

Pinch out the growing tips of young plants when they are about 2 in. (5cm) tall. They will be even bushier if this is repeated again a few weeks later but flowering will be delayed.

In areas where they are of borderline hardiness it is worth taking cuttings in late summer to winter in a coldframe or cold or cool greenhouse.

Height: 6–12 in. (15–30cm).

## Varieties to look for
Popular hybrids include "Joyce's Choice' with soft apricot flowers, "Lilac Belle," and "Salmon Supreme." Reliable species are *D. barberae* ("Blackburn Apricot" and "Ruby Field" are particularly good varieties), and *D. vigilis* with soft pink flowers.

## Soil and site
Well-drained soil, in full sun. Zone 8.

## Propagation
Take cuttings in spring or late summer.

# Felicia amelloides
*Blue marguerite*

A bushy perennial with sky-blue daisy flowers with yellow centers, carried well above the foliage throughout summer.

In areas where they would be of borderline hardiness they may survive if covered, or by being moved to a coldframe. Otherwise take cuttings and store for winter in a frost-free greenhouse.

Height: 1 ft. (30cm).

## Varieties to look for
"Read's Blue" is a strong blue, "Variegata" has leaves edged in creamy-white. "Read's White" is white with a yellow center.

## Soil and site
Undemanding regarding soil, but grow in full sun in a sheltered position (the flowers close in shade). Zone 9.

## Propagation
Take cuttings in summer.

# Tubs are tops

*Use tubs and pots to clothe your patio and bring height and interest to a paved area. Large ones containing trees or large shrubs can remain in position as permanent features, while others can be moved around and replanted regularly for seasonal interest.*

Most tubs and pots hold a greater depth and volume of soil than window boxes and baskets, so larger plants can be grown … and there is scope for imaginative plant combinations. Always use a good potting soil, and for plants that are to remain in the container for more than a season choose a soil-based mixture. This will have a greater natural reserve of nutrients than a soilless mixture, and weight is not a consideration if the containers are standing on a paved area.

**Right: Silvers, grays and whites can look good together. The gray foliage of a helichrysum can soften the edge of a container while blending beautifully with white argyranthemum (marguerite).**

## Trees in tubs

Trees add a vertical dimension to the planting and, after a year or two, they will give your patio a sense of maturity that one filled with seasonal plants alone would lack.

Even relatively tall trees, such as the prettily variegated *Acer platanoides* "Drummondii," can be grown successfully in a tub. The root restriction and nutritional restraints have a similar effect to that of container size and root restriction on a bonsai – though to a lesser extent, of course.

Compact Japanese acers, such as *A. palmatum varieties*, are ideal as they are naturally small and slow-growing.

A laburnum can also look pleasing in flower, covered with its long golden tassels, but rather boring for the rest of the year.

Some conifers make pleasing shapes, but go for one with distinct branches rather than the close-cropped mound habit typical of many dwarf conifers. Try some of the pines, such as *Pinus mugo*.

## Shrubs make sense

The choice of shrubs that can be grown successfully in containers is vast. As deciduous shrubs look decidedly unattractive for many months of the year, place the emphasis on evergreens.

Pride of place has to go to flowering evergreens, like rhododendrons, azaleas, and camellias (use a ericaceous – acid – compost for all three). Some of the skimmias have attractive flowers, and many have bright red berries that last for months. Laurustinus (*Viburnum tinus*) is uninspiring in summer, but when covered with small white flowers (sometimes pinkish, according to variety)

from autumn right through until spring it is always welcome. Any plant that flowers continuously for almost six months has to be worth considering.

Phormiums (not reliable in cold areas) and yuccas have an "architectural" quality that makes them particularly appealing in a formal setting. There are varieties with colorful variegation, so they don't have to look dull. But beware of yuccas: the leaf ends are often like spines, and present a serious hazard to children and unsuspecting adults!

## Seasonal containers

Seasonal summer bedding plants and spring bulbs bring variety and color in a way that

permanent plantings can't. Be sure to include some tubs and pots that you replant at least twice a year. It is often possible to add a few flowers around the base of permanent plants such as trees and shrubs, but choose shallow-rooting plants so that you do not disturb the main planting.

## Permanent planting

Try a permanent planting of alpines in a pot or shallow container (a collection of sempervivums is always impressive, especially if you add a few small pieces of rock for effect).

A pot planted with non-woody evergreens can also be pleasing: try a mixed group of *Carex hachijoensis* "Evergold," a variegated *Ajuga reptans, Euphorbia amygaloides* "Purpurea," and *Arum italicum* "Marmoratum" with its white-veined leaves.

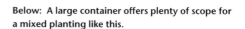

Below: A large container offers plenty of scope for a mixed planting like this.

# How to plant in a tub

*For a spectacular display, choose a large ornamental pot and cram it with bright summer flowers. Here's how easy it is.*

**Above: The secret of a successful tub planting is to create a mound of color, unless the container itself is a feature – when restrained planting may be more appropriate.**

**1** Only use containers with drainage holes, but cover these with pieces of broken pot, large pieces of chipped bark, or even broken plastic tiles, to prevent the soil from washing through.

**2** Use a good potting soil – this is essential for success. Ordinary garden soil is likely to be disappointing. Add a slow-release fertilizer and water-absorbing granules if you sometimes leave your plants for a day.

**3** Fill almost to the rim, but leave 1 in. (2.5cm) to allow space for watering. Place the central plant first, preferably something large, bushy, and imposing, such as a fuchsia or an argyranthemum.

**4** Plant densely around the edge. Include a few trailers such as the gray-leaved *Helichrysum petiolare* or colorful cascading pelargoniums. Plant the root-balls at an angle to encourage early trailing.

**5** Top up with more potting soil if necessary, firming the root-balls well. Water thoroughly. Keep in a shaded and sheltered position for a few days, if possible, before placing in full sun.

**6** Within weeks your tub will begin to look mature as the plants start to grow into each other and gaps are filled in. To keep it looking good, water daily, liquid feed as soon as necessary, and deadhead the plants.

# Fuchsia

Fuchsias need no introduction, but there are many species and a great number of hybrids, not all suitable for patio containers.

The frost-tolerant hybrids (hardy down to zone 7) are best grown in borders. Triphylla hybrids are more pleasing in summer bedding schemes than in pots.

Most trailing or cascading hybrids are ideal patio plants, whether in baskets or hanging pots, or tumbling over the edge of a window box. There's an enormous choice of half-hardy bushy fuchsias ideal for containers of all kinds, and much depends on personal taste. Double and semi-double flowers are popular, but singles can also be very striking if they bloom prolifically.

Pinch out the growing tips of young plants to encourage bushiness. The more often this is done, the bushier they will be, but slower coming into bloom. Standards and other formal shapes require special formative training, and standards require more than one growing season to form an attractive plant.

Winter tender types (most of which are hardy in zone 10 or above, though they may survive mild winters in zone 9) as dormant plants in a frost-free greenhouse or frame.

Alternatively, take cuttings in autumn and winter as green plants on a sunny window sill or in a greenhouse.

Regular feeding during the flowering seasons is essential, however, to sustain a long season of prolific blooming in a container.

See pages 74–75 for more details on the different types of fuchsia.

## Varieties to look for

Consult a specialty fuchsia catalog or book if you wish to study the merits of the many different varieties.

These are just a few of the first-rate patio varieties: "Cascade," a trailer with white and carmine flowers trailing; "Florabelle," a semi-double, with purple and red flowers, cascading; "Genii" with golden-green leaves, small cerise-red and reddish-purple flowers; "Golden Marinka" with red flowers, variegated golden foliage, trailing; "Marin Glow." flowers white and purplish-blue, makes a good standard; "Pacquesa," red and white, makes a good standard; "Swingtime" with large red and creamy-white flowers, arching habit. The dwarf variety "Tom Thumb" also makes a pleasing container plant.

## Soil and site

Best in fertile soil with a high humus content (provided by adding well-rotted manure or garden compost, for example), but will grow satisfactorily in most soils, and any good potting soil will be adequate.

## Propagation

Take cuttings at any time from spring to autumn. Late summer and early autumn is a good time to root cuttings to store for winter as an insurance against losing the parent plant.

Fuchsias can be raised from seed, but most give unpredictable results and may be slow to flower. "Florabelle" is totally reliable and flowers come true to type. It can be in flower within 14 weeks from sowing. Sow in warmth under glass in late winter or early spring.

## BUYING FUCHSIAS

Garden centers stock plants in spring and early summer, but specialty fuchsia nurseries will have a larger selection. Young plants can also be bought by mail order.

If you have a greenhouse heated for other plants, save money by buying young rooted cuttings in late winter or early spring and growing them to maturity. Otherwise it is best to buy larger plants ready to go into the garden – even if they cost more.

# A touch of the exotic

*One of the great advantages of growing plants in containers on patios and balconies is that you can include plants normally too tender to be used outdoors except in frost-free areas.*

Provided you can take the containers indoors or into a greenhouse for the winter, you can grow many wonderful plants that will give your garden an exotic feel.

## Inside out

Many house plants can spend the summer outdoors provided you give them a sheltered position (which is why patios are ideal), and acclimatize them carefully. If possible stand them in a coldframe for a week or two, or at least cover them with horticultural fleece for a couple of weeks – cold winds will mean disaster for some of them. Equally harmful is direct sun, which can damage even cacti and succulents if they have become accustomed to conditions in the home.

After a couple of weeks of protection and shade outdoors, most of them will be perfectly happy in a sunny spot. Be guided by the conditions the plant likes in the home – if full sun should be avoided indoors, choose a lightly shaded position outdoors. If they are best in a sunny window, give them full sun outdoors.

Some of the exotic-looking plants that can be grown successfully on a sheltered patio or balcony for the summer are crotons (codiaeums), bananas (dwarf varieties are practical for a pot), indoor yuccas, oleanders (*Nerium oleander*), and marantas and calatheas, but beware of sun scorch with these two.

If you have some attractive foliage plants, like palms and philodendrons, these will add to the "warm climate" atmosphere, but be sure to acclimatize them carefully and avoid direct sun until the leaves have toughened.

## Succulents

Tender cacti and succulents are very reliable provided they have been acclimatized very carefully, but they don't usually mix happily with the "forest" type of plants mentioned above. They are better arranged together in a group or planted to make a summer cactus garden in a container (you can leave them in their pots and just plunge them into coarse grit or sand).

Mother-in-law's tongue (*Sansevieria trifasciata* "Laurentii") is remarkably tough, and a large specimen in a pot can make a stunning feature on its own.

## Oranges and lemons

In warm regions where frosts are rare or seldom severe, citrus fruits can be grown very successfully outdoors, and they make handsome tub plants. If you have a or frost-free greenhouse (it does not have to be warm) to move them into for the winter, they will make impressive patio trees in tubs or large pots.

Go to a specialty nursery for advice about which types and varieties are likely to do well in patio containers in your area.

**Above: Mediterranean plants such as *Nerium oleander* are sure to give your patio a sense of the exotic.**

**Left: Cacti and succulents make good patio plants for the warmer months, especially if artistically arranged like this.**

Below: *Glechoma hederacea* (syn. *Nepeta glechoma*).
Right: *Helichrysum petiolare* (syn. *H. petiolatum*) "Limelight," also known as "Aureum."

## Glechoma hederacea (syn. Nepeta glechoma)

*Ground ivy*

The variety usually grown is "Variegata," which has kidney-shaped leaves irregularly edged white. This hardy perennial is really a vigorous ground-cover plant for shady places, but it will trail if planted in a basket or at the edge of a window box. It can be rampant and may need trimming back frequently.

### Varieties to look for
"Variegata" is the only one worth growing.

### Soil and site
Undemanding, but grows most rapidly in moist but well-drained soil, in sun or shade. Zone 6.

### Propagation
Divide in spring or autumn or take cuttings in spring. Its stems root readily where they come into contact with soil.

## Helichrysum petiolare (syn. H. petiolatum)

Much used as a foliage plant in baskets and other containers to break up the flowers visually and add useful contrast. The normal species of this tender perennial is gray, but there are yellowish and variegated varieties.

Not frost-hardy, and old plants are difficult to extricate from a mixed planting to pot for winter. Take cuttings in late summer or early autumn and winter these in a sunny, frost-free place.

Height: 1 ft. (30cm), or trailing.

### Varieties to look for
The species itself is very effective as a gray foliage plant, but "Variegatum" is worth considering where a combination of gray and green is desired, and "Limelight" (syn. "Aurea") is a pleasing lime green.

### Soil and site
Well-drained soil, in full sun. Will grow well in any good potting soil. Zone 10.

### Propagation
Take cuttings, from spring to autumn. Take them toward the end of the season to store for winter for the next season.

### TIP TO TRY
The spreading prostrate stems of *Helichrysum petiolare* can be used in many ways. On the ground they can be allowed to spread between colorful flowers, where they will often emerge among the blooms to create an enchanting effect.

In baskets and containers, plant at an angle at the edge so that they readily cascade and mask the container itself.

At the edge of a lawn or in a container with plants that find it difficult to compete, trim back long shoots to keep the plant within its allotted space.

# Wonderful window boxes

*Use window boxes to exploit the potential of wasted space. The favorite position is on window sills, but can be used effectively on bare walls or on low boundary walls.*

Use window boxes creatively. The impact will be much greater if all the boxes on one wall have matching plants – four of the same will look much stronger visually than four different plantings. If you have just one or two boxes, and want something different, try an herb window box, or a box filled with alpines, perhaps "landscaped" with a few small pieces of rock and the surface covered with stone chips. For the summer you could even have a cactus-garden window box. Most of us want a colorful display, however, and the more color-packed and overflowing the better. There are plenty of suggestions for suitable plants in these pages, but the plants

you choose should reflect your personal taste. Decide also whether you want a color theme: blue and gray, yellows, or red and gray, for example (all these can be stunning), or a display with as many colors and different types of flowers as possible.

Don't dismiss tried and tested plants like those suggested below. A long flowering season and an ability to compete with other plants in confined conditions are qualities needed for a good window box plant. Each year novelties and "new" plants are marketed by growers. Often they have been around for a long time, but not promoted for use in containers. Experiment with these cautiously – some will be superb, others may be disappointing in the climate in your area, or they may lack the qualities of established favorites.

### Reliable summer favorites
*Lobularia maritima* (formerly *Alyssum maritimum*)
*Begonia semperflorens*

*Begonia* x *tuberhybrida* (tuberous-rooted, including pendulous varieties)
*Fuchsia* (compact bush and cascading types)
*Glechoma hederacea* "Variegata"
*Hedera helix* (ivy, small-leaved)
*Impatiens* (Busy Lizzie)
*Lobelia erinus*
*Pelargonium* zonal (flowering and foliage types)
*Pelargonium* trailing (ivy-leaved and cascading)
*Petunia*
*Tagetes patula* (French marigold)
*Verbena*
*Viola* x *wittrockiana* (pansy)

### Well worth a try
*Argyranthemum* (marguerite)
*Brachycome iberidifolia*
*Calceolaria integrifolia* (syn. *C. rugosa*)
*Cineraria maritima*, now *Senecio cineraria*
*Diascia* (many kinds)
*Felicia amelloides*
*Heliotropium peruvianum* hybrids

**Right: Spring displays can look good for months, especially a mixed planting of popular bedding plants. Opposite: Make the most of window boxes in spring – they can look as good as this. Here polyanthus, hyacinths, muscari, and dwarf narcissus "Tête-à-Tête" nestle together with ivy for contrast.**

*Lantana camara*
*Nicotiana* (compact, day-opening varieties)
*Salvia splendens*

## Hardy annuals to sow in situ

These generally have a much shorter flowering season than normal bedding plants, but they are a cheap way to provide single-subject boxes of summer color.
*Anchusa capensis*
*Iberis umbellata* (candytuft)
*Tropaeolum majus* (nasturtium; choose a very compact variety)

## For an autumn display

*Dahlia* Lilliput type
*Dendranthema* (chrysanthemum), dwarf bedding type

## For a spring display

*Aurinia saxatilis,* formerly *Alyssum saxatile* (gold dust)
*Aubrieta deltoidea*
*Bellis perennis* (double daisy)
*Erysimum* formerly *Cheiranthus* (wallflower; choose a dwarf variety)
Dwarf bulbs such as crocuses, hyacinths, and scillas.

## How to plant a spring window box

Spring-flowering window boxes often look disappointingly sparse, or have a frustratingly short-lived display. Try this method of planting to cram in plenty of color over a relatively long period.

**1** Choose a deep window box so that you can use plenty of potting soil and pack in plenty of bulbs. Cover the drainage holes with pieces of broken pots, large pieces of chipped bark, or broken plastic tiles.

**2** Use a good potting soil for best results, though old soil from summer containers, or garden soil, can be used if necessary if you plan to discard the bulbs after flowering. Place a 2 in. (5cm) layer in the bottom.

**3** Place the larger bulbs, such as dwarf tulips, hyacinths, or dwarf narcissi, first. Leave space between them as more bulbs will be planted over the top, but plant close enough together for a bold show.

**4** Add sufficient potting soil to cover the first layer of bulbs, leaving just the tips of the bulbs showing to act as a guide. Then place small bulbs such as crocuses and scillas between the first layer.

**5** Cover the second layer of bulbs with more potting soil, but leave about ½–1 in. (1.2–2.5cm) of space at the top for watering. Firm the soil gently between the bulbs to remove any large air pockets.

**6** Plant some spring bedding plants to finish it off. Pansies and double daisies (*Bellis perennis*) are ideal. Try to make the planting holes with your fingers to minimize damage to the bulbs.

Below: *Impatiens* "Aslia," a New Guinea hybrid impatiens.
Right: *Laurentia axillaris* (syn. *Isotoma axillaris*).

# Impatiens
*Busy Lizzie*

The normal Busy Lizzies widely used for bedding are also excellent container plants, and look good in single-subject or mixed baskets as well as window boxes, tubs, and pots. Other types that are not so reliable in the rough and tumble of ordinary bedding schemes can make delightful patio plants. Double varieties, for example, can be appreciated in a raised container in a way that is seldom possible at ground level: these bloom less profusely but the individual flowers are charming.

New Guinea hybrids also make striking container plants. These have larger flowers than the normal varieties, and the foliage is usually bronze or variegated and generally bolder. Not frost-hardy. Seed-raised plants are usually discarded at the end of the season, but a few can be potted and taken indoors to flower for a little longer.

Those propagated vegetatively can be propagated from cuttings taken in late summer or early autumn and wintered in a light, frostproof place.

Height: 6–15 in. (15–38cm).

### Varieties to look for
New varieties are introduced annually, so consult current catalogs for the best bedding Busy Lizzies. In garden centers New Guinea hybrids may have this generic label rather than varietal names, but you should be able to judge from the foliage and flower whether a particular plant is suitable.

### Soil and site
Undemanding, but best in a fertile soil, in sun or partial shade. Full shade is tolerated, but the plants will be "leafier" with fewer flowers. Zone 10.

### Propagation
Some of the double and New Guinea hybrids have to be propagated from cuttings; others can be raised from seed. Take cuttings at any time, but in late summer or autumn to produce young plants to winter under glass. Sow seed from late winter to mid spring, in warmth under glass.

# Isotoma
*see Laurentia*

# Laurentia axillaris (syn. Isotoma axillaris)

This tender perennial makes a charming summer patio plant, and can be raised from seed if necessary. It is sometimes listed under its older name of isotoma. It's a member of the campanula family, and has masses of small, blue, star-shaped flowers. It forms a mound of blue blooms, ideal for baskets and patio containers.

Take cuttings in autumn to provide plants to store for winter; otherwise discard and raise fresh plants from seed.

Height: 9 in. (23cm).

### Varieties to look for
There are several: "Blue Stars" is a good seed-raised one, "Shooting Stars" is a pure white variety. "Fairy Carpet" is a variety usually raised from cuttings.

### Soil and site
Well-drained soil, in full sun.

### Propagation
Sow seed in warmth under glass in mid-winter. Can also be raised from cuttings, which can be taken in late summer or early autumn to provide plants to store for winter in a light, frost-free place.

# On the scent

*Stimulate the olfactory senses as well as the visual ones — it will add another dimension to your patio gardening. Be sure to add some night-scented plants, which often have the strongest perfume, to make sitting out on a summer evening even more enjoyable.*

Scent is perceived differently by different people. What may seem a delightful fragrance to one may be offensive to another. The detected strength of a fragrance also varies with the individual. Faint scents, like that of sweet alyssum (*Lobularia maritima*)

may be quite pronounced to one person, almost undetectable to another. Your choice of scented plants must be a matter of personal preference, but most of the plants suggested here have a strong and distinctive scent that the vast majority of gardeners should find attractive. The night-scented stock, honeysuckle, or a very fragrant rose, have almost universal appeal.

You should not plant too many fragrant flowers that bloom at the same time in close proximity. Choose a day-flowering and a night-scented plant to juxtapose, not two that will compete and mask each other's scents.

Fragrant foliage can be used more lavishly, as mostly the aroma is only released on contact, when you brush against the plant or deliberately squeeze a leaf.

Above: *Lonicera periclymenum.*
Center: *Melissa officinalis "Aurea."*
Top: *Lonicera periclymenum "Serotina."*

## Flowers to scent the air

### For spring
*Iris danfordiae*
*Matthiola incana* (Brompton stock)
*Cheiranthus cheiri* (wallflower)

### For summer days
*Lobularia maritima* (formerly *Alyssum maritimum*)
*Dianthus* (carnation and pink, some types)
*Lavandula* (lavender)
*Lilium* (some)
*Nicotiana alata* (ornamental tobacco, some types)
*Reseda odorata* (mignonette)
Roses (some types)

### For summer evenings
*Brugmansia* (formerly datura)
*Lonicera periclymenum* (honeysuckle)
*Nicotiana alata* (ornamental tobacco, some types)
*Matthiola bicornis* (night-scented stock)

### For winter
*Mahonia lomariifolia* (and hybrids such as "Charity")
*Sarcoccoca hookeriana* (Christmas box)
*Viburnum* x *bodnantense*

## Fragrant foliage
*Choisya ternata*
*Aloysia triphylla*, formerly *Lippia citriodora*
*Melissa officinalis* (lemon balm)
*Pelargoniums* (various types)
*Rosmarinus officinalis* (rosemary)
*Thymus* (thyme, most species)

Below: *Lilium* 'Little Girl'
Bottom: *Lysimachia nummularia.*

# Lilium

*Lily*

Many hybrid lilies can be used very successfully as patio plants, but bear in mind that they will have a short flowering season of perhaps a few weeks. It is best to grow them in their pots on a spare piece of ground, then bring them onto the patio to flower. Move them to a spare piece of ground to die down naturally after flowering.

Varieties as tall as 3 ft. (90cm) can be grown successfully in a large tub such as a half barrel without staking, but dwarf hybrids that grow to about 1–2 ft. (30–60cm) are more suited to small patio pots.

Water freely and feed regularly once buds start to form. Watch for greenfly and lily beetle, which may spread virus diseases as well as weakening or damaging the plants.
Height: 1–3 ft. (30–90cm).

### Varieties to look for

New varieties are introduced every year, so consult bulb catalogs for the latest varieties suitable for the patio. Examples of very compact varieties are "Mr. Ed," which is white and reaches 1½ ft. (45cm), and "Orange Pixie," which is pale orange and grows to 1 ft. (30cm).
Some of the scented species are very pleasing and can be

successful in a large tub, among them *L. longiflorum* with its huge white trumpets.

### Soil and site

Moisture-retentive, fertile soil, in full sun or partial shade. In pots any good potting soil is adequate, especially if the plants are fed. Good drainage is essential. Most hybrids are hardy in zone 5 or 6 or above.

### Propagation

For just a few extra plants, divide a large clump, but for many plants propagate from bulb scales.

# Lysimachia nummularia

*Creeping Jenny*

An extremely versatile evergreen or semi-evergreen trailer or ground cover. It will tolerate dry conditions, yet grows in damp soil and even in shallow water; it manages to put in a good show whether in full sun or shade. It will grow along the ground to provide ground cover or trail over the edge of a patio wall to produce a curtain of foliage and bright yellow flowers. It can be used effectively in baskets and any container that benefits from a cheerful trailer.

It will become straggly with age, so be prepared to cut back any stems that are not well clothed with leaves. As old plants can become sparse and new ones are easy to propagate, replant as often as necessary.
Height: 3 in. (7.5cm).

### Varieties to look for

The ordinary species has yellow flowers and green leaves. "Aurea" has golden flowers and foliage.

### Soil and site

Undemanding but best in moist soil, in full sun or partial shade. Zone 4.

### Propagation

Can be raised from seed or cuttings, but the easiest method is to divide plants growing along the ground, which root freely as they spread.

# Nepeta glechoma

*see Glechoma hederacea*

# Summer screens

*Annual climbers are unsuitable as screens where you want to mask something all year round, such as an ugly wall or fence, but many are ideal for a summer screen on the patio or other part of the garden where you might need the extra light after the plant dies in autumn.*

## Climbers to start under glass

Tender climbers have to be started in warm conditions and can be planted outdoors only when there is minimal risk of frost, and after gradual acclimatization. Most of them are well worth the effort, some being fast growers, others particularly beautiful.

*Cobaea scandens* (cathedral bells, cup-and-saucer vine)
Dense foliage cover; large blue or white flowers.

*Eccremocarpus scaber* (Chilean glory vine).
Thin foliage cover, but bright red, orange, or yellow flowers.

*Mina lobata*
Reasonable foliage cover. Very conspicuous flowers that shade from yellow to red, changing color as they mature. A plant that almost always attracts attention.

## Climbers to sow in situ

These no-fuss plants can be sown where they are to flower, but check the seed package for detailed instructions. Some are hardier than others and can be sown sooner.

*Humulus japonicus* (Japanese hop)
Leafy plant providing dense foliage cover. "Variegatus" is blotched and streaked white, and is more attractive. Flowers insignificant.

*Lathyrus odoratus* (sweet pea)
Modest foliage cover, but superb flowers. Popular for colors and scent.

*Tropaeolum majus* (nasturtium)
Dense foliage cover. Bright flowers, mainly in shades of yellow and orange.

*Tropaeolum peregrinum* (canary creeper)
Good foliage cover; bright yellow flowers.

**Above right:** *Cobaea scandens* usually has purple-blue flowers, but "Alba" is a white variety.

**Above:** The canary creeper (*Tropaeolum peregrinum*) is a quick-growing annual with plenty of foliage.

**Right:** *Mina lobata*, a striking climber that always catches the eye, is now more correctly called *Ipomoea lobata*.

71

# Blaze a bright trail

*Trailing plants are invaluable for hanging baskets and window boxes, but use them freely to soften the walls of raised beds, and to mask the edge of tubs.*

Many excellent trailers can be raised from seed, but some of the best have to be propagated from cuttings. Some of these, such as ivy-leaved and cascade pelargoniums, are easy to propagate and winter at home. Others, like Surfinia petunias and *Scaevola aemula*, are more difficult to maintain through winter without a suitably heated greenhouse, but they are readily available as plants from garden centers and by mail order in spring.

## Trailers from seed

*Fuchsia* "Florabelle"

*Hedera helix* (ivy), small-leaved
*Lobelia* (trailing)

*Pelargonium* (seed-raised cascading and trailing varieties such as "Breakaway" and "Summer Showers")

*Petunia* (Wave series, such as "Pink Wave" and "Purple Wave" – a seed-raised type similar to the Surfinias raised from cuttings)

*Silene pendula*

## Trailers from cuttings

*Fuchsias* (cascading types)

*Glechoma hederacea* "Variegata"

*Helichrysum petiolare*

*Lotus berthelotii*

*Lysimachia nummularia* "Aurea"

*Monopsis lutea*

*Pelargonium* (ivy-leaved and cascade types)

*Petunia* (Surfinia and Million Bells types)

*Plectranthus*

*Scaevola aemula*

*Verbena* (cascade types)

## Osteospermum
*Cape marigold, African daisy*

Evergreen, semi-woody perennials with large daisy-shaped flowers, in shades of pink, purple, yellow, and white. It is usually hybrids that are grown as container plants. They have a spreading habit of growth, so they are best in large tubs, and the display is often better in the second season.

Deadhead to prolong flowering. The hybrids mentioned will survive some frost, but in cold areas they are best given winter protection in a coldframe or greenhouse, or cuttings taken to winter in a greenhouse as an insurance against losses.

The plants described used to be listed as dimorphothecas. Height: 1½–2 ft. (45–60cm).

### Varieties to look for
"Buttermilk" is pale yellow, "Nairobi Purple" bright purple, "Polar Star" and "Weetwood" are good whites. There are also variegated varieties, such as "Golden Sparkler," with white flowers, and "Gweek," with pink flowers.

### Soil and site
Well-drained soil, in full sun. Zone 9.

### Propagation
Take cuttings of named varieties in late summer. Seed-raised plants should be sown in warmth under glass in spring.

## Pelargonium
*Bedding geranium*

Pelargoniums are indispensable patio plants: trailers are perfect for hanging baskets and window boxes, zonal pelargoniums are ideal for tubs and pots, in mixed plantings or used alone. See pages 78–79 for details of pelargonium types.

Although most will tolerate a slight frost, they should be lifted and moved to frost-free positions for the winter before the first frost occurs. Seed-raised varieties are usually discarded at the end of the season, but all can be wintered as cuttings rooted in late summer or autumn.

### Varieties to look for
See pages 78–79 for examples of popular varieties.

### Soil and site
Well-drained soil, in full sun or partial shade. Zone 10.

### Propagation
Take cuttings in spring or late summer and early autumn. Take them at the end of the season to store for winter as young plants; then the old ones can be discarded.

Many zonal pelargonium varieties are raised from seed – sow in mid or late winter in warmth under glass.

PATIO AND CONTAINER PLANTS

# Know your fuchsias

*Fuchsias are some of the most popular patio and garden flowers, but there are many different kinds and many hundreds of different varieties. The possibilities are even greater because they can also be trained into a variety of shapes, which is one reason that these are such collectable plants.*

Whether you want just a couple for a hanging basket or a collection of them for a border, fuchsias have lots to offer … not least a profusion of beautiful blooms from early summer until the first frost.

Fuchsias vary in their hardiness. Some will stand quite low winter temperatures and survive to grow another year, even though the top growth is killed. In mild areas where frosts are absent or not severe, these same plants will go on getting larger every year, and some make tall plants and beautiful flowering hedges. Others are best regarded as tender and kept in the greenhouse for the winter and placed outside only for the warmest months.

The other great joy about fuchsias is that they are so easy to propagate: you can root cuttings easily from spring to autumn with a high success rate. That means that, within a year or two, you will have as many fuchsias as you can probably accommodate, with plenty to pass on or to exchange with friends.

Bush-shaped fuchsias are easy to grow, but some of the trained forms, such as standards, take skill to train from a cutting.

## Hardy species

The most popular frost-tolerant species, which can be left outdoors down to hardiness zone 8, is *F. magellanica*. Although the purple-and-red flowers are small, it makes a bushy shrub to about 5 ft. (1.5m) in a season if cut down to ground level: it will grow much larger where it is not cut back. This is a superb plant for the shrub or mixed border, flowering for months until cut back by frost.

There are many good varieties of it, such as the variegated *F. m.* "Variegata" and "Versicolor." *F. m.* var *gracilis* has more pendulous growth but still grows to about 4 ft. (1.2m) or more. "Aurea" is a superb variety for a dull corner, where its yellow leaves always look refreshing.

## Hardy hybrids

"Riccartonii," a very free-flowering plant with scarlet tube and sepals and dark purple corolla, is sometimes listed as a variety of *F. magellanica*, but is now considered to be a hybrid. Two other old and very popular hardy hybrids are "Madame Cornelissen" with crimson tube and sepals, crimson corolla, semi-double flowers; and "Mrs. Popple" with scarlet tube and sepals, deep purple corolla, single flowers.

## Bedding hybrids

Most fuchsias can be used in the garden for the summer and brought in before the first frost. A good fuchsia catalog will indicate the type of growth habit and whether they make good bedding fuchsias.

Some of the *F. triphylla* hybrids, such as "Gartenmeister Bonstedt" with its orange flowers and dark, reddish foliage, are very effective with other summer bedding plants. This type of fuchsia is distinctive, with long tubes, short sepals, and a small single corolla.

## Home and greenhouse

Fuchsias flower well in a greenhouse; some will perform even better than if planted out-

Left: Large plants are worth keeping from year to year, pruning as new growth starts in spring. Pinching out the tips of young shoots to encourage bushy growth should be started soon after the cuttings root. They benefit from regular feeding in spring and summer.

doors, but they are best regarded as short-term house plants. The poor light and warm, dry atmosphere does not suit them and they generally deteriorate rapidly indoors. They do, however, make attractive conservatory plants where light and humidity are better.

## For the rock garden

There are a few really dwarf frost-tolerant varieties suitable for the rock garden and even for window boxes. "Tom Thumb" has red sepals with a mauve corolla and "Lady Thumb" has carmine pink sepals, and a white corolla veined pink. Both are popular varieties that grow to about 1½ ft. (45cm).

### JARGON BUSTER

**Bush** *This refers to the shape and not the size. The growth is upright rather than cascading, and much-branched, to create a rounded outline.*
**Calyx** *The group of four sepals.*
**Corolla** *The collection of true petals in front of the colored petal-like sepals. Depending on the number of petals, the flower is described as single, semi-double or double.*
**Pyramid** *A shape sometimes used for vigorous varieties, broad at the base and narrowing toward the top.*
**Sepal** *The colored, usually reflexed, petal-like growth at the back of the flower, emerging from the tube.*

Pyramid

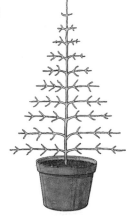

## Cascaders

Trailing varieties are ideal for hanging baskets, but they are also effective at the front of a large window box. Although a single specimen of an upright variety is sufficient in the center of a mixed basket, several trailers are best planted in a single-subject basket. Unless the basket is small, place about three plants around the edge, with the root-ball planted at an angle to encourage the shoots to cascade over the side.

There are many trailing varieties, but "Cascade" (white sepals flushed pink, deep crimson corolla) is one of the finest for baskets.

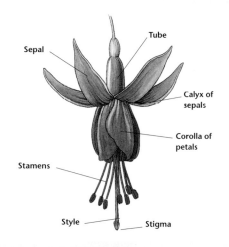

**Standard** *A plant with a long, straight stem without side-shoots, with the head of growth at the top. This can have bushy and upright growth or have a trailing habit if the variety is a trailer.*
**Trailer** *A plant with lax, arching growth that tends to cascade over the edge of the container.*
**Tube** *The tubular part of the flower between the flower stalk and the usually reflexed petal-like sepals.*

## Petunia

Seed-raised petunias have always been popular patio plants, but those raised from cuttings, such as the Surfinia range, are outstanding for baskets and containers of all kinds. They have spreading or trailing growth ideal for tumbling from a basket or over the edge of a patio wall, and they continue to bloom prolifically until cut back by frost.

Deadheading will help to prolong flowering. Discard at the end of the season – although surfinias are perennials they are difficult to maintain through winter in a heated greenhouse and it is better to buy fresh plants annually.

### Varieties to look for

Surfinia petunias (available in a range of colors) are outstanding but best bought as plants each year. There are also many superb seed-raised varieties that should not be overlooked. New ones are introduced annually, so study current catalogs for up-to-date varieties.

### Soil and site
Undemanding regarding soil, in full sun or partial shade. Zone 10.

### Propagation
Sow seed in warmth under glass in late winter or early spring.

## Scaevola aemula

A tender perennial trailing plant with usually violet-blue fan-shaped flowers, on long, trailing stems, suitable for hanging baskets, urns, or trailing over the edge of a raised patio bed.

Undemanding if fed and watered regularly throughout the summer. The plants require frost protection in winter, but as they become large after a summer's growth it is usually more convenient to take cuttings to store for winter. Height: trailing.

### Varieties to look for
They may not always be named and differences are usually minor, but "Blue Fan" and "Blue Wonder" are reliable varieties to look for. "Petite" has tiny, pale blue flowers.

### Soil and site
Moisture-retentive, fertile soil, in full sun or light shade. Any good potting soil will be adequate if kept well watered. (Zone 10.)

### Propagation
Take cuttings in spring or in late summer. The latter will provide small plants suitable for wintering in a frost-proof greenhouse or very sunny window sill.

# Sutera cordata "Snowflake"

This tender perennial is much more likely to be found under its old name of bacopa than as a sutera. Its small white flowers are uninspiring individually, but the trailing stems are covered with them, making the plant ideal for trailing over the edge of containers. Height: trailing.

## Varieties to look for
"Snowflake" is the only variety likely to be found.

## Soil and site
Moisture-retentive, fertile soil, in full sun. Zone 10.

## Propagation
Take cuttings in early spring, or in late summer to keep for winter in a frostproof greenhouse.

# Verbena

Seed-raised verbenas are discussed on page 33; the ones described here are raised from cuttings. Although many seed-raised varieties make excellent container plants, some of the vegetatively propagated kinds make bigger and bolder plants with a more robust and spreading habit – ideal for containers.

Colors are mainly pinks, blues, and purples, sometimes attractively shaded.

Although these hybrids will continue growing and flowering even in low temperatures at the end of the season, they are best regarded as tender. Lift and keep plants in a frost-free frame or greenhouse during winter, or take cuttings.

Height: 1 ft. (30cm)

## Varieties to look for
"Sissinghurst" is an outstanding pink variety; "Homestead Purple" a robust plant for planting in a mixed tub.

## Soil and site
Undemanding but best in well-drained soil in full sun. Zone 10.

## Propagation
Take cuttings in spring from wintered plants, or in late summer and early autumn for storing for winter in a light and frost-free place.

## USING VERBENAS
Seed-raised varieties are usually compact, bushy plants ideal for summer beds. They can be used in containers, especially window boxes and tubs, but are most useful for summer bedding schemes.

Many of those raised from cuttings are vigorous and spreading, and are best at the front of an herbaceous or mixed border or in a large tub.

Other verbenas, such as the Tapien range, have vigorous prostrate growth, and are suitable for hanging baskets or tumbling over the edge of patio tubs.

# Know your pelargoniums

*Pelargoniums, still sometimes called bedding geraniums, are an amazingly versatile group of plants.*

The zonal pelargoniums, cascading and ivy-leaved kinds, are indispensable summer bedding plants that flower prolifically even with minimal attention. The Regals make beautiful house plants, and scented-leaved species will bring a touch of spice and fragrance to your life indoors and out. You can even use the scented leaves of some kinds in the kitchen.

The pelargoniums most widely used for garden decoration are the zonals, which have a dark circular zone around the leaves. Usually they are grown for the sheer brilliance and abundance of their flowers, which bloom non-stop from early summer until the first frost (and even beyond if grown indoors). They are reasonably drought-resistant, which is another reason why they are good container plants.

Enthusiasts grow varieties that have to be raised from cuttings, but for massed bedding or containers, seed-raised varieties are usually used. These are relatively inexpensive to buy as plants in spring or early summer, and you can raise your own if you prefer. Where a large number are grown, it is normal to discard them at the end of the season to save the time, space, and trouble involved in attempting to keep them through winter. But you can take cuttings to winter in the greenhouse or on the window sill if you prefer.

You may find the seed-raised varieties listed as "geraniums" in seed catalogs. Sow them early so that they come into bloom in early summer rather than at the end of the season. New varieties are introduced every year, and they are constantly being improved, so consult current catalogs for the best of them.

There are also varieties of ivy-leaved and cascading pelargoniums that can be raised from seed. These used to be inferior to the type raised from cuttings, but modern varieties are well worth growing.

**Left: The Cascade or Balkon type of pelargoniums have tumbling growth and masses of flowers that almost hide the leaves. They are ideal for window boxes.**

## Focus on foliage

Although a dark zone on a green leaf is the typical leaf marking for bedding pelargoniums, there are varieties with golden or boldly variegated leaves that are grown mainly for foliage effect. These are often neglected, yet they look great massed in beds or as isolated plants in mixed containers.

There are dozens of highly desirable varieties, but tried and tested very old favorites include "Mrs. Quilter," yellowish leaves with bold brown zone and pink flowers; "Caroline Schmidt," green leaves edged white and red flowers; and "Mrs. H. Cox," a tricolor with zones in a range of colors.

## Fragrant foliage

Scented-leaved pelargoniums are often grown as potted plants for the home or sun room, but you can use them outdoors in the summer. They are not beautiful in flower, however, so use isolated plants here and there where you can brush against them or squeeze a leaf. You are more likely to do this if they are in a raised bed or a container.

"Lady Plymouth" is a popular variety to use outdoors because it's quite bushy and has citrus-scented cream-edged leaves. *P. crispum* "Variegatum" has prettily variegated, small, and crinkled lemon-scented leaves. For a very bushy plant, too large for a small container, try *P. graveolens*, the plant from which "oil of geranium" is extracted.

Left: Zonal pelargoniums make ideal bedding plants and do well even in very dry summers.

Below: Ivy-leaved pelargoniums are suitable for baskets, pots, and window boxes. This is "Rouletta."

There are dozens of varieties to experiment with. Some rose-scented, some spicy, while cedar, pine, peppermint, nutmeg, and orange are among the adjectives used to describe some of the other scents.

## JARGON BUSTER

**Angel** These are described as miniatures, but they will grow to 1½ ft. (45cm). They resemble Regals in leaf and flower shape, but both flowers and leaves are small.

**Cactus-flowered** Varieties with quilled and pointed petals, rather like those of spider chrysanthemums.

**Continental ivy-leaved** These are popular in many countries in mainland Europe, and are now widely grown elsewhere. They may be found listed under different names, such as Balkon, Decora, or Cascade types. The flowers are small, but they bloom prolifically.

**Double** A variety with eight or more petals.

**Finger-flowered** Similar to a Stellar, with narrow petals.

**Irene varieties** Varieties with semi-double flowers, bred for garden bedding.

**Ivy-leaved** Varieties of P. peltatum, with small, glossy, ivy-shaped leaves, and cascading growth.

**Regal or Martha Washington** These plants, with relatively large flowers in late spring and early summer, are varieties of P. x domesticum.

**Rosebud or Noisette varieties** Many-petalled varieties that can only open as far as a rosebud shape.

**Semi-double** A variety with five, six, or seven petals.

**Speckles** Varieties with flecked and speckled petals.

**Stellar** Varieties with star-shaped leaves and flowers, originally raised in Australia. Startel varieties are seed-raised, though you can take cuttings, of course.

**Tulip-flowered** The flowers never fully open, but stop when the petals have created a shape similar to a tulip.

**Unique** There are many different varieties, despite the generic name. They make quite large plants outdoors in summer. The flowers are small and slightly resemble a Regal. Some have aromatic leaves.

**Vari-petalled** A term used for varieties with multicolored flowers, striped, dotted, or edged with a different color.

**Zone** The circular darker-colored band on the leaf of zonal pelargoniums (P. x hortorum).

Left: Mini-cascade pelargoniums make good container plants, and are thriving in this cattle trough.

# Beautiful Border Perennials

Large borders devoted solely to herbaceous plants may be unfashionable except in very large gardens, but border plants are as desirable as ever.

If your garden is small, you may prefer to use herbaceous plants in a mixed border containing some shrubby plants and annuals, but if you have space for an island bed or a border of herbaceous plants you will be able to grow some of the most striking plants in the garden.

The term *border plants* rather than *herbaceous plants* is used here because not all plants used in such borders are truly herbaceous (in the sense that they die back to the ground for winter). There are non-woody evergreens, such as bergenias, hellebores, some irises and delightful plants like *Carex hachijoensis* "Evergold."

Indeed, it is a positive advantage to include a sprinkling of these plants to ensure some winter interest.

Some border plants can even be used in containers; others make pleasing ground cover in front of shrubs; a few – like red-hot pokers (kniphofia) or bear's breeches (acanthus) – can be used as isolated specimens to form focal points. There's always space somewhere for a few choice border plants.

# Features

Below left: *Acanthus mollis.*
Below middle: *Achillea "Coronation Gold."*
Bottom: *Alchemilla mollis.*
Right: *Anemone hybrida* (syn. *A. japonica*).

## Acanthus mollis
*Bear's breeches*

Striking semi-evergreen grown for its tall spikes of unusual white and purple hooded flowers in mid and late summer. Large wavy-edged leaves are also a feature.

Height: 4 ft. (1.2m).

### Other species
*Acanthus spinosus* is similar but the leaves are deeply cut and spiny.

### Soil and site
Deeply cultivated fertile soil, in full sun or partial shade. Zone 6.

### Propagation
Take root cuttings in winter, or sow seed in spring or summer.

### ● TIP TO TRY
Try cutting a few spikes for indoor decoration – they make a really stunning display.

### ●TIP TO TRY
Try cutting a few achillea heads for indoor decoration – they should last 7–10 days. Cut them when the florets are fully open, or when the majority of the florets on the cluster have opened. You can also dry them for winter decoration!

## Achillea filipendulina
*Yarrow*

Bold border plant, with flat heads of pale yellow flowers on tall stems from mid summer to early autumn, above feathery, divided foliage.

Height: 3–4 ft. (90–120cm).

### Varieties to look for
"Gold Plate" (deep yellow) and "Cloth of Gold" are the varieties

usually grown. The hybrid "Coronation Gold" (deep yellow but more compact) is another outstanding variety.

### Soil and site
Well-drained soil, in full sun. Zone 4.

### Propagation
Divide in spring.

## Alchemilla mollis
*Lady's mantle*

The pale green lobed leaves are an attractive feature from spring to autumn, especially when droplets of rain or dew are captured on the hairy surface. The sprays of small yellow-green flowers from early to late summer are surprisingly attractive for their size.

Useful as individual border plants, but also an attractive summer ground cover. This charming plant will self-seed freely… sometimes into

unlikely places, such as crevices in paving. Despite self-seeding it is not invasive and is easy to control.

Height: 1 ft. (45cm).

### Similar species
There are kinds that are more dwarf for rock gardens, but they lack the impact of *A. mollis.*

### Soil and site
Well-drained but moisture-retentive soil, in sun or partial shade. Zone 4.

### Propagation
Divide in autumn or early spring, or sow seed in spring.

### DID YOU KNOW?
The "flowers" are actually yellow-green calyces and not proper petals…but you wouldn't know unless you examine the plants with a magnifying glass.

## Anemone hybrida (syn. A. japonica)

Late-flowering plants to enhance the border between late summer and mid autumn. White and pink are the dominant colors, most with single flowers but some are doubles. Height 2–4 ft. (75–120cm).

### Varieties to look for

Nomenclature is confused: some varieties of *A. x hybrida* are distributed as *A. japonica*, but *A. hupehensis* varieties are similar and some varieties may be listed under that name. The varietal name should, however, enable a particular one to be tracked down. Good performers are *A. hupehensis* var. *japonica* "Bressingham Glow" (rosy-red semi-double); *A. h. j.* "September Charm" (rose-pink); *A. x hybrida* "Honorine Jobert" (single white); and *A. x h.* "Königin Charlotte", syn. "Queen Charlotte" (semi-double pink).

### Soil and site

Fertile, moisture-retentive soil, preferably in partial shade though full sun is tolerated. Zone 6.

### Propagation

Divide in early spring, or take root cuttings in winter.

## Aquilegia
*Columbine*

Cottage-garden plants with distinctive, spurred flowers in a wide range of colors. The hybrids, flowering in late spring and early summer, are the most widely grown.
   Height: 2–3 ft. (60–90cm).

### Varieties to look for

"McKanna Hybrids" and "Mrs. Scott Elliott Hybrids" both have very long spurs and a good range of contrasting colors.

### Soil and site

Moisture-retentive soil, in sun or partial shade. Zone 3.

## Propagation

Divide plants in early spring or autumn, or sow seed in mid or late summer.

## Aster novi-belgii
*Michaelmas daisy*

Invaluable autumn-flowering plants with daisy-like flowers in many shades of blue, pink, red, and white. Unlike the tall Michaelmas daisies that are varieties of *A. novae-angliae*, along with some of the *A. novi-belgii* varieties, these are much more compact with most in the 2–3 ft. (60–90cm) range, and dwarfs about 1–1½ ft. (30–45cm), making them more

useful plants for a small border. Water in very dry weather, and watch for mildew which is a major problem for these plants in some gardens. Tall varieties require staking.
   Height: 1–4 ft. (30–120cm).

### Varieties to look for

There are hundreds of varieties. Reliable ones include "Audrey," semi-double, pale blue, 1 ft. (30cm); "Fellowship," semi-double, pink, 4 ft. (1.2m); "Jenny," double, rose-red, 1½ ft. (45cm); "Lady in Blue," semi-double, blue, 1 ft. (30cm); and "Little Pink Beauty," clear pink, 15 in. (38cm).

### Soil and site

Well-drained but moisture-retentive soil, in full sun. Zone 2.

### Propagation

Divide or take cuttings in early spring, or divide in autumn after flowering.

# Mixed borders

*Where space is limited, a mixed border with both shrubs and border plants makes sense. You can choose the best of both to create a border with a long period of interest, and there is more scope for some super plant combinations.*

A mixed border always has a structure, even in winter and if most of the shrubs are deciduous. Woody plants provide height and shape, and there even may be small patches of color from those that flower in winter. With early bulbs and perhaps winter-flowering hellebores, and the brave *Iris unguicularis*, the border should not look totally bleak even through the coldest months.

### Designing a mixed border

The best mixed borders appear well-integrated, with plants of different kinds blending together. Try to avoid positioning a row of shrubs at the back with the border plants in front: that's just what it will look like.

Use some tall border plants toward the back, like red-hot poker with its stiff orange and yellow poker spikes, and *Crambe cordifolia,* which will create a cloud of white like a giant gypsophila above the other plants. Use a few small shrubs like *Caryopteris x clandondensis*, hardy plumbagos (ceratostigmas), shrubby potentillas, and Russian sage (*Perovskia atriplicifolia*) toward the front of the border. Sun roses (helianthemum) can be placed at the front edge of the border.

If the border is a large one, almost any shrub or border plant can be used, but where space is at a premium, perhaps in a small border, choose plants that integrate well. Place the emphasis on shrubs that look as though they could almost be herbaceous plants, like perovskias and shrubby peonies, and use border plants that will stand their ground against the woody and usually more dominant shrubs.

The suggestions given here are a good starting point, but you will want to include your own favorites.

Don't overlook the importance of foliage. Choose shrubs with bright or interesting foliage rather than those with dull leaves. A golden *Philadelphus coronarius* "Aureus" will make a bright background early in the year, though the color deteriorates as the season progresses; and by cutting out one third of the oldest stems each year after flowering you can restrain its height. The golden privet (*Ligustrum vulgare* "Aureum") serves a similar purpose and can be kept compact by regular pruning.

Gray-leaved *Brachyglottis* and B. *"Sunshine"* (both formerly *Senecio*) look tasteful in a mixed border, and their yellow daisy flowers do not look out of place. A clump of the low-growing *Pachysandra terminalis* "Variegata" can be used to bring a bit of relief to a dull spot within the shade of a taller shrub.

**Left: Mixing different kinds of plants can create a border that looks surprisingly natural. Here the plants include foxgloves (*Digitalis purpurea*), primulas, an acer, and meconopsis.**

## Good shrubs for a mixed border

*Brachyglottis grayii* formerly *Senecio grayii*
Gray foliage, yellow daisy flowers. Evergreen.

*Calluna*
Heather, needs acid soil. Evergreen.

*Caryopteris* x *clandonensis*
Blue flowers above gray leaves. Does well on chalky soils.

*Ceratostigma willmottianum*
Bright blue flowers from late summer.

*Choisya ternata* "Sundance"
Yellow evergreen foliage, white flowers in late spring.

*Cistus*
There are several kinds, varying in height, with bright single white, pink, red, or purple flowers in early summer. Evergreen.

*Cornus alba* "Sibirica"
Red winter stems.

*Cornus stolonifera* "Flaviramea"
Yellow winter stems.

*Cytisus*
There are several small brooms, such as *C. x kewensis* and *C. x praecox* "Allgold," that are low-growing and covered with yellow flowers in spring.

*Daphne mezereum*
Purplish flowers in late winter and early spring.

*Erica carnea*
Winter-flowering heather. Evergreen.

**Right: Don't be afraid to use bold plants. These red Oriental poppies (*Papaver orientalis*) blend surprisingly well with the stiff spikes of the red-hot pokers (kniphofia).**

**Opposite top: This very attractive mixed planting includes lavenders, crocosmias, and geraniums.**

**Left: This tuberous red dahlia has to be lifted and replanted annually, but it blends perfectly with the herbaceous plants.**

*Fargesia murieliae* formerly *Arundinaria murieliae*
A bamboo with yellow stems. Evergreen.

*Hebe*
There are many kinds, most forming a neat mound of growth. Some are not very hardy, so check with your supplier which are likely to survive where you live. Evergreen.

*Helianthemum nummularium*
Low-growing and covered with a mass of red, pink, or yellow flowers in late spring and early summer. Evergreen.

*Hypericum moserianum* "Tricolor"
Variegated and multicolored leaves, yellow flowers.

*Lavandula*
There are many lavenders, all compact enough for a mixed border.

*Ligustrum vulgare* "Aureum"
The golden privet. Evergreen.

*Pachysandra terminalis* "Variegata"
Low-growing ground cover for shade. Variegated evergreen.

*Paeonia suffruticosa* (tree peony)
Peony-shaped flowers on large, woody plants.

*Perovskia atriplicifolia*
Blue flowers in late summer and early autumn, gray leaves.

*Philadelphus coronarius* "Aureus"
Yellow leaves in spring and early summer. Needs regular pruning to remain compact for a border.

*Phloemis fruticosa*
Yellow flowers. Gray-green evergreen.

*Phormium*
There are many hybrids with attractively variegated sword-like leaves, but check hardiness in your area. Evergreen.

*Pleioblastus auricomus* formerly *Arundinaria viridistriata*
An outstanding low-growing bamboo with green and yellow variegated evergreen leaves.

*Potentilla fruticosa*
Mounds of yellow or orange flowers for months in summer.

*Rosemarinus officinalis*
Blue flowers in spring. Aromatic gray-green evergeen foliage.

*Santolina chamaecyparissus*
Dwarf shrub with gray foliage and yellow flowers in summer. Evergreen.

# Know your carnations and pinks

*Carnations and pinks are famed for their scent as well as their beauty, and no traditional herbaceous border is complete without them. There are many kinds, however, and some are more suitable for the border than others.*

Carnations and pinks can be grown in most gardens, but they do particularly well in alkaline (chalky) soils. If the ground is on the acid side of neutral, it's worth adding limestone in the planting area to make it more alkaline.

## Border carnations

These are derived from *Dianthus caryophyllus*, and generally have a relatively short peak of flower in mid summer, though a few blooms will continue to be produced until the end of summer. The flowers are usually heavily scented, and normally self-colored though some are picotees (petals outlined in a darker color). Unfortunately they require staking to keep the flowering stems upright.

Above: Some pinks, like this one from the Allwoodii Alpinus group, can be used in the rock garden or toward the front of a border.

Left: Border carnations mix well with other summer flowers, and here are being grown with cosmos.

Below: "Doris" is one of the best-known modern pinks, an outstanding plant that blooms reliably and prolifically over a long period.

## Old-fashioned (Old World) pinks

These are believed to be descended, at least in part, from *Dianthus plumarius*. There are selfs (single colors), bicolors (outer zone one color, the eye or central zone a different one), laced (central zone extended to form a loop around the edge of each petal), and fancies (irregular markings).

Old-fashioned pinks flower in early summer so the season is short in comparison with modern pinks, but the scent is usually strong.

## Modern pinks

These originated with crosses between the old-fashioned pink and perpetual-flowering carnations (which flower over a long period but are generally regarded as greenhouse plants). In flowering terms these are an improvement on the old-fashioned pinks, as they bloom during early and mid summer and often again in early autumn.

They come in all the same forms as old-fashioned pinks.

## Astilbe hybrids

The plants most often grown for their decorative plumes of red, pink, or white summer flowers are mainly hybrids of *A. x arendsii* and *A. chinensis*. The ferny foliage makes an attractive backdrop for the long-lasting flowers. Water freely in dry weather, and mulch to conserve moisture.

Height: 1–3 ft. (30–90cm).

### Varieties to look for

"Fanal," deep red, 1½ ft. (45cm), and "Sprite," pink, 1 ft. (30cm) are some of the best of the larger varieties. *A. chinensis* var. *pumila*, 9–12 in. (23–30cm) makes an attractive drift of raspberry-red flowers over a long period.

### Soil and site

Moist soil, in shade or partial shade. Zone 6.

### Propagation

Divide in early or mid spring.

## Bergenia
*Elephant ears*

One of the few non-woody evergreens that's really showy all year round. The large, leathery leaves make an excellent ground cover; with some varieties they turn an attractive purple-red in winter. Showy pink or white flowers appear in early spring, with the occasional flower at other times.

Height: 1–1½ ft. (30–45cm).

### Species and hybrids

Two particularly reliable species are *B. cordifolia* "Purpurea" with red flowers and purple-tinted winter foliage, and *B. purpurascens* with dark green leaves that turn red in winter, and red flowers. "Bressingham White" has pure white flowers and "Silberlicht" (syn. "Silverlight") has white flowers, sometimes pink. All are attractive hybrids.

### Soil and site

Undemanding regarding soil, in sun or partial shade. Will even tolerate full shade, though flowering will suffer. Zone 4.

### Propagation

Divide in spring or autumn.

## Chrysanthemum maximum
*see Leucanthemum x superbum*

## Delphinium

Traditional back-of-border plant, grown for its blue flower spikes, though there are also creamy-yellow varieties. The varieties grown as border plants are usually hybrids that flower in early and mid summer. Tall varieties require staking.

Height: 5–8 ft. (1.5–2.4m).

### Varieties to look for

There are lots of varieties, many stocked by just a few nurseries. For good varieties, consult the catalogs of delphinium specialists. The Belladonna group varieties are shorter: 3–5 ft. (1–1.5m) and more branched.

### Soil and site

Deeply-dug fertile soil, in full sun. A sheltered site is beneficial. Zone 3.

### Propagation

Cuttings from the base of the plant in mid spring, or division in early or mid spring. Seed-raised varieties are easy and mixtures are easy to germinate.

## ●TIP TO TRY

Astilbes can be used as short-term house plants. Try potting one in spring and growing in a temperature of at least 50°F (10°C), in good light. Keep the soil moist at all times. Plant outdoors again when flowering is over.

# Variety through variegation

*Attractive variegated plants are much rarer in herbaceous perennials than among shrubs, so you may have to search harder for suitable plants. They are best used sparingly to break up what might otherwise be dull areas of the border.*

When the flowers have finished, too many variegated plants too close to each other look odd. It's better to have a bold splash of one variegated plant, with perhaps three or more specimens together, than three different kinds in close proximity.

The list given here provides suggestions for what to grow as punctuation points in the border, but keep your eyes open for others. Remember that you can use plants like variegated phormiums and even yuccas to great effect, even if they are not herbaceous plants. Also included in the lists of suggested plants are some grasses, bamboo, and sedges. These look pleasing in any herbaceous or mixed border, retaining their shape and structure during the cold months.

Right: Foliage can create dramatic effects, like this *Hakonechloa macra* "Alboaurea" and *Hosta* "Halcyon."

Below: Hostas are among the best variegated herbaceous plants. This one is *Hosta ventricosa* var. *aureomaculata*.

## Make a splash with variegated foliage

These are just some of the variegated foliage plants suitable for herbaceous or mixed borders. Some of them are readily available; others you may have to search out or send for by mail order.

*Acorus gramineus* "Ogon"
Rush-like, with green and gold bands along the length of the evergreen leaves.

*Ajuga reptans*
Bugle is a ground cover with blue flowers, but it's usually grown for its colored, variegated foliage. Best grown as a drift at the front of a border. "Variegata" has gray-green and cream leaves, but there are varieties with reddish-purple foliage ("Atropurpurea"), and bronze and red leaves ("Multicolor"). Evergreen.

*Carex hachijoensis* "Evergold"
A sedge with evergreen grass-like foliage longitudinally striped yellow and green.

*Erysimum linifolium* "Variegatum" formerly *Cheiranthus*
A variegated form of perennial wallflower, with cream-variegated leaves topped by lilac flowers.

*Convallaria majalis* "Variegata"
A variegated lily-of-the-valley. Grow it as a carpet at the front of the border. The fragrant flowers appear in mid and late spring.

*Hosta*
Perhaps the most popular variegated border plant. See Know Your Hostas, page 91.

*Houttuynia cordata* "Chameleon"
An amazingly versatile plant that will grow in water or boggy ground, yet still perform well in a border or container. The green, cream, and red variegation makes it one of the best variegated plants for the front of a border.

*Iris pallida* "Variegata"
Sword-shaped upright evergreen leaves edged white. Blue flowers in summer.

*Lamium galeobdolon* "Hermann's Pride"
A non-invasive deadnettle, with silver-and-green finely patterned leaves. Useful for shade.

*Liriope muscari* "Variegata"
One of several variegated varieties of this useful evergreen, with blue flowers in autumn.

*Phlox paniculata* "Norah Leigh"
Unlike most border phlox, this is grown for its variegated foliage rather than its pink flowers. "Harlequin" is another variegated variety, this time with bolder purple flowers.

*Polemonium caeruleum* "Brise d'Anjou"
An outstanding Jacob's ladder, with yellow-edged leaves, topped by violet-blue flowers in summer. Best in shade or partial shade.

*Pulmonaria saccharata*
The spotted leaves of this lungwort look best in spring. There are several good varieties with spring flowers in shades of blue and pink.

*Saxifraga* "Aureopunctata" (syn. *S. umbrosa* "Variegata")
Low-growing rosettes of yellow-variegated evergreen leaves. Sprays of small pink flowers in late spring and early summer.

## Striped grasses

Variegated grasses are especially useful because they bring a different kind of "texture" to the border, often being tall and spiky. These are all striking in a border:

*Cortaderia selloana* "Aureolineata" (syn. "Gold Band")
A tall grass with yellow-variegated leaves and large silvery flower plumes in autumn.

*Hakonechloa macra* "Alboaurea"
A low-growing grass with green-striped yellow leaves that appear to cascade.

*Miscanthus sinensis* 'Zebrinus'
A tall grass with distinctive horizontal yellowish-white bands. Striking fan-shaped flowerheads in autumn.

Opposite: There are even variegated grasses for the border, like *Miscanthus sinensis* "Zebrinus."

Left: Try *Houttuynia cordata* "Chameleon" where you want really striking low-growing variegated foliage.

Below left: *Dicentra spectabilis.*
Right: *Euphorbia griffithii* 'Fern Cottage."
Bottom: *Echinops ritro.*

## Dicentra spectabilis
*Bleeding heart*

Locket-shaped flowers above attractive ferny foliage make this a popular border plant for late spring and early summer. The flowers are normally pink and white, but "Alba" is all white. *D. spectabilis* dies down by mid summer.

Height: 1–1½ ft. (30–45cm).

### Other species
*Dicentra formosa,* with bright green leaves and narrower pink flowers, and *D. eximia,* with gray-green foliage, are similar, and there are superb hybrids, such as "Luxuriant" and "Stuart Boothman."

### Soil and site
Well-drained, but humus-rich soil, in partial shade. Zone 6.

### Propagation
Divide in late winter, while the plants are still dormant.

### DID YOU KNOW?
The common name of bleeding heart alludes to the locket-shaped pink or red flowers.

## Echinops ritro
*Globe thistle*

Although not a true thistle, this striking plant has thistle-like leaves and flowers. The gray-green foliage is not spiny despite its appearance. The drumstick thistle-like purplish-blue flowerheads appear in late summer.

Height: 4 ft. (1.2m).

### Other species
Some varieties distributed as *E. ritro* are considered by experts to be more correctly *Echinops bannaticus* – the popular "Taplow Blue" is an example.

### Soil and site
Well-drained soil, in full sun. Zone 3.

### Propagation
Divide in early spring or autumn, or take root cuttings in winter.

## Euphorbia griffithii

One of many spurges suitable for the border. The orange-flame "flowers" are at their best in late spring and early summer.

Height: 2½ ft. (75cm).

### Other species
*Euphorbia polychroma* (syn. *E. epithymoides*) is another desirable border species, with bright green leaves and heads of yellow bracts in mid and late spring.

### Soil and site
Well-drained soil, in full sun. Zone 5.

### Propagation
Take cuttings from the base of the plant in spring.

### DID YOU KNOW?
The red or yellow "flowers" on these plants are really modified leaves called bracts – just like small versions of the red bracts on the popular poinsettia, which is also a kind of euphorbia. The true flowers are small and insignificant.

Bracts can be as colorful as flowers and are often longer lasting.

# Know your hostas

Below left: One of the most widely grown variegated hostas is *H. undulata albomarginata*, better known as "Thomas Hogg," which is undemanding and easy to grow.

*Hostas have a huge following, and there are societies for enthusiasts to join. But most gardeners recognize them simply as some of the best foliage plants for the border.*

There are many hundreds of varieties, and those described here are just a small selection.

It is the sheer versatility of this group of plants that fascinates many gardeners, as well as their handsome foliage. They will grow in shade (even under trees) or in full sun. They thrive in moist ground but will tolerate very dry conditions too. They make ideal border plants; small ones are suitable for the rock garden, and they make impressive container plants. Flower arrangers love the foliage too. The Japanese even eat the leaf stalks!

### Big leaves

There are some big hostas, best planted where there is space to show them off. *Hosta sieboldiana* grows to about 3 ft. (90cm), and has an even bigger spread. The heart-shaped leaves are puckered, deeply ribbed, and are bluish-gray but tend to turn a dull green in full sun. *H. sieboldiana elegans* has even larger leaves, usually bluer in color.

"Krossa Regal" is smaller but still stately in stature, growing to about 2½ft. (75cm). The slightly wavy-edged leaves form a dense, arching clump.

"Royal Standard" (rich green) and *H. sieboldiana* "Bressingham Blue" (blue-green) both grow to about 3 ft. (90cm) and make a bold statement in the border, while "Big Daddy" grows to about 2½ft. (75cm).

### Small leaves

"Ginko Craig" has small, lance-shaped leaves, edged white, and grows to about 10 in. (25cm). Its strong horizontal growth and low height make it an effective ground cover.

Smaller is *H. tardiflora*, with lance-shaped leathery leaves about 6 in. (15cm) long. It makes a plant about 10 in. (25cm) tall.

Even tinier, for the rock garden rather than the herbaceous border, is *H. venusta*, which has leaves only about 1 in. (2.5cm) long!

### Blue leaves

You have to use a little imagination here, but in comparison with the green varieties, these definitely do look blue. Varieties to look for include "Big Daddy," "Blue Moon," "Bressingham Blue," and "Hadspen Blue."

### Golden leaves

There are fewer varieties with all-gold leaves than with gold variegation, and they can be more difficult to place. Impressive varieties include "Sun Power," "Midas Touch," and "Zounds" (the puckered foliage of the last two tolerates sun better than most yellows).

Some reliable variegated varieties are almost all gold, so should also be considered here. *H. fortunei* "Gold Standard" is delicately edged dark green, but the dominant impression is of a golden variety, and it's first-rate.

### Variegated leaves

There's a huge range of hostas with variegated foliage and they come in all sizes; you could fill a garden with them. Some of the popular varieties that have stood the test of time are: *H. undulata unvivittata* with a white central splash; "Shade Fanfare" with a broad creamy-yellow edge; and *H. undulata albomarginata*, which has a broad cream edge.

### Fragrant flowers

Usually flowers are a secondary feature of hostas but some, such as "Honeybells," are worth growing for their flowers alone.

Many are pleasantly fragrant including "Honeybells," *H. plantaginea* and hybrids such as "Royal Standard," "Sugar and Cream," and "Summer Fragrance."

Below left: *Geranium endresii.*
Bottom: *Helenium autumnale.*

## Geranium endressii

One of dozens of excellent border geraniums, this one is a pretty semi-evergreen suitable for ground cover. The rose-pink flowers are borne throughout summer.

Height: 1½ ft. (45cm).

### Varieties to look for
"Wargrave Pink" is often sold as a variety of *G. endressii*, but botanists now consider it a variety of *G.x oxonianum*. Whatever it's sold as, it is a first-rate plant. Look also for "A. T. Johnson" with pink flowers tinged silver. *Geranium endressii album* has white flowers, which look best in a shady position.

### Soil and site
Undemanding regarding soil, but best in sun or partial shade. Zone 5.

### Propagation
Divide in spring.

## Helenium autumnale
*Sneezeweed*

Late-flowering mid-border plants. Although there are dwarf varieties, most grow tall and will require staking, especially in an exposed position. Flowering time is between late summer and mid autumn.

Height: 3–4 ft. (90–120cm).

### Varieties to look for
"Butterpat" is a popular yellow, while "Moerheim Beauty" is an orange-red.

### Soil and site
Undemanding regarding soil, but best in full sun. Zone 3.

### Propagation
Divide in early spring or late autumn.

## Helleborus niger
*Christmas rose*

Not a true rose, of course, but the white flowers resemble a single wild rose in shape. The leaves are evergreen, but when the flowers appear depends on the severity of the winter. They bloom any time from early winter to early spring. If flowers are required for cutting, protect them with a covering.

Height: 1 ft. (30cm).

### Other species
*Helleborus viridis*, the green hellebore, flowers in late winter and early spring, with the purple, pink, or white *H. orientalis*, the Lenten rose, usually blooming in late winter but sometimes earlier. Green-flowered hellebores are very pleasing and surprisingly bright when flowering in late winter and spring. Good ones to try include H. viridis and H. foetidus, the striking hellebore.

### Soil and site
Well-drained but moisture-retentive soil, in partial shade. Zone 3.

### Propagation
Divide in spring, or sow seed in early or mid summer.

● **TIP TO TRY**
Cut a few Christmas roses to decorate the home. Although they will only have short stalks, they look pretty in a small arrangement, or simply floated on water. They will last up to a week if cut soon after opening.

# Using evergreens

*Your borders will look attractive and interesting all winter long if you include a few evergreen border plants.*

The number of non-woody evergreens is fairly small, but the ones suggested here are just a few of those available. Next time you're shopping for border plants, keep an eye open for plants that retain their foliage through winter.

Don't space out the evergreens around the border so that they remain as isolated plants when the rest die down in autumn. Arrange them in several groups to create pockets of winter interest.

Remember that some ferns are evergreen too (see page 97).

### Green
*Acanthus*
*Bergenia*
*Epimedium* (various)
*Helleborus* (many, some winter-flowering)
*Iris unguicularis* syn. *I. stylosa* (winter flowering)
*Liriope muscari*
*Persicaria affinis* formerly *Polygonum affine*
*Sisyrinchium striatum*

### Gold
*Acorus gramineus* "Ogon"
*Carex hachijoensis* "Evergold"

### Gray
*Dianthus* (carnation and pink)

### Reds/purples
*Ajuga* (various)
*Bergenia* (varieties that color in winter, such as "Bressingham Ruby")
*Euphorbia amygdaloides* "Purpurea" (syn. "Rubra")
*Heuchera* "Palace Purple"
*Ophiopogon planiscapus* "Nigrescens" (almost black leaves)

Above: The leaves of some bergenias turn reddish in winter, like "Sunningdale," seen here among winter heathers. Bergenias are especially useful because they have attractive flowers in spring as well as bold evergreen foliage.

Left: Some interesting euphorbias are evergreen, among them *E. amygdaloides* "Purpurea," sometimes sold under the name "Rubra." It makes a valuable contribution to the border the year round.

Far left: Bergenia growing round the base of a stone container planted with helichrysum.

# Fantastic foliage

*A foliage plant will be attractive for at least six months of the year, a claim that can be made for few flowering plants. Bold foliage plants will also bring a different kind of visual "texture" to your borders, and can act as a visual link to hold together the design as the more transient flowers come and go.*

The beauty and seemingly endless variation of leaf shapes, patterns, and colors, make them vitally important as garden features. Variegation is discussed on page 88–89, and hostas, which have an amazing range of texture, shape, and color, are featured on page 91. Ferns, which are among the most fascinating plants to study for symmetry and beauty of leaf form, are discussed on page 97. The plants described here are just a few of the many grown for color, texture, or size.

## Color

Gray is not the drab color it sounds – at least not in horticultural terms. It helps to break up bright colors, and is often a refreshing change from the multitude of greens.

Verbascums can be dramatic in leaf and flower. Many, like *V. bombyciferum*, are biennial and in the first year grow a handsome rosette of large gray leaves, the spike of yellow flowers being produced in the second season.

There are many silver-leaved border plants among the artemisias, and they grow in an attractive and symmetrical way that always makes for a neat-looking plant. Among the popular species are *A. ludoviciana* and *A.* "Powis Castle."

Black leaves sound particularly unattractive, yet the very dark grassy leaves of

*Ophiopogon planiscapus* "Nigrescens" obviously hold a fascination, judging by the number of them planted.

Dark purples and reds are also attractive. *Euphorbia amygdaloides* "Purpurea" (syn. "Rubra") makes a vivid show with maroon stems and dark evergreen foliage. *Heuchera micrantha* var. *diversifolia* "Palace Purple" is another evergreen with very dark leaves.

## Texture

The popular lady's mantle (*Alchemilla mollis*) always delights with its ability to hold rain or dew in large drops on the surface of its hairy pale-green leaves.

The woolly silvery leaves of *Stachys byzantina* (syn. *S. lanata*) have a felted texture and a special fascination.

Feathery and fern-like leaves contribute their own sense of texture to the border,

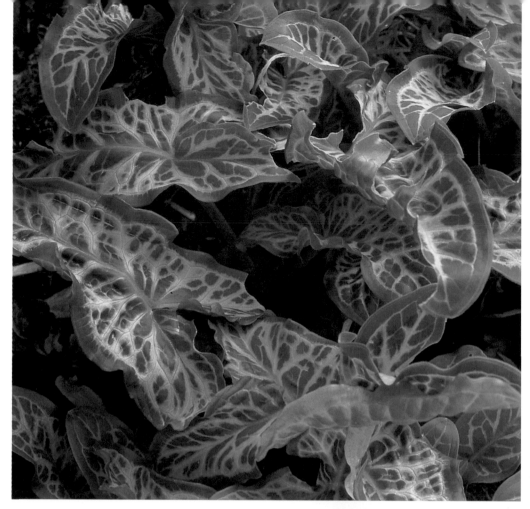

**Right:** *Arum italicum* is full of interest. In winter there are wonderfully variegated leaves, with strange green or creamy-white flower spathes to look forward to in spring, followed by spikes of red berries in autumn.

especially if there's a mass of the foliage. Bleeding hearts (dicentras) are particularly attractive in late spring and early summer when the pink, red, or white locket-shaped flowers dance above the soft, divided foliage, but long after the flowers have died the mat of frond-like foliage will continue to please.

## Size and shape

The rodgersias need a damp position out of full sun to do really well, but you can grow them in the herbaceous or mixed border if you keep the roots moist. They are worth the effort. The palmate (hand-shaped) leaves are big and well displayed. Two imposing species are *Rodgersia aesculifolia* and *R. podophylla*. Sprays of white or pinkish flowers are a bonus.

Even bigger and bolder, but again demanding moist shade to do well, is *Astilboides tabularis* (formerly *Rodgersia*

*tabularis*), with circular leaves almost 3 ft. (90cm) across and seeming to perch on the centrally placed stalk like a plate balancing on a stick in a circus act.

Acanthus leaves were depicted in classical architecture, which gives an indication of their worth. The heavily indented leaves of *Acanthus. mollis* are up to 2 ft. (60cm) long; those of *A. spinosus* have wickedly sharp spines. The leaves are almost evergreen, a useful bonus.

Bergenias have thick leathery evergreen leaves that make an impenetrable ground cover. They are grown as much for their pink, red, or white spring flowers as for their foliage, but the leaves of many varieties turn reddish or purple in winter – they look superb in winter sunshine or in juxtaposition with plants like green-flowered hellebores – two that come to mind are *Helleborus viridis* and *H. foetidus*.

If you have a shady position where you can grow a trillium or two, you'll not only have striking white or purple three-petaled

flowers in spring, but a plant with leaves distinctively arranged in threes.

## Interesting patterns

Leaves that are attractively marbled are usually eye-catching, and if they also have a distinctive arrow-head shape like *Arum italicum*, they make even more desirable border plants. The white-veined leaves are followed by green or creamy-white flower spathes, then in autumn by a spike of red berries.

**Opposite left:** Rodgersias do best in moist soil with some shade. Here *R. podophylla* is showing off its "architectural" merits by flanking a flight of steps.

**Opposite right:** The rosettes of woolly gray foliage of many verbascums are reason enough to grow these plants, but the flowers are striking too. This is *V. bombyciferum*.

**Left:** These are two foliage plants for a moist position with some shade. *Rodgersia aesculifolia* is backed by *Rheum palmatum*, which will have a tall and dramatic flower spike.

# Big and bold

*Every garden needs at least a couple of big or bold plants to act as focal points or as "statements" within a border.*

Bold plants act as punctuation points that arrest the eye and prevent the border from being taken for granted. In a large garden they help to tie the garden together visually.

## Feathers and plumes

A focal point plant does not have to be bright and colorful. Sometimes sheer size is enough, and in a shaded area a white plant can be more conspicuous than a colored one.

The goat's beard or *Aruncus dioicus* (formerly *A. sylvestris*) looks like a large white spiraea. Individual flowers are tiny, but the plumes are big and bold, and reach 6 ft. (1.8m). They stand out well with dark trees or shrubs in the background. This is a plant for a big garden, where its mid summer flowers and large leaves help to fill up a space.

The 6 ft. (1.8m) plumes of *Macleaya microcarpa* and *M. cordata* are pinkish-buff, so a lighter background is needed as a backdrop.

The visual effect of *Crambe cordifolia* is more cloud-like but no less imposing. The small white flowers are fragrant, but the first thing you notice is the hazy mound of white, about 6 ft. (1.8m) tall and almost as much across. It looks like a giant gypsophila.

## Imposing grasses

The pampas grass in its various forms and varieties is perhaps the best-known of the large grasses. *Cortaderia selloana* will send its silvery-white plumes up to 7 ft. (2.1m), and as the evergreen clump gradually expands in girth this is not a plant to go unnoticed. It is often planted in isolation, but can look rather stark. Placing it in a border means the base is masked by more interesting plants. If that's too tall, "Pumila" is a more compact variety to try.

*Arundo donax* is another giant, only suitable for the back of a large border, and this time grown for foliage effect only. Sometimes called the giant reed, it grows up to 20 ft. (6m) where conditions suit it.

**Above: The towering yellow spikes of the aptly-named** *Ligularia* **"The Rocket" seldom fail to impress.**

**Left: The large umbrella-like leaves of** *Gunnera tinctoria* **(syn.** *G. chiliensis***) make a superb focal point.**

A more realistic option for most gardens is the various varieties of *Miscanthus sinensis*. "Zebrinus" has horizontal creamy stripes on the leaves (more noticeable as the season progresses), and attractive fan-shaped flower heads in autumn. At only 4 ft. (1.2m), this is a more modest plant, but still makes a large clump. Other miscanthus have similar stature and are grown mainly for their flowers.

Two grasses that are undistinguished out of flower but stunning once the long-lasting flower spikes appear are *Deschampsia caespitosa* (tufted hair grass) and *Stipa gigantea* (golden oat). The deschampsia grows to about 3 ft. (90cm), while the stipa will reach 8 ft. (2.4m). Both look like stunning fireworks as the autumn sun catches their flowerheads.

## Conversation piece

*Rheum palmatum* "Atrosanguineum" is a kind of ornamental rhubarb that always attracts attention. The leaves resemble a large rhubarb, and the tall crimson flower spikes reach 6 ft. (1.8m) or more.

## Launching rockets

Some big or bold plants have tall flower spikes that seem to demand attention. The popular red and orange red-hot pokers (kniphofias) simply demand attention. But even these are outdone by the foxtail lily (*Eremurus robustus*) which push their rocket spikes to over 7 ft. (2.1m).

*Ligularia przewalskii* and L. "The Rocket" are shade-loving plants with long yellow-flowered spikes about 6 ft. (1.8m) tall, which really do look like the trail of a rocket.

# Fancy ferns?

*Ferns dropped out of favor against the competition for brighter and bolder plants, but now they are returning.*

It comes as a surprise to many novice gardeners that there are so many kinds of hardy ferns for the garden. A further surprise is how easy and undemanding they are to cultivate. Also many of them will thrive in places where other plants struggle, and they are evergreen.

The majority of them will thrive in shade. Some will do well in dry shade beneath trees, though others are moisture-lovers. One of the grandest of all, the 4 ft. (1.2m) royal or regal fern (*Osmunda regalis*) is at its best when grown in boggy or waterside conditions. There are ferns that grow in dry walls and others that demand high humidity around their flimsy fronds. But the vast majority of readily available hardy ferns are undemanding and easy to grow, and those mentioned below can be used in the herbaceous border if you find a suitable spot for them. Better still, create a fern bed or border.

## The show-offs

A number of ferns are particularly showy, especially where they are planted in a drift for a more spectacular display. One of the most attractive is the ostrich feather or shuttlecock fern (*Matteuccia struthiopteris),* which looks like a giant shuttlecock when its fronds have unfurled. This one is best in moist shade.

If you live in a mild and sheltered area where winter frosts are rare or not severe, it may be possible to grow a stunning tree fern such as *Dicksonia antarctica*. This evergreen tree-like fern has a stout trunk with palm-like fronds, and will grow to 15 ft. (4.5m) or more. At this size, it is clearly not suitable for the middle of your border, but you may be able to find a spot in the garden where it can become a focal point.

The royal or regal fern (*Osmunda regalis*) is another big fern that will grow to 6 ft. (1.8m), but it's a waterside plant rather than one for the border.

## Easy and reliable

Start with easy ferns, like the male fern (*Dryopteris filix-mas*, a semi-evergreen), polystichums such as semi-evergreen *Polystichum. setiferum*, the evergreen common polypody (*Polypodium vulgare*), or sensitive fern (*Onoclea sensibilis*). Some of these have varieties with variations in leaf shape, so there are plenty to choose from.

The ostrich feather or shuttlecock fern (*Matteuccia struthiopteris*) is a particularly pleasing fern.

Below left: *Hemerocallis* "Golden Chimes."
Right: Bearded iris hybrids.
Bottom: *Hosta sieboldiana.*

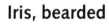

# Hemerocallis

*Day lily*

Versatile and colorful plants with trumpet-shaped flowers in shades of yellow, orange, and red. Though each bloom lasts only about a day in a perfect state, there is a constant succession of them over a long period through the summer months.

Height: 1½–3 ft. (45–90cm).

### Varieties to look for

Mainly hybrids are grown, and there are hundreds of them – many stocked by just one or two specialty nurseries. Among the widely available and particularly pleasing varieties are "Golden Chimes," which is yellow, 2½ ft. (75cm); "Marion Vaughn," which is pale yellow, 3 ft. (90cm); "Stafford" with red flowers, 2½ ft. (75cm); and "Stella de Oro" with orange-yellow flowers, 1½ ft. (45cm).

### Soil and site

Fertile, moisture-retentive soil, in full sun. Zone 4.

### Propagation

Divide in early spring or mid or late autumn.

# Hosta

*Plantain lily*

Popular foliage plant, many attractively variegated or with golden or "blue" foliage, some with attractive flowers. Slugs and snails are common problems. Be particularly vigilant in spring, as most of the damage is done when the new leaves unfurl. The main groups are described in more detail on page 91.

Height: 6–36 in. (15–90cm).

### Varieties to look for

See page 91 for a selection of some of the best varieties.

### Soil and site

Undemanding, but best in moisture-retentive soil in sun or

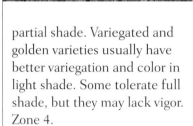

partial shade. Variegated and golden varieties usually have better variegation and color in light shade. Some tolerate full shade, but they may lack vigor. Zone 4.

### Propagation

Divide in early spring.

### DID YOU KNOW?

Hostas are usually thought of as foliage plants, but some have quite large and conspicuous flowers, and a few have the bonus of fragrance. They are even used by flower arrangers as cut flowers. Cut when most of the flowers on the spike are still buds, with just a few open; they should continue to open once cut over three or four days, then last about another four days in reasonable condition.

# Iris, bearded

The tall bearded border irises are derived from *I. pallida* and related species. Most of those grown are used for herbaceous and mixed border decoration. The flowering season is relatively short, in early summer.

Height: Miniature dwarf varieties grow to 8 in. (20cm); standard dwarf 8–16 in. (20–40cm); intermediate 16–28 in. (40–70cm); and tall 28 in. (70cm) or more.

### Varieties to look for

There are hundreds of varieties, many stocked only by specialty nurseries. Study their catalogs for available varieties.

### Soil and site

Well-drained, neutral soil, in full sun. Mainly Zone 5.

### Propagation

Divide the rhizomes in early or mid summer, when flowering has finished.

# Fragrant flowers

*Scent will enhance the visual beauty of your borders, but you will have to choose and position fragrant plants carefully to make the best of them.*

The very nature of a herbaceous or mixed border makes it difficult to appreciate scented plants. The fragrance has to be very powerful to carry from the back of a border, for example, and plants with aromatic foliage have to be positioned at the front to be appreciated. There are relatively few strongly-scented border plants that are not truly herbaceous in the sense that they die back to the ground for the winter, if we exclude bulbs. But that does not mean you can't introduce scent from other sources. Use bulbs like lilies and summer hyacinth (*Galtonia candicans*) and clumps of scented annuals such as sweet peas and ornamental tobacco (nicotiana).

Below: Lily-of-the-valley (*Convallaria majalis*) is synonymous with scent, and it makes a super low-growing carpeting plant for a shady position.

Beware of books and catalogs that describe scented plants in a loose way. Alliums, calendulas, and African and French marigolds do have a smell, but few of us would compare those "scents" with the sweet fragrance of sweet peas or lilies.

## Plants to try

*Convallaria majalis* (lily-of-the-valley)
*Crambe cordifolia*
*Dictamnus albus* (burning bush)
*Filipendula hexapetala*
*Filipendula ulmaria*
*Monarda didyma* (aromatic leaves)
*Oenothera biennis*
*Oenothera missouriensis*
*Paeonia lactiflora* (good ones for scent include "Duchesse de Nemours" and "Sarah Bernhardt")
*Paeonia emodi*
*Phlox maculata*
*Phlox paniculata*

Left: Peonies are border favorites, and some are fragrant. This is *Paeonia* "Duchesse de Nemours."

# Strange and wonderful

*It's fun to grow a few unusual plants, and they always make a good conversation piece when showing visitors around your garden.*

Sometimes it's worth growing plants that are not especially beautiful, may even smell unpleasant, or don't have long-lasting and beautiful flowers … if they bring some other quality to the garden. Most visitors love to be surprised or amazed, and a few plants with interesting features or peculiarities make for a more interesting garden.

The arum family provides some of the most dramatic plants to grow. The dragon arum (*Dracunculus vulgaris*) is one of the boldest for a border. It grows to about 3 ft. (90cm) with mottled stalks and white-streaked leaves, and in late spring or early summer produces a blackish-maroon spadix from its deep maroon-purple spathe. The whole flower is over 1 ft. (30cm) long. Its performance doesn't stop there: the flower's putrid smell of rotting flesh attracts beetles and flies from all around!

The voodoo lily or monarch of the East (*Sauromatum venosum*), is widely sold as a gimmick plant to grow indoors without soil or water, but it can also be used in the garden, where you can enjoy the foliage that follows the flowers. The spathe emerges and grows at an amazing rate, to a height of about 1 ft. (30cm), then peels back to reveal a skin of brownish-purple and yellow, with a spadix in the middle sticking up like a poker. But take care if you plan to examine it closely … the smell is truly nauseating. Grow a clump for real impact.

Not all interesting arums are large. Try growing the mouse plant (*Arisarum proboscideum*) at the front of a border. It produces a carpet of arrow-shaped leaves about 4 in. (10cm) high, among which you will find the flowers in spring. They have a spathe that is drawn out into a tail up to 6 in. (15cm) long. The whole flower resembles a mouse.

Above: The voodoo lily (*Sauromatum venosum*) has strange flowers produced before the leaves, but don't get too close … the smell is overpowering.

## JARGON BUSTER

*Aroid*  A group of plants with a flower stem (spadix) enclosed within a spathe (see below).

*Spathe*  A petal-like leaf, which peels back when mature to expose the spadix that contains the flowers.

*Spadix*  A spike (straight or curved) or club-like structure which contains many individual and often insignificant flowers. This is initially enclosed in the spathe.

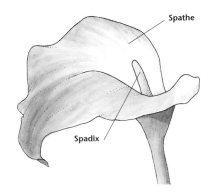

Spathe

Spadix

Above: The dragon arum (*Dracunculus vulgaris*) looks strange and mysterious … and smells putrid!

Right: The voodoo lily (*Sauromatum venosum*) produces large, striking foliage once the flowers die down.

# Kniphofia
*Red-hot poker*

Focal-point plants with tall, stiff poker-like flower spikes, though sizes and flowering times vary with species or variety. Some flower as early as mid summer, others as late as mid autumn. In areas where kniphofias are of borderline hardiness, protect the crowns with a mulch in winter.

Height: 3–6 ft. (90–180cm).

## Varieties to look for

Hardiness varies, so it is advisable to check with your garden center to see which varieties are likely to survive the winter if you live in a borderline hardiness area.

However, the following are well-proven varieties: "Little Maid" has creamy yellow flowers in mid summer to mid autumn, 2 ft. (60cm); "Royal Standard" has red-and-lemon flowers in late summer, 4 ft. (1.2m); and "Samuel's

Sensation" has deep orange flowers in late summer, 5 ft. (1.5m).

## Soil and site

Well-drained soil, in full sun. Best in a warm position. Most hybrids are Zone 7.

## Propagation

Divide in mid spring.

# Leucanthemum x superbum (syn. Chrysanthemum maximum)
*Shasta daisy*

Big, bold, white daisy flowers on stiff stems make the shasta daisy one of those border plants that stands out from a distance. Despite being white, it will hold its own with the more colorful summer flowers.

Height: 2½–3 ft. (75–90cm).

## Varieties to look for

"Aglaia" is semi-double, 3 ft. (90cm); "Esther Read" is double, 2 ft. (60cm); "Phyllis Smith" is single, 2 ft. (60cm);

## ● TIP TO TRY

In areas of borderline hardiness, winter the penstemons in a cold frame. If winters are too cold to leave outdoors, take cuttings in late summer or early autumn and winter in a frost-free place.

"Silberprinzesschen," (formerly "Little Princess") is single, 2 ft. (60cm); and "Wirral Supreme" is double, 3 ft. (90cm).

## Soil and site

Undemanding regarding soil, but best in full sun or partial shade.

## Propagation

Divide in early spring. Some varieties can be raised from seed – sow early spring to early summer.

## NOW YOU KNOW!

For years most of us have known the shasta daisy as *Chrysanthemum maximum*; then it was decided that the plants we grew in gardens under this name were really hybrids between *C. maximum* and *C. lacustre*, and should be known as *Chrysanthemum* x *superbum*.

Then most of the chrysanthemums were reclassified and the group into which the shasta daisies fall became known as leucanthemums. So now the correct name is *Leucanthemum* x *superbum*!

BEAUTIFUL BORDER PERENNIALS

Below left: *Liriope muscari.*
Right: *Nepeta x fassenii.*
Bottom: *Lupinus* "Russell Hybrids."

# Liriope muscari
*Lilytuft*

Evergreen foliage and small spikes of lilac-mauve bell-shaped flowers in autumn make this a very desirable plant despite its rather dull coloring. Once established, it is undemanding and tough.
   Height: 1 ft. (30cm).

## Varieties to look for
The ordinary species is the best for general planting, but for contrast try "Monroe White" (syn. "Alba") or one of the variegated kinds such as the attractive "Variegata."

## Soil and site
Light, sandy soil, in full sun or partial shade. Dislikes alkaline soils, but tolerates dry soils. Zone 6.

## Propagation
Divide in early or mid spring.

# Lupinus polyphyllus
*Lupin*

Eyecatching spikes of pea-type flowers in late spring and early summer. The color range is wide and there are many attractive bicolors.
   Height: 3–5 ft. (90–150cm).

## Varieties to look for
"Russell Mixed" is still the most trusted seed-range mixture, but named varieties, mainly propagated from cuttings, are available if a specific color is required.

## Soil and site
Well-drained soil, in full sun or partial shade. Zone 3.

## Propagation
Take cuttings of named varieties in early or mid spring. Sow seed of mixtures and seed-raised varieties in early or mid spring – they will flower the following year.

# Nepeta x fassenii
*Catmint*

Gray-green foliage and lavender-blue flowers, much loved by bees, make this a first-rate border or edging plant for early summer.
   Height: 1½ ft. (45cm).

## Varieties to look for
*N. mussinii* is similar (see box); "Six Hills Giant" is a hybrid that grows to about 2 ft. (60cm).

## Soil and site
Well-drained soil, in full sun or partial shade. Zone 4.

## Propagation
Divide in early or mid spring. Take cuttings of basal shoots in early or mid spring.

### NOW YOU KNOW!
The nomenclature of nepetas can be confusing. Plants named as *Nepeta mussinii* should now be categorized as *N. racemosa*, while *N. x fassenii* is a hybrid between *N. racemosa* and *N. nepetella*.
   The same variety may be found listed as belonging to one or other of these species, or simply as a hybrid. From a gardening viewpoint, it makes no difference to these excellent plants ... just be prepared to find them listed under different names in different places!

# Grasses are great

*Grasses are often ignored when a border is being planned, yet they have a considerably longer period of interest than most of the more popular border flowers. They don't have to be dull, as the illustrations show, and most of them can be kept under control easily.*

Most of the ornamental grasses mentioned here should not make a take-over bid for the border (which cannot be said of all grasses), and if you are in the least bit concerned, just plant in an old bucket with the rim level with the surface of the border soil.

## Plumes of white

The pampas grass (*Cortaderia selloana*) is widely planted as an isolated specimen, but

it makes a huge plant, too large for a small border. If you want to use a pampas grass where space is limited, try the variety "Pumila," which is only about 5 ft. (1.5m) tall, with a spread of about 3 ft. (90cm).

*Miscanthus sinensis* "Silver Feather" also forms a substantial clump and grows to about 6 ft. (1.8m) or so. Its sprays of white flowers in early autumn are not as spectacular as those of the pampas grass, but it is a useful all-round plant for the border.

Perhaps a more fascinating plant is the variety *M. s.* "Zebrinus," the zebra grass. The leaves have cream cross-bands (not so noticeable early in the year), and the fan-shaped flower heads are an arresting sight when caught in shafts of autumn sunlight against a dark background.

## Blue and gold

The blue fescue (*Festuca glauca*) is one of those mound-forming grasses that always looks neat and well-behaved. The silver-blue foliage looks great near golden foliage plants. "Blauglut" (also sold as "Blue Glow") is a particularly intense silver-blue.

The golden wood millet (*Milium effusum* "Aureum") is one of the best golden grasses, and always looks bright in the border. It's essentially a foliage plant, the flowers being uninspiring. It grows to about 1½ft. (45cm), and does not spread out of control. Seedlings are often found around the plant, but these can be potted and given to friends.

## Waving in the wind

Some grasses have tall and conspicuous flower spikes that tend to wave gently to flag their presence. These can look stunning in late summer and early autumn. Two particularly good ones to plant are *Stipa gigantea*, which grows to 6 ft. (1.8m) or more, and *Deschampsia caespitosa*, which is smaller at 2–2½ft. (60–75cm).

**Above:** *Miscanthus sinensis* grows tall but makes an eye-catching focal point where there is space for it.

**Center:** The golden grass *Milium effusum* "Aureum" is not invasive, though it may produce some self-sown seedlings.

**Left:** *Stipa gigantea* makes a superb border plant, but can grow tall when it's in flower.

## Paeonia lactiflora hybrids

*Border peony*

Spectacular for late spring and early summer interest, the individual blooms are often 4 in. (10cm) or more across, on stems about 3 ft. (90cm) tall.

Scarlet is the usual color, but there are many shades of red, as well as pink and even white.

Height: 2½–4 ft. (75–120cm).

### Varieties to look for

There are hundreds of varieties, many stocked by just a few nurseries, but among the best of the more readily available varieties are "Bowl of Beauty," semi-double pink and white, and "Sarah Bernhardt," double pink to white, scented.

### Soil and site

Deeply dug, well-drained but moisture-retentive soil, in full sun or partial shade. If possible, incorporate plenty of rotted manure or garden compost into the ground before planting. Zone 6.

### Propagation

Divide in early autumn.

## Papaver orientale

*Oriental poppy*

Spectacular blooms often 4 in. (10cm) or more across, on 3 ft. (90cm) stems in early summer.

Scarlet or vermilion are the common colors, but there are pinks and even whites.

Height: 3–4 ft. (90–120cm).

### Varieties to look for

Among the striking varieties are "Goliath," bright red; "Ladybird," vermilion with black center; "Mrs. Perry," salmon pink; and "Perry's White," white with purple center.

### Soil and site

Well-drained soil, in full sun. Zone 3.

### Propagation

Divide in early or mid spring, or take root cuttings in winter.

## Penstemon

Semi-evergreen perennials that flower over a long period throughout the summer. Most of those grown are hybrids, with spikes of hanging bells in shades of pink, red, and purple, often flushed or marked with white.

Height: 1½–2 ft. (45–60cm).

### Varieties to look for

There are many varieties, among the best being "Apple Blossom," pale pink; "Evelyn," rose pink, pale striped throat; "Hidcote Pink," pink; "Pennington Gem," pink and white; "Schoenholzeri," (syn. "Firebird"), red; and "White Bedder."

### Soil and site

Well-drained soil, in full sun. Zone 9.

### Propagation

Take cuttings in late summer or early autumn.

## Phlox paniculata

Invaluable flowers for the late summer border, bringing color and sometimes scent with large flowerheads on tall stems. The species itself is seldom grown, but there are many excellent varieties.

Below left: *Phlox paniculata.*
Below center: *Rudbeckia fulgida.*
Bottom: *Sedum spectabile.*
Right: *Stachys byzantina.*

Water the plants freely in dry spells.

Height: 4 ft. (1.2m).

### Varieties to look for

For flowers, consider the following: "Eventide," light mauve-blue; "Fujyama," white; "Mother of Pearl," white, flushed pink; "Prince of Orange," orange-salmon; "Prospero," pale lilac; "White Admiral," white. If variegated foliage appeals, try "Harlequin," reddish-purple flowers, and "Nora Leigh," pale lilac flowers.

### Soil and site

Fertile, well-drained but moisture-retentive soil, in full sun or partial shade.

### ● TIP TO TRY

Cut a few phlox flowers for indoors; they will last about a week in a vase or floral arrangement. But sear the end of the stem with a flame or immerse in boiling water for a few seconds, to seal it and prevent the loss of latex that will cause early wilting.

### Propagation

Divide in early spring or mid autumn, or take cuttings from the plant's base in early spring.

## Rudbeckia fulgida var. deamii

*Black-eyed Susan*

One of the treasures of the late border, and often the brightest plant in flower in early autumn. The eye-catching yellow daisy-type flowers have a contrasting black central cone.

Height: 2–2½ ft. (60–75cm).

### Varieties to look for

Rudbeckia f. var. sullivantii "Goldsturm," perhaps more

often seen simply as R. "Goldsturm," is also a very popular choice.

### Soil and site

Well-drained soil, in full sun. Zone 4.

### Propagation

Divide in early spring or mid autumn.

## Sedum spectabile

*Ice plant*

One of the most popular autumn-flowering border plants, with large flat heads of pink flowers loved by bees and butterflies. The succulent leaves are almost hidden by the mound of large flowerheads.

Height: 1–1½ ft. (30–45cm).

### Varieties to look for

There are several varieties in various shades of pink, as well as whites and a pink one with variegated foliage. One of the best is the vibrant rose-pink "Brilliant."

### Soil and site

Well-drained soil, in full sun. Zone 4.

### Propagation

Divide in early spring or mid autumn.

## Stachys byzantina (syn. S. lanata, S. olympica)

*Lamb's ears*

A useful ground cover for the front of a border, grown mainly for its evergreen silvery felted foliage. The foliage often looks shabby by the end of winter, but it helps to provide some year-round cover. Spikes of pink or purplish flowers in summer are a bonus, but not all varieties flower reliably.

Height: 1 ft. (30cm).

### Varieties to look for

"Silver Carpet" rarely produces flowers. "Primrose Heron" has yellowish-green new growth, which becomes light silver-gray by winter.

### Soil and site

Undemanding regarding soil, but best in full sun. Zone 5.

### Propagation

Divide in spring.

# The Appeal of Alpines

Whether you call them alpines or rock plants doesn't matter, and you don't even need a rock garden to plant them. Their diminutive size appeals to many gardeners and, of course, you can grow a large number of plants in a small area.

It is possible to grow a whole collection of houseleeks (sempervivums) in a small garden, whereas you would need a large garden indeed (not to mention an acid soil) to have a large collection of rhododendrons, for example.

A true rock garden is the ideal home for many of the plants described here, and it could be one of the garden's strongest focal points if well constructed.

The most stunning rock gardens are built on a natural slope, but if you have a flat garden a very convincing "rock outcrop" can be constructed (see page 111).

Don't be deterred from growing alpines just because you can't build a rock garden – just regard them as dwarf plants to be used where appropriate. Some of the keenest alpine specialists grow their plants in pots, often in an alpine house (a greenhouse with very good ventilation to keep the temperature down).

Raised beds also provide a wonderful opportunity for displaying alpines, as they are brought that much nearer to eye level. If alpines appeal to you, you should be able to find somewhere suitable to grow them!

## Features

THE APPEAL OF ALPINES

## Aethionema
*"Warley Rose"*

Pretty deep-rose flowers in mid and late spring, over a thick carpet of gray-green evergreen foliage.

Height: 6 in. (15cm).

**Varieties to look for**
"Warley Ruber" is similar but with darker flowers.

**Soil and site**
Well-drained soil, in full sun. Zone 7.

**Propagation**
Take cuttings of non-flowering shoots in mid or late summer.

## Alyssum saxatile
*see Aurinia saxatilis*

## Arabis alpina caucasica (syn. A. albida, A. caucasica)
*Rock cress*

An easy and reliable undemanding plant with downy gray-green leaves and white flowers in early and mid spring. The arabis is useful for clothing a rock bank or a large area in a big rock garden where it can be allowed to spread. Although evergreen, the leaves tend to die back in wet or unfavorable winters.

Height: 9 in. (23cm).

**Varieties to look for**
"Flore Pleno" is a double with larger flowers, but they are less freely produced. There are pink forms such as rosea, and "Variegata" has white flowers and cream-splashed leaves.

A different species, *A. ferdinandi-coburgi*, is often grown where a variegated plant is required. This has white-edged leaves and white flowers.

**Soil and site**
Well-drained soil, in full sun or partial shade. Zone 4.

**Propagation**
Divide in autumn or take cuttings in summer. The species and some varieties can be raised from seed sown in spring or early summer.

**GOOD COMPANIONS**
Aubrieta and arabis flower at about the same time and grow to a similar height, so make good companions. Try interplanting them as both tend to spread and sprawl.

## Armeria maritima
*Thrift, sea pink*

Evergreen tufts of grass-like foliage, topped with masses of drumstick-like flowerheads in pink, red, or white, in late spring and early summer. A useful plant for rock crevices.

Height: 9 in. (23cm).

**Varieties to look for**
"Vindictive" is an excellent bright red, "Alba" a good white. *A. juniperifolia* (syn. *A. caespitosa*) is another excellent rock plant, smaller but covered in pink or white flowerheads in mid and late spring. "Bevan's Variety" is an attractive pink.

**Soil and site**
Well-drained soil, in full sun. Zone 4 (*A. caespitosa* Zone 8).

**Propagation**
Take cuttings in spring or summer. Unnamed varieties can be raised from seed sown in summer or autumn.

# How to make a rock garden

*If you garden on a sloping site, build your rock garden into the hillside. You will have less soil-moving to do, and it will look more convincing.*

If your garden is flat, however, try building it by the method described here, in a sunny position where there is a natural backdrop at the back – don't make a mini-mountain in the middle of your lawn.

### Think of your back

Rocks are heavy and you could injure your back if you are not accustomed to lifting weights or do not use the right techniques. Whenever possible, move rocks on rollers and lever them into position with a pole or iron bar. If you do have to lift a heavy rock, enlist help and let your legs and knees do the lifting, not your back.

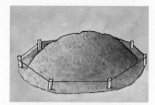

**1** Mark out the area for your rock garden with string. Mix your soil (equal parts soil, coarse sand, and peat or peat substitute, will suit the majority of alpines); then make a mound in your marked area.

**2** Remove the string and begin positioning the rocks, starting at the lowest level. Pack more soil behind the rocks and around the sides to ensure they are stable. Ensure the rock strata lines run in the same direction.

**3** Build up the rock garden a layer at a time, always keeping an eye on the strata so that they look as though they are part of the same larger underlying rock. Use a crowbar or pole to lever heavy rocks into position.

**4** Set each layer further back so that the sides slope, but leave a reasonably flat top – don't build it too high or into a peak. Pack the soil firmly to remove large air pockets, then finish off with a layer of coarse sand.

**5** Space the plants out while still in their pots before you start planting, and be prepared to move them around until you are completely happy with the arrangement. Don't forget to allow for growth!

**6** When you have decided on their positions, start planting. Scrape back some of the sand and make a hole a little larger than the root ball. You will find a narrow-bladed trowel easier to use.

**7** Adjust the planting depth if necessary, then trickle more of the soil mix around the root ball and tamp it well. Finish off by covering the exposed soil with sand, leveling it with the surrounding area.

Below right: *Aurinia saxatilis* (formerly *Alyssum saxatile*).
Bottom: *Aubrieta* hybrid.

## Aubrieta hybrids
*Rock cress*

One of the most widely planted of all rock plants, extensively used to cascade over the edges of raised beds, or planted in crevices in the face of a wall. Can even be used as an edging and carpeting plant. It may be too vigorous for a rock garden planted with choice alpines as neighbors. Cut back the long shoots with shears after flowering to keep the plants compact.

Ambrietas tend to deteriorate with age, so propagate new plants regularly.

Height: 4 in. (10cm).

**Varieties to look for**
Because excellent plants are easily raised from seed, many sold in garden centers are unnamed. These are unlikely to disappoint, but there are named varieties if a particular color is required. "Doctor Mules," violet-purple, and "Novalis Blue" are examples of impressive performers. There are also a doubles, such as "Bressingham Pink," and variegated varieties, such as "Lemon and Lime."

**Soil and site**
Well-drained soil, in full sun. Avoid acidic soils: does well on chalky soils. Zone 7.

**Propagation**
Divide in autumn, take cuttings in summer, or sow seed in spring or early summer and they should start to flower the following year.

**DID YOU KNOW?**
Most seed-raised varieties are mixed colors and the flower size may be inferior to named varieties raised from cuttings or by division, but "Novalis Blue" is an example of a seed-raised F1 hybrid that has particularly large medium-blue flowers. There are other seed-raised varieties that usually come true from seed, such as "Royal Red."

Aubrieta is one of the easiest rock plants to raise from seed.

## Aurinia saxatilis (syn. Alyssum saxatile)
*Gold dust*

Almost as popular as aubrieta, and used in the same situations, a carpet of bright yellow flowers smothers the foliage of aurinia in late spring and early summer. Trim back with shears when flowering has finished, to keep the plants compact.

Although listed under its correct name here, it is nearly always sold under its old name of *Alyssum saxatile*.

Height: 9 in. (23cm).

**Varieties to look for**
The species is an excellent plant, but try the variety "Citrina" for bright yellow-gold flowers, or "Dudley Neville" for an unusual buff-yellow. There are also variegated varieties if these appeal to you.

**Soil and site**
Well-drained soil, in full sun. Zone 3.

**Propagation**
Take cuttings in early summer. If named varieties are not required, sow seed in spring or early summer.

**GOOD COMPANIONS**
Although usually grown in a rock garden or wall, *Aurinia saxatilis* can be used imaginatively in beds as a short-term spring-bedding plant. Try planting it with aubrieta between tulips for a stunning effect. Move to the rock garden or discard when the bed has to be cleared.

# How to make a rock outcrop

*If you want a rock feature in a large lawn, rock outcrop beds will be more pleasing than a large rock garden looking like a mini-mountain. Sandstones work particularly well as outcrops, but limestones, slates, and even granites still look pleasing.*

Bear in mind that, once the plants have made a few years of growth, the amount of rock left exposed will probably be much less than half of what is visible right after construction.

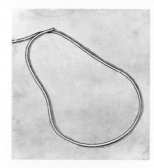

**1** Mark out the bed on your lawn using string. Do not make the bed too small – as there will be little height, it will appear even smaller from a distance. Stand back and look at it from further back.

**2** A group of outcrops can make more of a feature and have a bigger impact. Try three or five beds, leaving a path between them. It is easier to make an odd number of beds look more natural.

**3** Improve the soil to make it free draining and suitable for alpines. It may be sufficient to dig in a generous amount of coarse sand and peat or peat substitute. Mound the soil up toward the middle of the bed.

**4** Start with the largest rock first. This will be the key stone and will largely dictate the overall appearance. It can be placed in a high position or a low one, but make the hole for it deeper than the actual rock.

**5** Group the remaining rocks so that they look like natural outcrops. It's a good ideal to slope all the rocks backwards slightly, in the same direction. Bury them slightly so that they do not appear to sit on the surface.

**6** Apply stone chips to improve the appearance, but make sure they cannot stray on to the lawn as they may damage the mower. Plant one or two dwarf conifers or alpine shrubs to provide some height.

# Know your campanulas

*The campanulas, or bellflowers, are an important group of rock plants. There are many choice kinds that make charming and well-behaved plants.*

There are about 300 species of campanula, some annuals or biennials, some tender perennials, but those discussed here are all hardy perennials. Campanulas generally have bell-shaped flowers, but these vary from narrowly tubular to nearly saucer-shaped. The color is almost

*Campanula garganica* is covered with sprays of light blue starry flowers all summer long, above the tufts of neat foliage. It won't become a nuisance.

### Enthusiastic spreaders
*Campanula poscharskyana* (not to be confused with *C. portenschlagiana*!) has starry lavender to violet flowers in summer and into autumn, and its free flowering habit makes it attractive initially. Unfortunately is tends to stray and it may become regarded as a weed in time. *Campanula portenschlagiana* (syn. *C. muralis*) does not have an attractive name, but the flowers are really showy, with the plants smothered with upward-facing purple-blue bells all summer.

universally blue, sometimes tinted with pink, but whites are not unusual. There are uncommon exceptions, such as *C. thysoidea*, which is yellow.

They are nearly all very easy to grow, and in the rock garden have the advantage of flowering from summer onward, taking over when the first flush of spring flowers is over.

### Dainty and constrained
*Campanula cochleariifolia* is a dainty low-grower with small blue or white bells (which give rise to one of its common names, fairy thimbles) in mid and late summer. It grows to only about 3 in. (7.5cm) but spreads extensively by underground shoots.

### Show-offs
*Campanula carpatica* is showy enough to be sold as a potted plant for the home, and you can sometimes buy plants this way in flower. The large flowers are cup-shaped and upward-facing, and at their best in mid and late summer. The normal color is blue, but a white variety is widely sold. It grows to about 9 in. (23cm).

### Avoid the border bellflowers
Many campanulas are herbaceous border plants. These have a useful role in the border, but are far too large for a rock garden. Widely grown border kinds include *C. glomerata*, *C. lactiflora*, and *C. pyramidalis*.

## Campanula carpatica
*Bellflower*

There are dozens of excellent campanulas for the rock garden, but this is one of the most popular. The blue or white cup-shaped flowers are up to 2 in. (5cm) across and face upward, helping to make this a particularly bold campanula. The main flowering time is mid and late summer.

Height: 9 in. (23cm).

### Varieties and other species
"Blaue Clips" (syn. "Blue Clips") and "Weisse Clips" (syn. "White Clips") are particularly showy varieties, and can be raised from seed (they are sometimes grown as potted plants).

Another popular rock garden species is *C. garganica*, which has a profusion of star-shaped blue flowers that almost hide the foliage for most of summer. "Dickson's Gold" has golden leaves to contrast with the blue flowers (though the color is stronger out of direct midday sun).

A tiny gem, sometimes called fairy thimbles, *C. cochleariifolia* is a plant for rock crevices, forming a carpet of growth about 3 in. (8cm) high covered with small pendent blue or white bell flowers in mid and late summer.

### Soil and site
Well-drained soil, in sun or partial shade. Avoid acidic soil; campanulas do well on alkaline soil. Most rock campanulas are tough. Zones for the species above are: 3 (*C. garganica* 5, *C. cochleariifolia* 6).

### Propagation
Divide in spring or autumn, or take cuttings in late spring or early summer. All the campanulas mentioned above (except the golden form of *C. garganica*) can also be raised from seed – best sown in spring or autumn.

### BEWARE THE INVADERS
A few rock garden campanulas can become invasive and almost a garden weed. Beware of *Campanula portenschalgiana* and *C. poscharskyana*.

## Dianthus deltoides
*Maiden pink*

One of the most popular of the rock garden pinks, and a good crevice plant. Although pink is the usual color, there are red, and white, varieties. Flowering is early summer onward, and the leaves are evergreen.

Height: 9 in. (23cm).

### Varieties and other species
The species itself can be recommended, but for a bright crimson, "Leuchtfunk" (syn. "Flashing Light") is impressive, and "Alba" is white.

Many other dianthus are suitable for a rock garden, and these are just some: "Pike's Pink" has pink, semi-double flowers; "Inshriach Dazzler" is vivid carmine-pink; *D. alpinus* has pink, white, or purple flowers; and *D. gratianopolitanus*, (syn. *D. caesius*) is pink, fringed, and fragrant.

### Soil and site
Well-drained soil, in full sun. They do well on chalky ground, the natural habitat of most species. Zone 3.

### Propagation
Take cuttings in summer. Except for varieties that will not come true from seed, sow seed in early spring or summer.

THE APPEAL OF ALPINES

113

## Dryas octopetala
*Mountain avens*

A rock plant of many merits with evergreen leaves, attractive white flowers in late spring and early summer, and fluffy white seedheads in mid and late summer – these ensure that the plant remains attractive for a long period.

Height: 4 in. (10cm).

### Varieties and other species
The species itself is one of the best to grow, but "Minor" is also attractive and more compact. Among the other species, *D.* x *suedermannii*, with cream flowers, is one of the best.

### Soil and site
Well-drained soil, in full sun. Zone 2.

### Propagation
Take stem cuttings in summer, or sow seed of *D. octopetala* in summer.

## Erinus alpinus

Easy to grow and bright and cheerful, but usually short-lived. The starry pink flowers on short and wiry stalks are produced in late spring and summer, above a rosette of semi-evergreen leaves. This is a pleasing crevice plant, and can be used in a wall.

Height: 4 in. (10cm).

### Varieties to look for
The species itself is as pleasing as any of its varieties, but "Mrs. Charles Boyle" is another pretty pink, and *E. a. albus* is a striking white.

### Soil and site
Well-drained soil, in full sun or partial shade. Can flourish in impoverished soil. Zone 6.

### Propagation
Sow seed in autumn, but for selected forms take cuttings in early summer.

### ● TIP TO TRY
Gentians are notoriously fickle, so get to know their needs. The summer gentian *G. septemfida* resents being divided and is best raised from seed. The autumn *G. sino-ornata* performs better if divided every two or three years.

## Gentiana acaulis
*Trumpet gentian*

An outstanding alpine with beautiful upward-facing blue trumpet flowers, over 2 in. (5cm) long and almost stemless, in late spring and early summer. They are evergreen. Gentians can be demanding, and species such as *G. acaulis* and *G. verna* must have a suitable soil pH. They may also take a season or two to settle down before flowering well.

Height: 3 in. (7.5cm).

### Other species to look for
By growing other species too, it is possible to enjoy alpine gentians right through to mid autumn. *G. verna* is another for late spring and early summer, but it has smaller flowers.

### ● TIP TO TRY
*Erinus alpinus* looks good planted in a crevice in the face of a wall or raised bed. They thrive in poor soil, so there's no excuse for not growing them.

One of the easiest summer-flowering gentians to grow is *G. septemfida*, which has purple-blue trumpet flowers in mid and late summer. For autumn, try the beautiful intense blue *G. sino-ornata*, which blooms in early and mid autumn.

### Soil and site
Well-drained soil, in full sun or partial shade. *G. acaulis* requires an acid and moisture-retentive soil, while *G. verna* happily grows on chalky soils.

Those that demand an acid soil do well in peat beds but they thrive in an ordinary garden if the soil is specially prepared for them. Zone 3 (*G. sino-ornata* 6).

### Propagation
Divide in early spring (*G. acaulis* in early summer), or take cuttings in mid or late spring. Most species can also be grown from seed.

# The year-round rock garden

*Use this season-by-season planner to be sure that your rock garden always looks good.*

## Early spring

Adonis ameurensis
Androsace carnea
Anemone apennina
Aubrieta deltoidea
Aurinia saxatilis
(formerly *Alyssum saxatile*)
Chionodoxa luciliae
Erythronium dens-canis
Muscari armeniacum
Muscari botryoides
Narcissus bulbocodium
Narcissus triandrus and its varieties
and hybrids
Omphalodes cappadocica
Omphalodes verna
Saxifraga (Kabschia types)
Tulipa tarda
Tulipa kaufmanniana hybrids

## Mid spring

Adonis vernalis
Aubrieta deltoidea
Aurinia saxatilis
(formerly *Alyssum saxatile*)
Draba aizoides

Fritillaria meleagris
Primula auricula
Pulsatilla vernalis
Pulsatilla vulgaris
Ramonda myconi
Tulipa griegii hybrids

## Late spring

Aethionema "Warley Rose"
Armeria caespitosa
Armeria maritima
Dianthus species
Dryas octopetala
Erinus alpinus
Gentiana acaulis
Gentiana verna
Geum montanum
Iberis gibraltarica
Iris cristata
Linaria alpina
Lychnis viscaria
Potentilla verna
Pulsatilla alpina
Trillium sessile
Viola riviniana
(formerly *V. labradorica* "Purpurea")

## Early summer

Achillea chrysocoma
Androsace sarmentosa
Aster alpinus
Geranium dalmaticum
Gypsophila repens
Helianthemum nummularium
Leontopodium alpinum
Phlox adsurgens
Phlox douglasii
Saxifraga (Aizoon group)
Thymus serpyllum

## Mid summer

Campanula carpatica
Campanula garganica
Gentiana septemfida
Hypericum olympicum
Sempervivum

## Late summer

Ceratostigma plumbaginoides
Oenothera macrocarpa (formerly *O. missouriensis*)
Polygonum vacciniifolium
Sedum kamtschaticum
(formerly *S. floriferum*)
"Weihenstephaner Gold"
Silene schafta

## Early autumn

Colchicum autumnale
Colchicum speciosum
Crocus speciosus
Cyclamen neapolitanum
Gentiana sino-ornata
Sternbergia lutea
Zauschneria californica
Zephyrathes candida

## Mid autumn

Crocus kotschyanus
Cyclamen cilicium
Gentiana sino-ornata

## Late autumn

Crocus laevigatus
Erica carnea (early varieties such as list)

## Early winter

Helleborus niger

## Mid and late winter

All the following should be in flower by the time late winter is over, but how many of them flower in mid winter depends on the season and location:

Anemone blanda
Crocus chrysanthus
Cyclamen coum
Galanthus nivalis
Hepatica nobilis
Iris reticulata
Narcissus cyclamineus

There are many delightful rock garden primulas, including the pink *Primula x forsteri* "Bileckii" (syn. *Primula bileckii*) shown here in a trough.

# How to make a sink garden

*Sink gardens make attractive features in their own right, and if you choose the plants carefully it's possible to find space for perhaps a dozen plants.*

If you don't have an old sink to cover, use the same mixture to cast a sink using two boxes as molds. You can then make the trough shallower which improves the proportions.

Above: Stone sinks – genuine or manufactured – make an ideal home for a small collection of alpines. They look better if a few small rocks are used among the plants.

**Disguising a glazed sink**

**1** If you have an old glazed sink, you can coat it with "hypertufa," a mix of equal parts sphagnum peat (or a peat substitute such as coir fiber), coarse or fine sand, and cement. Clean the sink thoroughly first.

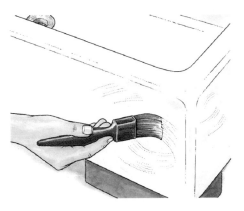

**2** Use hot water and a detergent to remove any traces of grease, then leave to dry. When the sink is clean and dry, brush a PVA adhesive on to the outside, top rim and about 2 in. (5cm) down the inside.

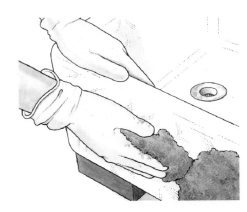

**3** Using gloves to protect your hands, slap on the hypertufa while the adhesive is still tacky. Press the separate applications together to create a seamless finish, but don't worry about a smooth surface.

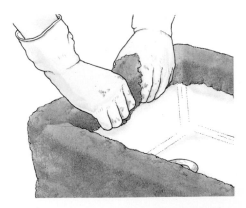

**4** Mold it over the rim, and extend it down the inside of the sink to below the final soil level. When the mixture has dried, brush it with a liquid fertilizer or rice water to encourage algae to grow.

## Planting a sink garden

It's even possible to create a miniature rock landscape if you approach it imaginatively and don't mind sacrificing some of the planting area for small rocks.

**1** Cover the drainage hole with broken pots or fine-mesh netting, and then add 3–4 in. (7.5–10cm) of coarse sand.

**2** Partly fill the trough with a gritty potting soil, then position any rocks that you plan to use.

**3** Top up with more gritty compost, then position the plants to make sure they are suitably arranged before planting.

**4** Firm all the plants in carefully, then cover the surface with coarse sand or stone chips to improve the appearance.

# Annual treats

*Annuals are especially useful in a recently constructed rock garden, to provide quick color and for filling in gaps while the permanent plants are becoming established.*

**Below: One of the better hardy annuals for sowing in your rock garden is** *Phacelia campanularia.*

Hardy annuals can be sown where they are to flower, but beware of self-sown seedlings which can sometimes be a problem in later years unless weeded out.

Don't dismiss some of the half-hardy bedding plants as gap-fillers. Gazanias and mesembryanthemums, for example, look perfectly at home on a sunny rock garden.

### Hardy annuals to sow

*Iberis* (candytuft)
*Ionopsidium acaulis* (violet cress)
*Limnanthes douglasii* (poached egg plant)
*Linaria maroccana* (toadflax)
*Lobularia maritima,* formerly *Alyssum maritimum* (sweet alyssum)
*Nemophila menziesii,* syn. *N. insignis* (baby blue eyes)
*Phacelia campanularis*

117

# Plants for paving

*Despite their small size, some rock plants are remarkably resilient and will even tolerate being trodden upon occasionally. Plant between paving sections to make the most of planting spaces that would otherwise go unused and unadorned.*

No plant will tolerate being pounded by feet several times a day, so plant in little-used crazy-paving paths, or toward the side of a path where only straying shoots are likely to be stepped on. If planting in an area paved for sitting, choose an area to one side where the expanse of paving can be relieved with minimal risk to the plants. In such a situation, many of the more succulent types of plants such as fleshy sedums can be used very effectively.

Right: Some low-growing annuals can be sown in the cracks between paving. *Limnanthes douglasii* will probably self-sow to provide plants in future years.

### Planting in crevices

Although many alpines are naturally adapted to growing in crevices with minimal soil or nutrients, you want your plants to get off to a good start.

Whenever possible, scrape out the existing soil from the crevice and expand the planting space as much as possible. Insert the plant roots, then pack in a good potting soil with the addition of a slow-release fertilizer. Water well after planting and until established. Losses are most likely in the weeks after planting.

If sowing seed, fill the excavated crevice with potting soil mixed with a generous amount of extra grit or sand, and sow a small pinch of seeds directly into this. Water and protect until the seedlings emerge, then thin to one plant. Continue to protect from crushing, and water in dry weather, until the plant is growing vigorously.

Left: A large area of paving can look boring, but a few tough alpines planted among the paving slabs can turn it into a pleasing feature.

### Plants for paving

*Acaena microphylla*
*Ajuga reptans*
*Arenaria balearica*
*Armeria maritima*
*Aubrieta deltoidea*
*Aurinia saxatilis* (formerly *Alyssum saxatile*)
*Campanula cochleariifolia*
*Campanula portenschlagiana*
*Erinus alpinus*
*Mazus reptans*
*Mentha requienii*
*Raoulia australis*
*Saxifraga* ("mossy" kinds)
*Sempervivums* (not to be walked on)
*Thymus serpyllum*
*Veronica prostrata*

Below left: *Geranium cinereum "Ballerina."*
Below right: *Gypsophila repens.*
Bottom: *Phlox subulata.*

## Geranium cinereum
*Rock cranesbill*

Easy to grow, this undemanding and cheerful plant is a prolific bloomer, flowering from late spring well into summer. The flower color varies from pink to crimson-purple, depending on variety. There is also a white.

Height: 6 in. (15cm).

### Varieties to look for
"Ballerina" has purplish-pink flowers with deep purple veins, *G. c.* var. *subcaulescens* is brilliant purple-magenta and its variety "Splendens" iridescent purple-red with darker veins. All are desirable additions to the rock garden.

### Soil and site
Well-drained soil, in full sun. Zone 5.

### Propagation
Divide in spring.

## Gypsophila repens

A dwarf version of the border gypsophila, with clouds of tiny but pretty white or pink flowers in summer.

Height: 6 in. (15cm).

### Varieties to look for
The species itself has white flowers, but there are pink varieties. "Dorothy Teacher" is a good all-round variety that ages to pink.

### Soil and site
Well-drained soil, in full sun. Does well on alkaline (chalky) soil. Zone 4.

### Propagation
Take cuttings in early summer. The species itself and the variety "Rosea" can be raised from seed.

## Phlox subulata
*Moss phlox*

A superb plant for late spring and early summer flowers, forming a ground-hugging carpet of lavender-blue, red, pink, or white flowers.

### ● TIP TO TRY
Try sowing the seeds in warmth under glass in late winter – some of the plants may flower in their first year.

### Varieties and other species
There are many good ones to choose from, but "Apple Blossom," pale pink, "Bonita," lavender-blue, "Red Wings," red, and "Temiskaming," magenta-red, are worth including.

*Phlox douglasii* (alpine phlox) is similar from a distance, but it flowers a little later than *P. subulata*, in early summer. Again there are many varieties, but among the best are: "Boothman's Variety," clear mauve, "Crackerjack," red, and "Red Admiral," crimson.

*Phlox stolonifera* with blue or pink flowers, spreads quickly.

### Soil and site
Well-drained but moisture-retentive soil, in full sun. Zone 3 (*P. douglasii* 5).

### Propagation
Take cuttings in mid summer.

THE APPEAL OF ALPINES

119

# Planting in wall crevices

*Dry stone walls and retaining walls (where the stones are held by gravity and not mortar) provide marvelous planting opportunities for more rock plants! You will be making use of planting spaces that would otherwise probably go unused, and this will soften the sometimes harsh visual impact of a stone wall.*

**How to plant in a dry stone wall**

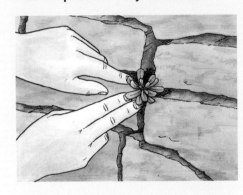

**1** Find a reasonably large crevice where the stone slopes backward (this ensures that moisture reaches the roots), and insert a small seedling or rooted cutting.

**2** Moisten some potting soil and press this into the crevice around the roots. It may be necessary to poke it in with a pencil or stick if the crevice is deep.

**3** The roots will eventually hold the potting soil in place, but if it tends to fall out after planting, try wedging a few small stones around the crevice to hold it in.

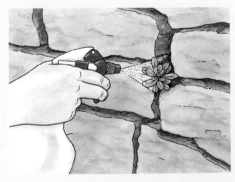

**4** Keep the plant watered until well rooted and established, especially if roots have been disturbed or damaged. The best way to do this is with a compression sprayer.

Ways with Water

# Ways with Water

Water is wonderful. Still water brings a sense of quiet tranquillity; moving water in the form of fountains, cascades or water spouts, a sense of life and vitality that stimulates both auditory and visual senses. An interesting water feature will be a dominant yet subtle focal point that draws attention and admiration, just as an open fire in a livingroom stimulates, attracts, and at the same time relaxes.

Water is a traditional design device used by garden architects through the centuries, but don't assume your garden is too small or your children too young to introduce a water feature. A small self-contained wall fountain, or a pebble fountain, can make a stunning feature ... and these take up little space and should be safe for toddlers too. A little water will make a big difference to your garden.

**Above:** A rather boring shady corner can be transformed by something as simple as a cut-down barrel and a simple water spout.

**Below left:** A simple circular pool can be striking in its simplicity. Avoid turbulent water, otherwise it will look restless rather than restful.

**Previous page:** The varied musical notes created by several trickling streams of water can work real garden magic.

**Right:** Wall masks provide the sight and sound of water in the minimum of space. The water can be allowed to cascade into a small pool beneath, but self-contained wall fountains are available that include a dish below the mask into which the water falls before being recirculated.

**Overleaf:** Streams can be natural or man-made – either way they show water at its most natural, and perhaps its most pleasing.

## Sowing seeds in a wall

Sometimes it is better to sow seeds. Aubrieta is an example of a plant that germinates readily in a wall, but you can also use trailing annuals for quick cover on a newly constructed or planted wall.

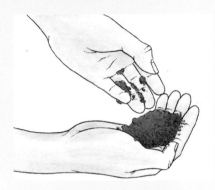

**1** Mix a small number of seeds with some soil, then moisten the mixture so that you can mold it into a ball.

**2** Press the moist soil into a crevice. If necessary push it in with a stick or pencil. Keep moist until the seeds germinate.

Right: Lewisias do not do not like wet crowns, and thrive best wall crevices. This is "Sunset Strain."

Below: Perennial candytuft (*Iberis sempervirens*) will grow like this once it has established a root-hold.

## Plants to try in wall crevices

*Aurinia saxatilis* (formerly *Alyssum saxatile*)
*Asplenium scolopendrium* (formerly *Phyllitis scolopendrium*)
*Aubrieta deltoidea*
*Campanula garganica*
*Campanula portenschlagiana*
*Corydalis lutea*
*Dianthus deltoides*
*Erinus alpinus*
*Gypsophila repens*
*Haberlea rhodopensis*
*Iberis sempervirens*
*Lewisia cotyledon* hybrids
*Lewisia tweedyi*
*Polypodium vulgare*
*Ramonda myconi*
*Saponaria ocymoides*
*Saxifraga cochlearis*
*Saxifraga longifolia*
*Saxifraga paniculata*
*Sempervivum tectorum* (and other species)

Left: *Primula "Wanda."*
Right: *Saxifraga "Cloth of Gold."*
Bottom: *Pulsatilla vulgaris.*

## Primula "Wanda"

Many types of primula can be grown in the rock garden, and even more varieties. This is one of the best-known hybrids, with crimson-purple flowers in spring.
Height: 3 in. (7.5cm).

### Other species to look for
Other spring-flowering primulas for the rock garden include *P. vulgaris sibthorpii*, purplish-pink, and auriculas (*P. auricula*), of which there are literally hundreds of varieties.

### Soil and site
Well-drained but moisture-retentive soil, in partial shade. Zone 6 (*P. auricula* 3).

### Propagation
Divide after flowering.

## Pulsatilla vulgaris (syn. Anemone pulsatilla)
*Pasque flower*

Always an eye-catching plant, with its purple, red, or white large upward-facing cup-like blooms with yellow centers, in mid or late spring. Silky buds add to the plant's appeal.
Height: 1 ft. (30cm).

### Varieties to look for
The most common – and perhaps the most attractive – flowers are those of the species itself and those of the red *P. v. rubra*.

### Soil and site
Well-drained alkaline soil, in full sun. Zone 5.

### Propagation
Take root cuttings in winter, or sow seed in early or mid summer.

### DID YOU KNOW?
The petals of *Pulsatilla vulgaris,* a member of the buttercup family, yield a green dye that was used to stain Easter eggs.

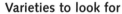

## Saxifraga
*Saxifrage*

This is one of the most important groups of rock plants, with many species and hybrids. There are many kinds differing greatly in appearance. See page 126 for examples of some of the most popular types.

### Varieties to look for
See page 126 for a selection of species and varieties.

### Soil and site
Well-drained soil, in full sun or partial shade. Most prefer alkaline (chalky) soils, but will grow in neutral soils too. The Encrusted saxifrages will tolerate full sun, but other types benefit from midday shade. Zone 6 (most kinds).

### Propagation
Divide after flowering, or detach non-flowering rosettes in late spring or early summer and treat as cuttings.

## Sedum spathulifolium

Apart from bright yellow flowers in early and mid summer, some of the most popular varieties are first-rate foliage plants for the rock garden.

Height: 3 in. (8cm).

### Varieties and other species

Choose one of the two varieties with the best foliage: "Cape Blanco" (syn. "Cappa Blanca") with silvery, almost white, foliage and "Purpureum" with leaves suffused purple.

*Sedum spurium* is worth including because its red, pink, or white, flowers are always striking in mid and late summer. "Schorbuser Blut" (syn. "Dragon's Blood") is a particularly fine variety.

*Sedum kamtschaticum* is always worth growing, with its orange-flushed yellow flowers in late summer and early autumn. Especially good are two of its varieties: S. *k.* var. *floriferum* "Weihenstephaner Gold" and S. *k.* var. *kamtschaticum* "Variegatum," with very striking cream-edged leaves.

### Soil and site

Well-drained soil in full sun. Zone 7.

### Propagation

Divide in early spring or mid autumn, or take cuttings from spring to mid summer. If specific varieties are not required, plants can also be raised from seed sown in spring. Seed of several good rock garden sedums is available from nurseries specializing in the more uncommon plants.

### CHOOSE WITH CARE!

There are many other sedums for the rock garden, but beware of any that can become weeds, such as *Sedum acre* – no matter how pretty the flowers. They will spread freely around the garden.

## Sempervivum
*Houseleek*

These amazing plants can seemingly grow on bare rock and even roofs – they just need a modicum of soil or debris in which to set up home. Although flowering plants, they are grown primarily for foliage effect.

The fleshy rosettes come in many different shapes, sizes, and colors. Some have a cobweb covering. Some enthusiasts grow large collections of them…in the rock garden, in sink gardens, or in pots.

Height: typically 1–2 in. (2.5–5cm) for the rosettes, but flower spikes can be 6 in. (15cm) or more tall.

### Species and varieties to look for

There are hundreds of species and hybrids from which to choose, but most are stocked only by specialty nurseries. These are just some of the best of the widely available houseleeks: S. *andrachnoideum* has small rosettes covered with web-like hairs, "Commander Hay" forms large rosettes, with green-tipped purple-red leaves, S. *tectorum* has green, purple-tipped leaves, deep pink or pale purple flowers.

### Soil and site

Undemanding regarding soil, though drainage must be good. Full sun is essential. Typically Zone 4 or 5.

### Propagation

Remove rooted offsets in early or mid spring or early or mid autumn."Othello," which has attractively colored ruby-red rosettes, is one of many fine hybrids grown for their foliage.

# Miniature bulbs

Below left: Dwarf forms of familiar flowers are often ideal for the rock garden. This miniature daffodil is the charming *Narcissus triadrus albus*, which is about 4 in. (10cm) tall.

*The rock garden is an ideal place to grow those delightful miniatures of the bulb world, like snowdrops and angel's tears narcissi.*

There are many less commonly planted small bulbous plants offered in specialty catalogs, but you might feel reluctant to plant them in a border where they may look insignificant, and the rock garden is an ideal place to show off many of them.

The term "bulb" has been used loosely here, and includes corms and tubers – but they are all plants you can purchase from a garden center or specialty bulb supplier.

Right: Hardy cyclamen make charming rock garden plants. This one is *Cyclamen hederifolum* (syn. *C. neapolitanum*), which flowers in autumn when color in the rock garden is scarce.

## Plants to try

### Alliums

The large globular lilac-white to mauve flowerheads of *A. karataviense* are always eye-catching. Many other alliums are worth a try, two popular ones being the yellow *A. moly* and *A. oreophilum*. They flower mainly in early summer.

### Anemones

*Anemone blanda* and its varieties are widely available and inexpensive to buy. They are predominantly blue, but there are pinks and white.

### Bulbocodium vernum

An eye-catching plant for early to mid spring. The rosy-violet cup-shaped flowers resemble an autumn crocus (colchicum), and appear before the leaves.

### Chionodoxa luciliae

This easy-to-grow bulb flowers prolifically in early and mid spring. It bears starry blue flowers shading to white in the center.

### Colchicums

These produce quite tall leaves in spring, so they need careful positioning, but the flowers

Left: Dwarf tulips that are low-growing and early-flowering are useful rock garden plants, but plant them in bold drifts for maximum impact.

appear separately in autumn and these grow to about 6 in. (10cm). They flower in late summer to mid autumn, depending on species and variety. *C. autumnale* and *C. speciosum* are the ones usually grown.

### Crocuses
All the small-flowered spring crocuses, such as *C. chrysanthus* varieties, are suitable, but make a point of including autumn-flowering species such as *C. speciosus*. It has light mauve to purple flowers.

### Cyclamen, hardy
Try to plant at least two kinds, to spread the period of interest. *C. coum* flowers in late winter to mid spring. *C. hederifolium* (syn. *C. neapolitanum*) in late summer and into autumn.

### Galanthus nivalis
The snowdrop needs no introduction, but there are many varieties, and you could have a whole collection of them!

### Irises
Many kinds of iris can be grown in the rock garden, but of the bulbous spring-flowering ones *I. danfordiae*, with yellow flowers, and *I. reticulata* in shades of blue and purple, are the most popular.

### Narcissi
There are dozens of suitable species and varieties, but reliable and readily available are

*N. bulbocodium* (the hoop petticoat daffodil), *N. cyclamineus*, (strongly reflexed petals like a cyclamen, and long, narrow trumpet) *N. triandrus albus* (angel's tears).

### Rhodohypoxis baurii
These plants, which have a corm-like rhizome, are excellent plants for a rock garden or for troughs. Rose-red is the dominant color, but they also come in various shades of pink as well as white.

### Sternbergia lutea
Useful for autumn interest, it has flowers that look like yellow crocuses. Unfortunately it can be slow and difficult to establish.

### Tulips
A specialty catalogue will reveal many tulips suitable for a rock garden, but early, dependable, and readily available is the yellow and white *Tulipa tarda*, a beauty in mid or late spring.

# Plants for troughs

*Androsace* (most kinds)
*Antennaria dioica* "Minima"
*Arenaria purpurascens*
*Armeria caespitosa*
*Dianthus alpinus*
*Draba* (most kinds)
*Dryas octopetala* "Minor"

*Gentiana saxosa*
*Gentiana verna*
*Iberis saxatilis*
*Myosotis rupicola*
*Oxalis enneaphylla*
*Phlox subulata*
*Polygala calcarea*

*Primula farinosa*
*Primula marginata*
*Saxifraga* (many types)
*Sempervivum* (smallest kinds)
*Thymus serpyllum* "Minor"

Left: *Sempervivum tectorum.*

Above: *Phlox subulata* "Redwings."

# Know your saxifrages

Below: No rock garden is complete without a few saxifrages. They are at their best in spring, and many of them spread readily, tumbling over the rocks in the process.

*This is an invaluable group of plants for the rock garden, but they vary in appearance and ease of cultivation. Some can be demanding to grow and are best grown in pots in an alpine greenhouse, but the vast majority will do well in the rock garden.*

This is a large group of plants (there are about 370 species), so there are plenty for the enthusiast to collect! This can be a confusing group of plants to understand, however, as catalogs and books may use terms that are unfamiliar to most gardeners. The nomenclature is complex too, with plenty of changes to plant names to add to the pitfalls waiting for the unwary.

Don't let any of this deter you. Just grow what you like the look of, but try to check on the plant's requirements. Some need full sun, others shade, some really require chalky (alkaline) soil, others are much less demanding.

The plants mentioned here are just some of the more popular kinds, but specialty suppliers will list a much wider range.

## Some saxifrages to try

### Saxifraga x apiculata
A kabschia or cushion saxifrage with yellow flowers freely produced in early spring. Best in partial shade or full sun.

### Saxifraga "Cloth of Gold"
A mossy saxifrage with soft rosettes of bright golden foliage and white flowers in summer. The color is most intense when put in a shady position.

### Saxifraga cochlearis
An encrusted or silver saxifrage with very attractive lime-encrusted leaves. Pure white

flowers in late spring and early summer. Best in partial shade or sun.

### Saxifraga cotyledon
An encrusted or silver saxifrage with tall arching sprays of white flowers in early and mid summer above rosettes of very ornamental leaves. Best in partial shade or sun.

### Saxifraga paniculata (syn. S. aizoon)
This is one of the easiest of the encrusted or silver saxifrages to grow. It has pale creamy flowers in early summer above small silvery leaf rosettes. Best in partial shade or sun.

### Saxifraga "Pixie"
A mossy saxifrage with rose-red flowers in mid or late spring. Best in partial shade.

## JARGON BUSTER

*Experts divide saxifrages into a number of different groups, called Sections, most of them with names only experts recognize or use. There are, however, a few terms that are widely used in catalogs and books, and you should understand these:*

*Aizoon saxifrages* see Encrusted saxifrages.
*Cushion saxifrages* A term sometimes applied to Kabschias.
*Encrusted saxifrages* (known as the Aizoon Section) form a rosette of flat or slightly incurving leaves that are almost invariable gray-green and are often interestingly encrusted with dots of lime around the edge. The flowers are generally small and white, and may be spotted.
*Engleria saxifrages* see Kabschia
*Kabschia saxifrages* form a rosette of stiff, pointed leaves, which are usually silvery and are often pitted with lime around the edges. They are free-flowering with open, five-petaled flowers, solitary or in small sprays. Engleria Section plants are similar but are usually taller with the flowers more or less pendent and enclosed in colored inflated calyces.
*Mossy saxifrages* make cushions of usually green foliage that is moss-like in appearance from a distance. Some have golden foliage, and most have attractive flowers in spring or summer.

# Veronica prostrata
*Rock or prostrate speedwell*

A superb carpeting plant that will spread to 1½ ft. (45cm) or so, and a mass of flowers from late spring often until mid summer. Although blue is the normal color, there are pinks and whites.
  Height: 4 in. (10cm).

## Varieties to look for
The species itself is the best choice if there is space for only one and a blue flower is required. Try "Rosea" or "Mrs. Holt" for a pale pink and "Alba" for a white. "Trehane" is striking with its violet-blue flowers set against yellow to yellowish-green leaves.

## Soil and site
Well-drained soil, in full sun. Zone 5.

## Propagation
Divide in early spring.

## BEWARE THE INVASION
Although *V. prostrata* is a superb plant for a large rock garden, it can be too rampant for a small space. Do not plant it close to choice but restrained plants that could be taken over by the veronica.
  Other vigorous rock garden veronicas include *V. filiformis* and *V. cinerea*.

Top: *Saxifraga "Pixie," one of the mossy saxifrages.*
Above right: *Veronica prostrata.*

# Viola riviniana "Purpurea" (formerly V. labradorica purpurea)

A charming and utterly reliable plant for the rock garden, though it can be invasive in a mild sort of way (the stray plants are easily removed).

Tiny purple flowers resembling small pansies are backed by striking dark purple-green leaves.

## Varieties to look for
This is the one usually grown, though there is a white form. It is almost always sold under its old name of *V. labradorica purpurea*.

## Soil and site
Well-drained but moisture-retentive soil, in full sun or partial shade. Zone 2.

## Propagation
Take cuttings in mid summer. If you do not mind green leaves, the species can also be raised from seed.

# Beautiful Bulbs

Bulbs – which here include corms and tubers as well as true bulbs – bring us some of our most beautiful flowers that it's hard to imagine our gardens being without. But there are gems for the rock garden, plenty to grow in pots, and choice specialties for the enthusiast to discover.

Any losses are usually due to pests or diseases (mice and other vermin find many of them an attractive meal), but usually you can leave the hardy kinds undisturbed to grow into bigger and better clumps year after year. Finally they will become so congested that they have to be lifted, divided, and replanted.

They're also exceedingly easy plants to grow. With few exceptions, if you plant a flowering-sized bulb you can be sure of flowers. Most of the hardy bulbs, corms, and tubers are particularly tough, though the frost-sensitive ones may have to be lifted and protected for the cold months. Even some of these can be left in the ground if deeply penetrating frosts are rare where you live and you don't mind taking a risk.

# Features

Below left: *Allium cristophii.*
Below right: *Allium giganteum.*
Bottom: *Amaryllis belladonna.*

# Acidanthera bicolor
*see Gladiolus callianthus*

# Allium cristophii
# (syn. A. albopilosum)
*Star of Persia*

One of the gems of the early summer border, and a favorite with flowers arrangers too. Large ball-shaped flower heads about 6 in. (15cm) across, made up of as many as 80 lilac-pink star-like flowers, appear in early summer. The short stems make the heads look even larger.

Height: 1½ ft. (45cm).

## Other species to look for
Apart from *A. giganteum* (see below), some of the boldest border species include *A. aflatunense* with 4 in. (10cm) heads of pinkish flowers on 2½ ft. (75cm) stems in late spring and early summer; *A. moly,* loose heads of bright yellow flowers in early and mid summer on 1 ft. (30cm) stems; and *A. oreophilum* with rose-colored flowers on 1 ft. (30cm) stems in early summer.

## Soil and site
Well-drained soil, in full sun. Zone 7 (*A. aflatunense* and *A. oreophilum* 8).

## Propagation
Remove bulb offsets when the leaves die down, or sow seed in summer or autumn if a slower method is acceptable.

# Allium giganteum
*Ornamental onion*

A giant among the ornamental onions, and a large clump of them makes a stunning border feature. The ball-shaped heads of lilac-purple flowers are about 6 in. (15cm) across, carried on tall stems.

Height: 5 ft. (1.5m).

## Varieties to look for
There are no varieties, but "Globemaster" is a hybrid that also makes a bold and impressive border display.

## Soil and site
Well-drained soil, in full sun. Zone 8.

## Propagation
Remove bulb offsets when the leaves die down, or sow seed in summer or autumn if a slower method is acceptable.

## ● TIP TO TRY
Some alliums make striking cut flowers and do not smell strongly of onion or garlic if they are not bruised. With a vase life of about 14 days, they will out-perform many other cut flowers.

Try drying the flower heads of *A. cristophii* for "everlasting" arrangements.

Bottom: *Anemone blanda.*
Right: *Camassia leichlinii.*

## Amaryllis belladonna

*Belladonna lily, Jersey lily*

This beautiful border bulb is the only species, and not to be confused with the popular hippeastrum widely grown as a potted plant and commonly called amaryllis. The pale pink trumpet flowers appear on bare stems in early and mid autumn, the strap-shaped leaves appearing after the flowers.

Where frosts occur, protect the bulbs by covering the soil with a 6 in. (15cm) mulch (remove again when frosts are unlikely). Be patient; they may need two or three years to settle down before flowering well.
Height: 2½ ft. (75cm).

### Varieties to look for

There are just a few varieties, with colors that range from wine-red through pink to white.

### Soil and site

Well-drained soil, in full sun. Zone 9, but can be grown in zones 7 and 8 if given a warm position, perhaps by a sunny wall.

### Propagation

Remove bulb offsets in summer once the leaves turn yellow. Although it is possible to raise them from seed, they take many years to flower and the results are variable.

## Anemone blanda

One of many excellent spring-flowering "bulbs" (actually tuberous rhizomes), they are easy to grow and naturalize well if conditions are right.

The flowers are normally blue but there are pinks and whites, forming a carpet of flower in early and mid spring.
Height: 4 in. (10cm).

### Varieties and other species to look for

"Radar" is an attractive rosy-purple, "Pink Star" a cyclamen-pink shading to silver-pink, "White Splendor" has large, glistening white flowers that last for weeks.

The wood anemone (*A. nemorosa*) resembles a white *A. blanda*, but is best in a woodland garden.

### Soil and site

Well-drained but moisture-retentive soil, in partial shade. Zones 5–9.

### Propagation

Divide the rhizomes after the top growth has died down, or sow seeds in autumn.

## Camassia leichlinii

A tall, spiky plant which is good for the border or for naturalizing in grassy areas such as an orchard. The spikes of white or blue flowers bloom in early and mid summer.
Height: 3 ft. (1m).

### Varieties and other species to look for

There are double and semi-double forms, but these are uncommon. The similar *C. quamash* (syn. *C. esculenta*) is readily available, with blue, purple, and white varieties.

### Soil and site

Moisture-retentive soil rich in organic matter, in full sun or partial shade. Does well in heavy soil. Zone 3 (*C. quamash* zone 5).

### Propagation

Remove bulb offsets in early autumn. Sow seed in summer but be prepared to wait four or five years for flowering.

# Spring spectacular

Below: Bulbs look more natural if several kinds are grown together. After a few years the large clumps begin to merge into a wonderful carpet of color.

*For most gardeners, bulbs are almost synonymous with spring. The leaves often emerge by mid winter, and the first flowers from autumn-planted bulbs can be expected by late winter.*

The daffodil comes into its own in early spring and, from then on, there is a succession of spring-flowering bulbs that will bloom through until late spring. Despite the vast number of bulbs planted each autumn, however, the results seldom look quite as breathtaking as those catalog pictures, unless you plant for a spring spectacular the way the professionals do.

Bulbs can be expensive, especially new varieties or those that are difficult or slow to propagate. Many individual varieties are bought by amateurs perhaps half-a-dozen at a time (in the case of very expensive bulbs, often single specimens are bought). If you plant these in a border and leave them to multiply, they will make very impressive clumps after a couple of seasons ... but as most of us space the new bulbs out to make our money appear to stretch further, the impact is lost.

If you look at photographs in catalogs or observe the displays in show gardens, you will find that they are crammed in so that the bulbs are almost touching. It's how you can achieve the effect of an established clump even though the planting is new. The way to have a spectacular spring display of bulbs is to plan carefully and plant for a bold display.

## Cover the ground

If your pocket is deep, you can plant a whole bed or border densely with bulbs. If you are gardening on a budget, make the most of spring-flowering biennials such as double daisies (bellis), forget-me-nots (myosotis), or pansies. You can buy these as inexpensive plants in autumn, or raise them yourself from seeds for a minimal cost.

Use spring bedding plants like these to cover the bare ground. If the bulbs are planted sparsely, they will show up better against a carpet of foliage, with the flowers looking far more attractive than they would against a background of soil. You will also be able to stretch the weeks of color beyond the short time that bulbs are at their best.

## Plan for succession

The best way to overcome the drawback of a short flowering season is to plant different varieties of the same kind of plant, so that as

Left: To create impact in spring beds that are to be replanted with summer flowers, interplant tall bulbs such as tulips with wallflowers and forget-me-nots.

one fades another is coming to its peak.

If you buy bulbs in a garden center, infor-

mation about flowering times may not be displayed, but if you buy from a bulb specialist they usually indicate which ones are early, which mid-season, and which late. Even though you can't predict precise dates as that will depend on the season, they will remain constant in the order in which they flower.

The problem with planting for succession is that the garden never looks as spectacular as it would if all the bulbs were in bloom together. Interplanting with spring bedding plants helps to overcome this, especially if their flowering period spans from early to late. Even if they are not in bloom, the carpet of foliage avoids "flat" areas where bare soil points to plants that have passed their prime.

## Short-and long-term

Avoid short-term planting. For bulbs that have to be lifted because they are not frost-hardy it may be inevitable, but most hardy bulbs can be planted and left undisturbed to

multiply on their own.

If you try to plant one bulb that you can leave to grow in a permanent position for every one that has to be short-term (perhaps because they must be lifted for summer bedding or are in containers), your garden will look more impressive every year.

Try planting large drifts in the herbaceous or mixed border. Don't worry too much about bare patches during the summer; it may be possible to plant shallow-rooting annuals over the top (but don't cut the foliage off the bulbs prematurely).

The area under deciduous trees is an ideal place to plant bulbs. They bring a carpet of color in spring when the light is good; the ground probably remains unplanted anyway because the canopy of leaves in summer makes the area dry and shady.

## Be odd

If planting a small number of bulbs, plant in a group rather than a row, and plant an odd number. Six bulbs will generally look less natural and less pleasing than five or seven.

## Be bold

Large drifts are more effective than a number of small clumps. If you can't afford many bulbs, buy the usually cheaper mixtures or a larger quantity of one kind, rather than a half-a-dozen bulbs of a dozen varieties — which will usually be more expensive.

Enthusiasts simply like to grow lots of different species or varieties, but it's still worth concentrating the color in a few areas. Twenty small clumps dotted around the garden will have less impact that the same number of bulbs in a single bed or border.

Above: Snowdrops, crocuses, and *Leucojum vernum* bring welcome color to a border in spring.

Left: For a more formal style, plant in blocks or drifts, like the tulips and muscari in this border.

Bottom: *Chionodoxa luciliae.*
Right: *Colchicum speciosum.*

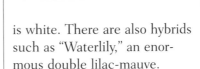

## Chionodoxa luciliae
*Glory of the snow*

Surprisingly striking plants for their small size, the blue, star-shaped flowers on short stems appear in late winter or early spring. They multiply freely and naturalize well – they will form a carpet of flowers in short grass or between other plants such as low-growing heathers.

This is a plant of cold areas, where it normally flowers as the snows recede. In warm zones where the ground does not freeze it may not flower well unless chilled.

They are best planted where they can be left to multiply.
Height: 6 in. (15cm).

### Varieties and other species to look for
There are pink varieties such as "Pink Giant," but some experts consider these to be varieties of *C. forbesii.*

*C. gigantea*, with large violet-blue flowers, is usually listed as a separate species, though some botanists consider it to be a larger form of *C. luciliae.*

### Soil and site
Well-drained soil, in full sun. Zone 4–9.

### Propagation
Lift and divide established clumps as the leaves begin to die down; otherwise allow the plants to seed themselves (which they usually do anyway) and transplant the seedlings.

## Colchicum autumnale
*Autumn crocus, meadow saffron, naked ladies*

Interesting plants with large corms that are sometimes flowered "dry" indoors as a fun plant. If purchased shortly before flowering time, the beautiful flowers, resembling huge lilac crocuses, can appear within a couple of weeks. The leaves, which grow taller than the autumn flowers, do not emerge until spring.

Height in flower: 6 in. (15cm), leaves 10 in. (25cm).

### Varieties and other species to look for
"Album" is white, "Alboplenum" is a white double. "Pleniflorum" (syn. "Roseum Plenum") is a pink double. *C. speciosum* has flowers predominantly in shades of mauve, but "Album"

is white. There are also hybrids such as "Waterlily," an enormous double lilac-mauve.

### Soil and site
Well-drained soil, in full sun or partial shade. Zone 5 (*C. speciosum* zone 6).

### Special needs
Plants flowered "dry" indoors must be discarded or planted in the garden after they have flowered.

### Propagation
Remove the cormlets that form around the base of the corm. The species can also be grown from seed, but this is a slower method.

### ● TIP TO TRY
Naturalize a drift of colchicums in a lawn – they will be a focal point. But choose an area you can leave without mowing in spring and early summer until the leaves die back.

### NOW YOU KNOW!
Despite the common name of autumn crocus, these are not crocuses at all – they have only the shape of the flower in common.

One of the common names sometimes used is meadow saffron, but it is not the source of the spice of that name – saffron comes from *Crocus sativus.* A powerful drug called colchicine, that has been used in the treatment of gout among other things, is derived from the colchicum.

In some countries another common name is "naked ladies," while elsewhere they may be called "naked boys." Perhaps it depends on your viewpoint.

## Cyclamen coum

The miniature versions of the popular cyclamen are perfectly frost-hardy and will even grow beneath trees where few other plants thrive. The pink or carmine flowers (occasionally

● TIP TO TRY

Eranthis are sometimes difficult to coax into growth if the tubers have dried out, which is why they are best moved "in the green". If you buy dried tubers, try soaking them in water overnight before planting – they often root and grow more readily.

Below left: *Cyclamen hederifolium.*
Bottom: *Eranthis hyemalis.*
Right: *Erythronium "Pagoda."*

white) also bloom in winter and early spring, and the leaves are often attractively marbled. Best left undisturbed to self-seed and form large drifts or colonies.

Height: 3 in. (7.5cm).

### Varieties and other species to look for

There are many variations on the basic plant, the main differences being in flower color and leaf markings. *C. hederifolium* (syn. *C. neapolitanum*) is similar but it flowers from late summer to late autumn. Again there are many varieties, in a similar color range. By growing both species it is possible to have color and interest for much of the year in shady areas, which is where it is often appreciated most.

### Soil and site

Well-drained soil with a high organic content, such as a leafy soil, in partial shade. Zone 6.

### Propagation

Although the corms can be divided it is better to sow seed in late summer.

## Eranthis hyemalis
*Winter aconite*

One of the welcome signs of spring, blooming from late winter in a mild season in some areas. Although low-growing, the bright yellow flowers, resembling large buttercups, are set off by a green ruff of leaves. Can be difficult to establish if the ground is too dry. For the first season, water if necessary while the plants are growing. Leave undisturbed.

Height: 4 in. (10cm).

### Varieties to look for

"Guinea Gold" is a particularly fine form of the flower.

### Soil and site

Well-drained but moisture-retentive soil, in full sun or partial shade. Zones 5–9.

### Propagation

Divide and replant the tubers when the leaves begin to die down. Alternatively, sow seed in mid or late spring.

### GOOD COMPANIONS

Although they do not always flower at the same time, snowdrops, *Crocus tommasinianus,* and winter aconites make good companions, and they can all be naturalized in short grass.

## Erythronium dens-canis
*Dog's-tooth violet*

Curious-looking little plants with reflexed nodding flowers in mid and late spring, above mottled leaves. Colors range from purple through pink to white.

They are best naturalized at the edge of woodland or in front of trees or shrubs.

These small but beautiful plants must be given a suitable site to thrive, and they resent being moved once established. Choose a site with care and leave the plants undisturbed for as long as possible.

Height: 6 in. (15cm).

### Varieties and other species to look for

Examples from the color range are: "Lilac Wonder," "Pink Perfection," "Purple King," "White Splendor." Other species are available, some taller plants with bolder flowers. Some of the hybrids are especially worth considering: "Kondo" is pale yellow, and "Pagoda" is yellow and up to 1½ ft. (45cm) tall. Both are particularly impressive plants.

### Soil and site

Moist but not waterlogged soil, with plenty organic matter, in partial shade. They do not thrive where the tubers become hot and dry in summer. Zones 3–9.

### Propagation

Remove offsets from mature plants when the leaves die down in summer. *E. dens-canis* can be raised from seed though results are slow and usually variable. Sow in summer.

BEAUTIFUL BULBS

135

# Summer specials

*Summer-flowering bulbs are less widely planted than spring-flowering kinds, probably because there are so many other plants to grow for summer color. Yet if you don't plant some of the bulbs suggested here, you'll be missing out on some of the most spectacular flowers in the border.*

If tuberous plants like begonias are included, there are some wonderful bulbs that can be used for summer bedding, for containers, and in flower borders. And there are many imaginative ways in which summer-flowering "bulbs" can be used. Many are exceptionally useful for providing highlights among the other herbaceous plants, and you can use them to fill in those inevitable gaps that occur from time to time.

**Above: Gladioli are often grown as cut flowers, but they are imposing border plants too. Tall varieties require staking, but dwarf kinds do not require canes.**

Some border bulbs, such as crocosmias (corms), *Zantedeschia aethiopica* (rhizomes), and day lilies or hemerocallis (fleshy rhizomes), are sometimes sold growing in pots, along with the normal herbaceous plants, but all the plants mentioned here can be obtained from bulb suppliers.

The lily is sometimes said to be the queen of the border bulbs, and you will find a large selection of species and hybrids in garden centers as well as in bulb catalogs. The main types of lily are described on pages 148–149, but whatever type you choose to grow should do well in a border or in light shade among shrubs. They do best in light or partial shade, though most of them will put in an admirable effort even in full sun.

Plant in a group of at least five bulbs if you want them to make a statement among the other border perennials, but don't hesitate to pop in an isolated bulb or two wherever there is space between other plants. As lily stems and foliage are hardly attractive, it doesn't matter if these are hidden by lower-growing plants and only the flowers are visible.

### Drumsticks and balls

Ornamental onions (alliums) include some stunning border plants. The 6 in. (15cm) rosy-purple balls of *Allium giganteum*, on stems up to 5 ft. (1.5m) tall, are an arresting sight. Many other species have imposing drumstick flower heads, such as *A. rosenbachianum* at 3 ft. (90cm) and *A. sphaerocephalon* at 2–3 ft. (60–90cm), both an attractive purple.

Lower growing at about 1–1½ ft. (30–45cm), *A. cristophii* (syn. *A. albopilosum*) never fails to attract interested comment. The spherical heads are about 6–8 in. (15–20cm) across, studded with well-spaced, star-shaped purple flowers. This one's popular with flower arrangers because the flower heads dry well for winter decoration.

Dahlias are likely to be the brightest plants in the border in late summer and into autumn, but they come in many guises, from Lilliputs of about 1 ft. (30cm) to giants with flowers the size of dinner plates. The main types are described on page 146. These tubers need lifting for the winter to be stored in a frost-free place.

## Cool and classy

Arum lilies (zantedeschias) have big white, pink, or yellow spathes set among large green leaves. What they lack in color they make up for in their cool, aristocratic appearance. Unfortunately they prefer a winter temperature of at least 50°F (10°C), though *Zantedeschia aethiopica* is tougher and will survive winter outside where frosts do not penetrate to root level. "Crowborough" is considered to be a hardier variety, but this is still not a plant for cold areas.

## Tall spikes

Try to find space for a clump of summer hyacinths (*Galtonia candicans*). The 4 ft. (1.2m) stems have hanging bells along their length. It is best to lift the bulbs in autumn if the soil is liable to freeze deeply.

Gladioli are often appreciated more as a cut flower than a garden plant, as they do not blend easily with the other border plants. Grow in a large clump, and consider the miniatures, butterfly hybrids, or primulinus types for a garden display.

The species *Gladiolus* x *colvillei* and *G. communis byzantinus* (often sold as *G. byzantinus*) grow to about 2–3 ft. (60–90cm) and have smaller and looser flowers. The colors are less varied, but they look more at ease among border plants. The corms of all of them will have to be lifted in cold regions, but the two species mentioned can be left in the ground where severe penetrating frosts are unlikely.

## Bright and beautiful

Indian shot (cannas) are tall, beautiful, and have what it takes to impart a sense of the exotic. At 4–6 ft. (1.2–1.8m), even a single clump in the border will not go unnoticed. Most have bright red, orange, or yellow flowers, and the foliage is bronze or almost brown, sometimes variegated. Cannas have to be lifted for the winter and stored in a frost-free place in areas where frosts occur.

*Crocosmia masonorum* and its varieties and hybrids are first-rate border plants, forming a large clump of sword-shaped leaves topped with orange or yellow funnel-shaped flowers on arching sprays about 3 ft. (90cm) tall. They may need a winter mulch of straw or other protective material in cold areas.

**Above:** *Crocosmia masonorum* **is easy to grow and will multiply freely to form large clumps.**

**Left:** **The cool white spikes of** *Galtonia candicans* **bring stately elegance to a summer border.**

## Weird and wonderful

Arisaemas are arums with hooded spathes, and often highly exotic markings. *Arisaema candidissimum* has pale pink cowl-like spathes about 6 in. (15cm) long, delicately striped white. *A. consanguineum*, a taller plant up to 3 ft. (90cm), has a whip-like end to the spathe, which is striped maroon-purple and white. Just a single plant of either, placed where it can be discovered almost accidentally, will create that useful element of surprise and arouse curiosity.

The angel's fishing rod (*Dierama pulcherrimum*) needs a moist but not waterlogged position to do well. It will reward with arching sprays of pendulous pink bells, on stems that reach about 5 ft. (1.5m). Try a climbing lily – *Gloriosa rothschildiana* – on a warm patio. This exotic flower can be grown in a pot if necessary. It will be happy growing up a trellis.

# Know your daffodils

*Once daffodils were mainly yellow and most of those grown had a long trumpet. Nowadays you can buy daffodils and other narcissi in a bewildering array of shapes and sizes.*

Pinks and oranges are now commonplace colors, and in addition to those with short cups instead of trumpets, there are "orchid-flowered" varieties that do not even look like daffodils.

This summary of the main types will ensure that you are not bewildered by those complicated descriptions in the catalogs.

The classification of narcissi usually used in catalogs is based on one recommended by the Royal Horticultural Society. You will sometimes see them referred to as Divisions (for example Division 2, which means a large-cupped narcissus). Don't be deterred by this shorthand; the illustrations here will give you a good idea of what they look like.

See the Jargon Buster opposite for an explanation of the terms used for describing narcissi.

## Trumpet (Division 1)

These need no description – the traditional daffodils we all know and love, with a long trumpet, belong here. The technical definition is that the trumpet or corona is as long or longer than the perianth segments.

*Above :* **Daffodils are at their most spectacular when naturalized over a large area like this. Although few gardeners have the space for this kind of display, it may be possible to plant large drifts in a small orchard or even within a large lawn.**

138

## Cyclamineus (Division 6)

These hybrids reflect the *N. cyclamineus* characteristics, such as swept-back petals. They are shorter than the majority of ordinary daffodils. Some varieties flower early and are very suitable for containers. Most are compact at 9–15 in. (23–38cm).

## Jonquilla (Division 7)

Plants of garden origin that reflect the characteristics of *N. jonquilla*: there are several small fragrant flowers to a stem. They make good cut flowers.

## Tazetta (Division 8)

Plants of garden origin with the characteristics of *N. tazetta* dominant. They have clusters of several fragrant flowers on each stem. There are not as hardy as most narcissi, and some are used mainly for forcing for cut flowers or indoor decoration.

## Poeticus (Division 9)

Plants of garden origin showing characteristics of *N. poeticus*. They have fragrant, almost flat white flowers with a tiny cup. There is only one flower to a stem.

## Species and wild forms and hybrids (Division 10)

This division includes many gems for the rock garden, including the hoop-petticoat narcissus (*N. bulbocodium*), *N. cyclamineus* with its strongly reflexed petals like a cyclamen, and *N. canaliculatus*, with three or four sweetly scented white and gold flowers on 6 in. (15cm) stems.

## Split-corona (Division 11)

These very distinctive varieties have the corona split for at least one-third of its length. The segments are often folded back close to the perianth, and their unusual and exotic-looking appearance has given rise to other generic names for this group: orchid-flowered and butterfly narcissi.

## Miscellaneous (Division 12)

This is not just a "dustbin" for uninteresting varieties. Two outstanding dwarf daffodils have been placed here: "Tête-a-Tête" and "Jumblie," both multi-headed plants, early-flowering and suitable for forcing and growing in pots, and only 6–9 in. (15–23cm) tall.

## Large-cupped (Division 2)

Although these lack the long trumpet, the cup or corona is more than one-third the length of the perianth segments.

## Small-cupped (Division 3)

The cup or corolla on these varieties is much smaller – not more than one-third the length of the perianth segments.

## Double (Division 4)

Double flowers distinguish this group, but their appearance is very variable according to variety.

## Triandrus (Division 5)

The dominant characteristics of these garden hybrids reflect the *Narcissus triandrus* origins: a compact habit with more than one flower to a stem, with somewhat swept-back petals. They are generally short plants about 1 ft. (30cm) tall, sometimes shorter.

Triandrus hybrids generally flower in mid and late spring and perform well in pots and other containers as well as in borders.

### JARGON BUSTER

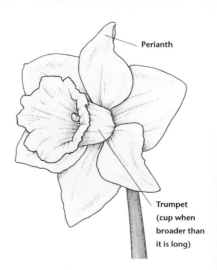

Perianth

Trumpet (cup when broader than it is long)

Above left: "Bridal Crown," an attractive white double variety. Doubles vary considerably in appearance.

Above: "Broadway Star," one of the split-corona varieties, sometimes described as orchid-flowered.

# Autumn delights

*Autumn-flowering plants help to make winter seem a little bit shorter. They flower toward the end of the season, just as everything else seems to be dying down.*

The colchicums will flower within weeks of planting, so the results can be almost instant. You don't need many autumn-flowering bulbs to transform the garden as the nights draw in and flowers in the garden become fewer. Their very scarceness makes the impact greater. A single clump of autumn crocuses (colchicums) in front of an otherwise gloomy shrub, a drift of miniature cyclamen (*Colchicum hederifolium*, syn. *C. neapolitanum*) beneath a tree, or a patch of bright yellow sternbergias among the brown autumn leaves scattered by the wind over a border ... all these are sufficient to lift the spirits as the gardening year comes to a low ebb.

Most autumn-flowering bulbs are very amenable and should multiply and give you a better show from year to year, so they make a worthwhile investment.

## Crocuses, true and false

There are more than a dozen true crocuses that you could plant to recreate memories of spring! But only a couple of them are likely to be readily available unless you go to a specialty supplier.

*Crocus kotschyanus kotschyanus* (syn. *C. zonatus*) is one of the first to flower in autumn, and rapidly increases into clumps. The color is pale lilac with a yellow zone or blotch in the throat. Also easy to grow, and widely available, is the delightful lilac or violet *C. speciosus* (there is also a white form). This one has an intensity of color that makes it especially attractive against the autumn leaves through which it often flowers.

Try *C. nudiflorus* if you want one to naturalize in grass. The orange stigma and rich purple petals make it surprisingly striking.

If you see what looks like a yellow spring crocus from a distance, it will almost certainly be a sternbergia. They are not crocuses

**Above:** Invaluable for late color, *Nerine bowdenii* blooms well into autumn, sometimes into early winter.

**Left:** Grow colchicums for early autumn color. This variety is "Conquest" ("Glory of Heemstede").

**Right:** The superb *Amaryllis belladonna* never fails to arrest attention, but it does require a warm position.

at all, but members of the amaryllis family. These look superb against a background of gravel or autumn leaves, but they are not as easy to grow as proper crocuses. They require a hot, sunny position and well-drained neutral or alkaline soil.

The colchicums are sometimes called autumn crocuses, but they are more closely allied to lilies. They are also much larger. Try them in clumps between other plants near the front of a border, or beneath trees and shrubs, or naturalize them in rough grass. Plant them in the rock garden with caution, as the leaves – which don't appear until spring – grow much taller than the flowers and may swamp small plants nearby.

The species commonly planted are *C. autumnale*, *C. byzantinum*, and *C. speciosum*, and their varieties. They come in shades of pink, lilac, and white. There are also doubles.

## Amaryllis and crinums
One of the most impressive autumn bulbs, sure to bring your herbaceous border back to life, is the exotic-looking *Amaryllis belladonna*. It needs a sunny spot though, and if you don't live in a warm part of the world

Below: Crocuses are associated with spring, but there are many autumn-blooming species too, such as the *Crocus kotschyanus* illustrated here. Plant where they can be left undisturbed to form large clumps.

it's best to plant it at the base of a sunny wall. It will bring new interest where wall shrubs and climbers are nearing the end of their season.

Don't confuse this plant with the tender hippeastrums, popularly called amaryllis and sold as house plants. The flowers are similar in shape, but this one is a true amaryllis. The leafless stems grow to 2–3 ft. (60–90cm), topped with up to six large, bright pink, fragrant flowers. The leaves appear after the flowers and remain until the following summer. Winter protection will be needed in cold areas.

Crinums are also very showy, with large funnel-shaped flowers in late summer and early autumn on 3 ft. (90cm) stems. They are generally tougher than the amaryllis, but choose *Crinum* x *powellii* unless you live in a mild area as this is hardier than most. It has up to 10 large pink or white blooms on each stem. Grow it in the herbaceous or mixed border, but if you live in a cold area it will be best in front of a sunny wall.

## Snowdrops and snowflakes
These autumn-flowering versions of the popular spring plants are not particularly showy, but worth planting for a little extra autumn interest.

The autumn-flowering snowflake, *Leucojum autumnale,* carries tiny, white, pendent bell-shaped flowers on plants 4–6 in. (10–15cm) high. It is best in a warm position in the rock garden.

A snowdrop called *Galanthus reginae-olgae* looks like a normal spring snowdrop but blooms at the opposite end of the year. It prefers more sun than the spring snowdrop.

## A final fling
The schizostylis, or kaffir lily, is a rhizomatous plant that deserves to be better known. It's easy to grow, and the red or pink flowers on 1½–2 ft. (45–60cm) spikes rising above the grassy foliage, stand out from across the garden from early to late autumn. It needs a moisture-retentive soil if possible, and may need winter protection in cold areas, but it's worth a little care. *Schizostylis coccinea* "Major" is the one widely grown, but there are other varieties, in various shade of pink and red.

Nerines often provide the last fling of really showy color at the tail-end of the year. *Nerine bowdenii* is the hardiest species, with 1½–2 ft. (45–60cm) stems topped with bright pink flower heads, the undulating petals giving them a spidery appearance from a distance. They are usually at their best in mid autumn, but may still be colorful in early winter.

Other nerines are grown, including *N. sarniensis*, but they require more warmth.

Even *N. bowdenii* is not the easiest plant to grow if you live in a cold area. Plant in front of a sunny wall if possible, and leave undisturbed to form large clumps. In cold regions a thick winter mulch over the surface may help (remove it in spring).

**Below left:** *Fritillaria imperialis.*
**Bottom:** *Galanthus nivalis.*
**Right:** *Galtonia candicans.*

## Fritillaria imperialis
*Crown imperial*

Outstanding border plants for mid spring, sure to attract attention and admiration. The orange-red or yellow nodding bells crowned with a tuft of green leaves, on tall stems, can hardly fail to impress.

The bulbs are fragile and easily damaged, and prone to rot. They are sometimes planted on their sides, on a bed of gravel or coarse sand, so that water does not lodge in the hollow crown.

Height: 3 ft. (90cm).

### Varieties and other species to look for
"Rubra Maxima" is red and very robust, "Maxima Lutea" is lemon-yellow; both are especially bold, but if variegated plants appeal, try "Aureomarginata".

*F. meleagris*, the snake's-head fritillary, is another very popular species, as delicate-looking

as the other is strong. The tiny nodding bells on slender 1 ft. (30cm) stalks are spotted in shades of pink, purple, or white.

### Soil and site
Well-drained, fertile soil, in full sun or partial shade. *F. imperialis* is best grown in borders, but *F. meleagris* will also grow well in short grass. Zone 4.

### Propagation
Remove offset bulbs in summer, or sow seed in mid or late summer (it can take more than five years before the seedlings flower).

## Galanthus nivalis
*Snowdrop*

The snowdrop needs no introduction: its nodding white bells mark the end of the worst of winter.

There are doubles as well as the more popular single form, and varieties with larger than normal flowers or with different amounts of green.

Although late winter is the typical flowering time, they sometimes bloom in mid winter, and in a cold year they may not flower until early spring.

Snowdrops need a year or two to become established and form imposing clumps. They succeed best where they can

be left to naturalize. Snowdrops do not usually do well where winter temperatures remain much above freezing.

Height: 6 in. (15cm).

### Varieties to look for
The species itself is difficult to beat for a general garden display, but "Flore Pleno" is one of the most widely grown doubles, and "Lutescens" is interesting because it has yellow patches at the apex of each inner petal.

### Soil and site
Moisture-retentive soil with plenty of organic matter, in partial shade. Zones 4–9.

### Propagation
Divide established clumps just after flowering. They can be raised from seed, best sown fresh as soon as it is ripe. There may be self-sown seedling around the parent plants that can be used.

## Galtonia candicans
*Summer hyacinth*

Despite their name, these do not much resemble hyacinths, and the common name is probably a reference to the fact that it used to be called *Hyacinthus candicans*. The widely spaced white bell-shaped flowers hang from tall, stiff stems, and they are best seen as a large clump.

Unless the bulbs have to be lifted in a cold region, leave in the ground and allow to form a large clump undisturbed for maximum impact.

Height: 4 ft. (1.2m).

### Other species to look for
*G. viridiflora* is similar but with pale green flowers.

### Soil and site
Well-drained, moisture-retentive soil, in sheltered position in full sun. Zone 5 (*G. viridiflora* zone 8).

### Propagation
Remove offsets in spring or autumn, or sow seed in early spring, although the seedlings take four or five years to flower.

# Winter wonders

*Winter is always a difficult period in the garden, and the few hardy bulbs that flower at this time help to bring a little relief to those drab days.*

The hardy bulbs tough enough to put in an appearance at this time tend to be small and best appreciated by close viewing, so it makes sense to plant them near winter-flowering shrubs and other winter-interest plants. Focusing the eye like this makes the most of these small bulbs.

Although only a couple of flowers are suggested here, many spring-flowering bulbs, such as snowdrops (*Galanthus nivalis*), winter aconites (*Eranthis hyemalis*), and *Crocus tommasinianus*, often start to flower in late winter. It depends where you live and the severity of the winter in a particular year, but plant plenty of these early bloomers because they will still bring early color before the main flush of spring flowers.

## What to plant for flowers

*Crocus laeviagus* flowers in mild spells from early to late winter.

*Cyclamen coum* will start to flower in mid or late winter in mild areas, slightly later elsewhere.

## One for foliage effect

Lords and ladies or cuckoo pint (*Arum italicum*) does not bloom in winter, but it does provide winter interest with its ornamental foliage. The arrow-shaped rich green leaves are strikingly marbled with cream-colored veins.

**Left:** The delightful dwarf cyclamen *C. coum* is amazingly tough and will bloom in late winter and through to early spring. Here large groups have been naturalized with snowdrops.

**Above:** *Crocus tommasinianus* is really tough despite its fragile appearance, and self sown seedlings help it to multiply freely where conditions suit.

BEAUTIFUL BULBS

143

Bottom: *Gladiolus callianthus* (formerly *Acidanthera bicolor murielae*).
Right: *Gladiolus* hybrid.

## Gladiolus callianthus (syn. Acidanthera bicolor murielae)

Invaluable for late border interest, the white flowers with their conspicuous maroon blotch in the center bring another flush of interest in late summer and early autumn. If you plant them close enough to the front of the border their scent can also be appreciated, though they are usually positioned mid-border.

Where possible, leave the corms in the ground to form large clumps, but where penetrating frosts are likely, lift and store the corms for the winter. In areas of borderline hardiness, they may survive most years protected by the soil, but losses can be expected in severe weather when frosts penetrate deeply. These types do not normally require staking.

Height: 3 ft. (90cm).

### Other species to look for
Other species gladioli ideal for the herbaceous border are *G. communis byzantinus*, syn. *G. byzantinus,* with purplish-red or purplish-pink flowers, in early summer, and *C.* x *colvillei* (salmon-pink, early summer) and its varieties such as "The Bride," white with greenish throat markings. These flower in late spring or early summer.

### Soil and site
Well-drained soil, in full sun. Zone 8 (*C. communis byzantinus* zone 6).

### Propagation
Remove the small corms that form around the base of the plant and grow them to flowering size.

## Gladiolus, large flowered
*Sword lily*

Large-flowered gladioli, and the smaller hybrids such as butterfly and primulinus types, are often grown as cut flowers, but they make an eye-catching display in the border if planted in groups – preferably with smaller and bushier plants in front to mask their leggy appearance.

Gladioli come in a huge color range. The tallest may require staking, but the shorter kinds usually stand straight if they are planted in a group and the position is not too exposed.

Most flower in mid or late summer, but flowering can be spread by using early, mid-season, and late varieties, and by staggering planting times.

Except in frost-free areas, lift the corms in autumn and store in a frost-free place until planting time to reduce the risk of losses. In areas of borderline hardiness, the corms may survive with the protection of the soil, but they may be lost in a severe winter when the ground freezes deeply.

Tall, large-flowered hybrids grow to about 3–4 ft. (90–120cm), primulinus varieties, which have loosely arranged florets, reach about 1½–3 ft. (45–90cm). Butterfly varieties, which have the florets closely packed on the stem, and often striking throat markings or blotches, grow 2–4 ft. (60–120cm) tall. Miniatures resemble the primulinus varieties in appearance, but are smaller and usually reach 1½–2½ ft. (45–75cm).

### Varieties to look for
There are very many varieties, most stocked by just a few suppliers, and the list of available plants is fluid, with new ones being introduced and old ones being dropped almost annually. As the performance of most is similar, it is best to choose varieties that you like the look of, or simply with a color that appeals.

### Soil and site
Well-drained soil, in full sun. Zone 9 (lower zones if lifted routinely for the winter).

### Propagation
Remove the small corms that form around the base of the plant and grow them to flowering size.

### ● TIP TO TRY
Try cutting species gladioli for indoor decoration. Their smaller size and less stiff appearance make them more suitable than large-flowered hybrids for many arrangements, though they do not last as long.

# Forcing the issue

*Get a foretaste of spring by forcing a few bulbs to flower indoors weeks or even months earlier than they would bloom in the garden.*

### Bulbs to try

Hyacinths are a popular choice, but tulips can be successful too if you choose varieties recommended for forcing. Some compact and small-flowered daffodils will also force well.

### Other bulbs to grow in water

Bulb specialists sell certain narcissi to grow and flower in water. "Paper White" (botanically *Narcissus papyraceus*) is the most popular. You need to grow a whole group of these together, so they are usually planted in a bowl filled with pebbles or marbles, to help keep the bulbs upright.

### The earliest flowers

Some bulbs are specially prepared for early flowering, and you should always choose these if you want the earliest blooms. They may be described as "treated," "pre-chilled," or "prepared".

## Bulbs in bowls and pots

**1** You can use bowls without drainage holes if you use a special bulb fiber and water very carefully; otherwise use a normal pot and potting soil. Plant an odd number of bulbs with the noses just above the potting soil.

**2** Bulb fiber should be moist but not wet. Water ordinary pots and allow to drain. Then place in a cold spot outdoors if possible. Slide into a plastic bag first to keep the bowl clean, then cover with about 2 in. (5cm) of gravel or sand.

**3** Check periodically, making sure the soil or fiber has not dried out. When the shoots are about 1–2 in. (2.5–5cm) tall, bring indoors to a cool, light spot. Put them in a warm position only when the buds have emerged.

## Hyacinth in a glass

**1** It's interesting to grow a hyacinth in a glass (buy a special hyacinth glass), and a fun project for children to try. Buy a good-sized bulb and fill the glass with water to just below the base of the bulb.

**2** Keep the bulb in a cold, dark place (or wrap the glass in aluminum foil) until a mass of roots has formed and a shoot is emerging. Check the water level occasionally and top up if necessary.

**3** Bring the bulb into the light when the shoot is about 1–2 in. (2.5–5cm) long, but keep cool. When the bud is beginning to show color, place in a warm room to flower.

# Know your dahlias

*Dahlias are diverse. There are miniatures, single flowered, and cactus-flowered plants, and the color range is enormous.*

There are miniatures that you can grow in a window box and giants 5 ft. (1.5m) tall with flowers 10 in. (25cm) or so across. There are single flowers, pompons, and ball-shaped flowers, cactus and semi-cactus flowers with quilled petals, and decoratives with their flatter and broader petals, to mention just some of them. With a color range that is nothing if not bright and varied, you are sure to find varieties to please.

Dahlias often start to bloom in mid summer, but the larger kinds don't put on a decent show until late summer. They will continue to bloom until cut back by the first frost. They are tuberous-rooted, and the dry tubers are widely sold by bulb specialists and seed companies as well as garden centers. Specialty dahlia nurseries usually sell young plants propagated from cuttings. Some bedding types are easily raised from seed sown in warmth in late winter or early spring.

**Single** The term is self-explanatory, each flower having 8–10 petals, with the central disc clearly visible.

**Anemone** Although the flowers are double, there are two kinds of petals: central ones are short and tubular, the outer large and flat.

**Collerette** There are three distinct parts to the flower: a central yellow disc, a collar of small petals, then the outer row of full-sized petals.

**Waterlily** These fully double flowers have broad, flat petals, giving the impression of a waterlily shape.

**Decorative** Decoratives are doubles with broad petals rounded at the end, usually curling inward slightly along their length.

**Ball** As the name implies, the whole of this double flower is rounded and ball-shaped. The petals are rolled for over half their length.

**Pompon** Like a small ball dahlia, pompons grow to 2 in. (5cm) across, and the petals are rolled for the whole of their length.

**Cactus** The double flowers have narrow, pointed petals, quilled or rolled backward; also may be incurving or straight.

**Semi-cactus** As their name implies, these are similar to cactus dahlias in appearance but they are not so spiky-looking. The petals have a broad base and curve backward.

**Orchid-flowered** Like a single dahlia, but with the petals rolled for at least two-thirds of their length.

**Dwarf bedding** Dwarf bedding dahlias usually have small single or semi-double flowers, though some are fully double. Normally raised from seed annually, even though the tubers can be saved.

**Lilliput** These grow little more than 1 ft. (30cm) tall, and have perfectly formed miniature single flowers. They can be used in the rock garden, pots, tubs, or window boxes.

# Hyacinthus
*Hyacinth*

Popular bulbs for forcing indoors, but also invaluable for spring bedding displays in the garden. They can also be naturalized in grass.

If the bulbs have been forced, do not attempt to force them a second time – instead discard or plant them in the garden.

Height: 9 in. (23cm).

## Varieties to look for
Dozens of varieties can be found in shops and bulb catalogs, in many shades of pink and blue as well as yellow and white. There are also double varieties, though these are not necessarily more showy as garden plants.

Well-proven varieties include "Anna Marie" which is rose pink; "Blue Jacket," bluebell blue; "Carnagie," pure white; "City of Haarlem," primrose yellow; "Delft Blue," soft blue; "Gipsy Queen," yellow flushed apricot; and "Ostara," navy blue.

## Soil and site
Well-drained, in sun or partial shade. Zone 4.

## Propagation
Not normally practical for amateurs. Professional growers use special techniques to stimulate the production of small bulbs around the base of the old one, which are then grown for several years until they reach flowering size.

# Ipheion uniflorum (formerly Triteleia uniflora)
*Spring star flower*

Charming for a mid or late spring display at the front of a border or in a rock garden, this low-growing plant produces a mound of pale blue star-shaped flowers for many weeks. The plants are best left undisturbed to form large clumps. The leaves have an onion-like smell if crushed.

Height: 8 in. (20cm).

## Varieties to look for
The species itself has pale blue flowers, but there are the following varieties: "Album" is

white, "Froyle Mill" is violet-blue, "Wisley Blue" dark blue.

## Soil and site
Undemanding regarding soil, but best in full sun or partial shade. Zones 6–10.

## Propagation
Remove offset bulbs as the leaves die down. Can be raised from seed, but offsets are produced freely and flower more quickly.

## NOW YOU KNOW!
This charming little plant has received a lot of attention from botanists, who have found reason to reclassify it several times. It has been a broadiaea and a millia, then *Triteleia uniflora* (a name under which it is still sometimes found in catalogs), and now it's *Ipheion uniflorum*!

# Iris danfordiae

One of the delights of early spring, with cheerful yellow flowers that are also sweetly fragrant. Try them in a raised bed to enjoy the fragrance. They also make attractive potted plants.

Unless planted deeply enough, the bulbs tend to split up into many small ones after flowering. This will not affect flowering the first year, and

could be beneficial for propagation, but is detrimental if plenty of flowers are required in the second year. Cover with at least 2 in. (5cm) of soil.

Height: 4–6 in. (10–15cm).

## Other species to look for
The other popular dwarf spring-flowering bulbous irises are *Iris histrioides* and *I. reticulata*, and their varieties and hybrids, which grow to a similar size and flower in early spring – a little earlier in favorable conditions. Both species have a number of varieties in various shades of blue and purple.

## Soil and site
Well-drained soil, in full sun or partial shade. They do well on chalky soils. Zone 5

## Propagation
Remove offset bulbs when the leaves have died down. They may require a couple of years to reach flowering size.

# Know your lilies

*Lilies have fascinated gardeners for thousands of years, and they are easier to grow than many gardeners imagine.*

Some of the species are demanding to grow, but most modern hybrids can be planted in the confident knowledge that you will be rewarded within months with some of the most magnificent flowers in the garden. Choosing which lilies to grow can be a bewildering task, but you won't go far wrong if you try any of the widely available hybrids — go for those that you find most appealing. Just check that the species or variety is lime-tolerant if you garden in chalky ground; otherwise try to give lilies the conditions they like best: a rich and fertile soil with good drainage, preferably one into which lots of garden compost or well-rotted manure has been incorporated. They enjoy flowering in the sun, but don't mind some shade and prefer to have their roots sheltered by other plants. This is useful, as the lower part of lily plants are uninspiring, so you can underplant with something pretty and enjoy the magnificent lily blooms above.

Modern hybrids are remarkably tolerant, however, and will bloom and multiply if grown in containers in sun or shade.

## Asiatic hybrids

This is one of the most popular groups for general garden decoration. The many varieties have been derived from various Asiatic species, and the best-known ones are characterized by their sturdy growth and early-blooming, upright "bowl-shaped" flowers — though there are Asiatic hybrids with trumpet and Turk's cap flower shapes. The main flowering period is early and mid summer. They are usually the earliest to flower and are ideal for large containers.

There are dwarf varieties, such as the Pixie range, which are ideal for patio pots or exposed positions in beds. They do not require support.

## Oriental hybrids

These were originally derived from crosses between *Lilium speciosum* and *L. auratum* — two excellent species for the garden. The bowl-shaped flowers, in mid and late summer, tend to face outward (rather than upward as in the Asiatic hybrids). They have the benefit of being very fragrant but suffer

the drawback of not tolerating limy soil.

There are dwarf Oriental hybrids suitable for pots or a small garden where the space is limited.

## Trumpet hybrids

The epitomy of the lily for many gardeners, these have long, trumpet-shaped blooms. They can be grown in large containers but usually look best in herbaceous or mixed borders. Most of them grow to about 4–5 ft. (1.2–1.5m). They are first-rate border plants, but can also be grown in large containers.

## Popular species

*Lilium regale* is one of the finest of all lilies for the border, for light woodland, or for growing in large clumps among shrubs. The large, fragrant trumpet flowers are flushed pinkish-purple on the outside; "Album" is all white.

**Above left: If you have space in the border for just one species, *Lilium regale* must be on your list.**

**Above: Lily hybrids come in bolder colors than most of the species. This is "Bellingham Hybrid."**

*Lilium speciosum* var. *rubrum* has large, sweetly scented white flowers with reflexed petals suffused pink and spotted with carmine. It blooms in late summer or early autumn, and is best in a herbaceous or mixed border. There is also an all-white variety.

*Lilium tigrinum* has heavily-spotted flowers in the shape of a Turk's cap. It looks bold in a border or light woodland, and is suitable as a cut flower for a large arrangement. The usual color is orange with dark spots, but there are yellow, pink, and white varieties.

## Classification

There is an international lily register which places each species or variety into one of more than 15 classifications; you may see these referred to in catalogs. If you just want a few magnificent lilies to grace your garden, however, don't concern yourself with these.

### Flower form

You will find three basic flower forms mentioned in catalogs: blooms may be described as having a bowl, trumpet, or Turk's cap shape.

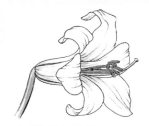

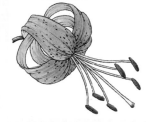

**Bowl-shaped**
flowers have flared petals, with no pronounced tube or trumpet.

**Trumpet-shaped**
flowers have the base of the petals fused to form a tube.

**Turk's cap**
flowers have strongly reflexed petals that are rolled and swept back.

# Iris, Dutch, English, Spanish

Popular as cut flowers, they deserve to be more widely planted for border decoration. All have typical iris flowers in a wide range of color, and grow 2–2½ ft. (60–75cm) tall. The three types will provide a succession of bloom from early to mid summer.

Dutch irises (hybrids between *Iris xiphium* and *I. tingitana*) flower first, in early summer.

Spanish irises (*I. xiphium*) flower a little later and follow the Dutch varieties.

English irises (*I. latifolia*, syn. *I. xiphioides*), span early and mid summer.

### Varieties to look for

Separate varieties are available, but there is little difference between them apart from color. For border display, mixtures are popular.

**Above: Dutch iris "Blue Champion."**
**Above right:** *Leucojum vernum* **var.** *carpathicum.*

### Soil and site

Well-drained soil, in full sun. Best in a sheltered position. Zone 5.

### Propagation

Remove offset bulbs when the leaves have died down.

## Leucojum aestivum
*Summer snowflake*

A cool-looking plant for a border or perhaps by the edge of water, with white bell-shaped flowers that are surprisingly conspicuous.

Height: 1½ ft. (45cm).

### Varieties to look for

"Gravetye Giant" is an improved form.

### Soil and site

Well-drained but moisture-retentive soil, in full sun.

### Propagation

Divide an established clump in early autumn.

# Perfect for pots

*When the summer bedding has finished, fill those vacant pots and other containers with bulbs for a superb spring display ... but don't forget that bulbs can also contribute to the summer display in patio pots.*

Concentrate on plants that will give a good display from the first season ... most bulbs used in containers are discarded or planted in borders after flowering, so avoid those that take a season or two to perform well. Snowdrops and winter aconites look superb when they have settled down and are flowering well, but bulbs or tubers planted the previous autumn will, at best, put in a modest performance. Hyacinths, daffodils, and lilies, on the other hand, are sure to put on an impressive display provided you buy good-sized bulbs and plant closely enough.

### Spring a surprise

Because spring bulbs are used so widely in containers of all kinds, they can be a little predictable. Try experimenting with unusual varieties or uncommon plants, a few of which are described below.

Crown imperials (*Fritillaria imperialis*) with their ring of orange-red or yellow bells on 3–4 ft. (90–120cm) stems, crowned with a conical tuft of leaves, make a stunning subject for a tub. Plant at least three bulbs, as a single stem looks slightly ridiculous. You will also need something around the base of the stems, and grape hyacinths (*Muscari armeniacum*) are ideal for this.

As well as the popular *Iris danfordiae* and *I. reticulata*, try a different species, such as the pale blue and yellow iris "Katherine Hodgkin," a hybrid between the blue *I. histrioides* "Major" and the yellow *I. winogradowii*. Because the more popular dwarf irises split up into smaller bulbs that take some time to reach flowering size, repeat flowering is uncertain, but don't hesitate to plant "Katherine Hodgkin" in the border after flowering – it blooms again readily.

Grape hyacinths (*Muscari armeniacum*) make reliable container plants, but generally look best in a mixed container, perhaps with double daisies (*Bellis perennis*) or primroses or polyanthus.

If you want a pot-full on its own, try the more compact but similar *M. azureum*. Or go for the distinctive two-tone *M. latifolium*, which has light blue flowers at the top of the spike and rich purple ones on the lower half.

Don't neglect the well-proven bulbs for containers, such as hyacinths, tulips, and daffodils. These are utterly reliable if you choose suitable varieties for the size of the container. You can still grow interesting variations, like those described below.

Opposite left: Choose compact tulips for containers, or
use other plants to "fill in" around the stems.

Opposite right: Tulips are beautiful container plants,
but choose a sheltered position for tall varieties.

Instead of the normal single hyacinth, you
could grow a double one such as the red
"Hollyhock." Or try one of the Multifloras,
which have several slender stems with more
loosely spaced bells, instead of the normal
tightly spaced single flower spikes.
Hyacinths look best in shallow containers.

Daffodils are better in deep containers, and
you may be able to pack in more than one
layer of bulbs (the upper layer being placed
between the noses of the ones below). The
trumpet daffodils are great, but try some of
the more interesting types: short-cupped are
attractive and there are some with stunning
color combinations, such as "Berlin," with a
primrose yellow perianth and a golden yellow
cup edged orange-scarlet, or "Salome" with a
white perianth with salmon-rose cup, tinted
copper at the rim.

Doubles are very variable in appearance,
but two-tone flowers like "Tahiti," yellow-
gold with bright orange, or "Unique," white
and chrome yellow, nearly always attract
attention.

Orchid-flowered daffodils are superb for
patio tubs – and seem to last a bit longer.
They have a split corolla, and some bear little
resemblance to the traditional daffodil.
Examples are "Cassata," soft yellow with ruffled edges, divided into six segments, folded
back against a white perianth, and "Tricolet,"
an amber-gold cup split into three symmetrical spade-shaped segments, against a pure
white perianth.

For window boxes and small containers,
keep to the dwarfs such as "Tête-a-Tête" and
"February Gold." Or splash out with a distinctive variety such as "Foundling," with
deep pink cup and white perianth.

You should avoid tall tulips unless you
can provide a sheltered position. Dwarf early-
double tulips do very well in containers, even
window boxes.

*Tulipa praestans* "Fusilier" is outstanding
for any type of container: each stem has from
two to four pure flame-scarlet blooms. Try it
in a shallow container with white *Anemone
nemorosa* or *A. blanda* "White Splendor."

For something a little different, try the
variegated varieties: "Unicum" is a variety
of *T. praestans* with cream-edged leaves.
Viridiflora tulips, such as the green, yellow,
and white "Spring Green" or green and yellow "Hummingbird" look classy and cool.

Fringed tulips and parrots (which have
more deeply lacerated petals) always look
good, but you may have to stake them.

## Summer specials

Lilies have to be the best summer-flowering
bulbs for pots and tubs. There are varieties
that grow no more than about 1 ft. (30cm)
which are ideal for pots, but most of the tall
varieties look superb in a patio tub or half-
barrel. See pages 148–149 for more
information on lilies.

Camassias are not often grown in containers, but the tall rich blue spikes of *C. quamash*
(syn. *C. esculenta*) make a superb show if you
plant enough to make a substantial clump.

Above left: Underplant tulips with spring bedding
plants to ensure that the container looks well filled.

Above: Pack bulbs close together for real impact, and
choose interesting containers to enhance the display.

## Autumn appeal

Nerines take a couple of years to start blooming prolifically, so these are best left in the
container permanently until they are too congested and need splitting. They should flower
in the first year, however, and they give a
superb display of bright pink flower right
until the end of autumn.

Dahlias are not normally regarded as container plants, but there are suitable dwarf
varieties. They start flowering in summer,
often look their best in early autumn, and
will continue until the first frost.

Although a short lived display, a container
packed with colchicums makes a breathtaking feature. Plant in a border after flowering, where they will bloom in future years.

BEAUTIFUL BULBS

# Know your tulips

Below left: The showy parrot tulips, with their large, fringed blooms, are best in a sheltered position.

Below: Parrot and single late tulips, here underplanted with double daisies (*Bellis perennis*).

*Provided you choose suitable varieties, you can have tulips in flower throughout spring – in the rock garden, beds, borders, and containers. Some can even be forced into flower pots in winter.*

Although tulips have a reputation for a short flowering period, if you choose a collection of varieties with care, you can enjoy them spread over a period or two or three months.

## Single early

With their classic tulip flowers, nicely pointed in bud, these are ideal for beds or borders. They flower in the first half of mid spring.

## Double early

Doubles are long-lasting in flower and their compact growth makes them ideal for a windy site. They flower in mid spring.

## Triumph tulips

Regard these as bridging tulips to fill the gap between single early and late-flowering tulips

– they are the result of hybridization between these types. There is an excellent color range and they normally bloom in the second half of mid spring and the first half of late spring.

## Darwin hybrids

This group of tulips is known for its large, oval flowers on tall, strong stems. They are excellent for bedding and flower in the second half of mid spring and the first half of late spring.

## Single late

Another group with classic tulip shape, but flowering in late spring. They tend to be tall and are best used for bedding or cutting. They flower about the same time as wallflowers, so choose these if you want synchronized flowering.

## Lily-flowered

Unmistakably distinctive, with pointed reflexed petals. They are generally tall-stemmed and best for bedding or cutting. The flowering period is late spring.

## Fringed

Another distinctive group, with showy flowers the petals of which are fringed at the top. They flower in late spring and make pleasing cut flowers.

Left: Lily-flowered varieties have a distinctive grace and elegance that sets them apart from other tulips.

Right: Single earlies have the classic tulip shape and are some of the first varieties to flower.

### Viridiflora

These "green" tulips have green as part of their coloring. They are probably more popular for cutting than for general garden decoration. Flowering time is late spring.

### Parrot

Exceptionally showy varieties, with lacerated and fringed petals. Better as a cut flower. Flowering time is late spring.

### Double late (peony-flowered)

Similar to double early varieties but slightly taller and flowering in late spring. Useful for both bedding and containers.

### Kaufmanniana hybrids

Among the earliest tulips to flower, in early spring. Most grow to about 8 in. (20cm), making them useful for an exposed site and for containers or the rock garden.

### Greigii hybrids

Similar to Kaufmanniana hybrids from a distance, but flowering in mid spring, and often with maroon-mottled foliage. They grow to about 10 in. (25cm) and are ideal for containers, the rock garden, and formal beds.

### Species tulips

There are dozens of readily available species worth growing in the garden. Among the best are: *Tulipa tarda*, yellow and white and low-growing; *T. praestans* "Fusilier," red with up to six flowers to a stem − excellent for containers or the rock garden; and *T. humilis* var. *pulchella* "Violacea" (formerly *T. pulchella violaceae*), with deep purple flowers.

## Lilium

*Lily*

Almost everyone can recognize a lily, even non-gardeners. There are many kinds, however, and just a few of them are described on pages 148–149.

Lilies are generally easy to grow, but most of the commonly grown types are best with cool roots and their heads in the sun, which makes them a good choice to plant among lower-growing border plants, or among shrubs. Height: 1–5 ft. (30–150cm).

### Species and varieties to look for

See pages 148–149 for suggestions.

### Soil and site

Most lilies grow well in ordinary well-drained soil, but they will be better if it is enriched with leaf mold, garden compost, or well-rotted manure. Some have a preference for lime, others will not grow well in an alkaline soil, so check when you buy.

The majority will grow happily in a pH of about 6.5. They grow best in partial shade but many can thrive in full sun.

Check hardiness when you buy, but most are tough and hardy down to Zone 5 or 6.

### Propagation

The easiest method is to divide large clumps when the foliage dies down, but for more plants a method of propagation using bulb scales can be used (consult a specialty book on lilies or propagation for information on how to do this).

The species, but not the hybrids, which provide variable plants,can be raised from seed, but the plants may take four or five years to flower.

Left: *Lilium* "Little Girl."

## Muscari armeniacum

*Grape hyacinth*

One of the easiest and most dependable bulbs if repeat flowering year after year is required. The compact spikes of tightly packed dark blue flowers are produced freely in mid or late spring, and the plants multiply rapidly. Left to multiply, grape hyacinths will make a bright and bold edging to a bed or border.

Height: 9 in. (23cm).

### Varieties and other species to look for
"Blue Spike" has double flowers on sturdy stems. *M. botryoides* is a smaller plant, with bright blue flowers, useful for interplanting with spring bedding plants, and for the rock garden. There is a white form, "Album."

### Soil and site
Well-drained soil, in full sun. Zone 4–10 (*M. botryoides* 3–10).

### Propagation
Remove bulb offsets, or simply divide large clumps, when the foliage dies down.

---

## • TIP TO TRY
Get your daffodils off to a good start by covering the bulbs with about 6 in. (15cm) of soil if it is light and well drained, about 5 in. (13cm) if it is heavy and poorly drained. If planted too shallowly they may produce leaves but few flowers in future years.

They will also perform better in future years if you feed them regularly after flowering until the leaves die down.

## Narcissus

*Daffodil*

Daffodils require no introduction, but there are many kinds, from miniatures for the rock garden to tall ones with long trumpets or large or small cups. Orchid-flowered varieties hardly look like daffodils. See pages 138–139.

Height: 4–24 in. (10–60cm).

### Varieties and species to look for
See pages 138–139 for a selection of some of the types available.

### Soil and site
Well-drained but moisture-retentive soil, in full sun or partial shade. They will flower especially well in full shade for a season or two, but will probably deteriorate very slowly – this will not matter for a seasonal display that is replanted annually. Zones 6–9 (most types).

### Propagation
Remove offset bulbs when the foliage dies down, or simply divide a large clump.

---

Left: *Muscari armeniacum.*
Bottom: *Narcissus "Double Event."*
Right: *Nerine bowdenii.*

## Nerine bowdenii

One of the treasures of autumn, bringing color for many weeks, and sometimes lasting until early winter. The spidery-looking pink flowers appear before the leaves.

In areas of borderline hardiness, plant near a sunny wall, and mulch in winter to help insulate the large bulbs.

Height: 1½ ft. (45cm).

### Varieties to look for
"Mark Fenwick" (syn. "Fenwick's Variety") is vigorous and flowers a little earlier; "Pink Triumph" has deep pink flowers.

### Soil and site
Well-drained soil, in full sun or partial shade. Zone 8.

### Propagation
Remove offset bulbs when the foliage has died down.

# Leave it to nature

*One of the most pleasing ways to grow bulbs is naturalized in grass.*

Choose bulbs for naturalizing carefully. Some popular bulbs do not naturalize readily, like tulips, while others, like daffodils, snow-drops, and crocuses, are ideal. Grassy banks are particularly suitable for nat-uralized bulbs, but you can even find a corner of a small lawn for dwarf bulbs like crocuses. Bear in mind that you must allow the leaves to die down naturally, and you should not mow the grass until this has occurred.

### Plants to try
*For spring*
*Anemone blanda*
*Anemone nemorosa* for shady areas
Crocus
*Fritillaria meleagris* (snake's-head fritillary)
*Galanthus* (snowdrops)

*Hyacinthoides hispanica* (Spanish bluebell) for shady areas
*Hyacinthoides non-scripta* (English bluebell) for shady areas
Narcissus (daffodil)

### For summer
Few summer-flowering bulbs are suitable for naturalizing as grassy areas are usually mown throughout the summer. Try the following where you can leave the grass long, perhaps in an orchard or wildlife area.
*Gladiolus communis byzantinus* (frequently sold just as *G. byzantinus*)

### For autumn
*Crocus sativus*
*Crocus speciosus*
*Colchicum autumnale* (the large leaves in spring can be a handicap in an ornamental lawn)
*Cyclamen hederifolium*

## Planting large bulbs

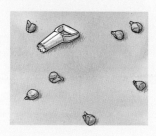

**1** Large bulbs, such as daffodils, have to be planted individually. Scatter them randomly first.

**2** Plant with a trowel or a bulb planter. A bulb planter will take out a core of soil, but is not as flexible when it comes to hole size and depth.

**3** Insert the bulb in the hole and replace the turf. It may be necessary to remove some soil from the base of the core.

## Planting small bulbs

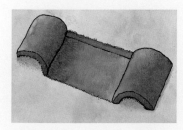

**1** Small bulbs, such as crocuses and snowdrops, are best planted by lifting a small area of grass. Make an H-shaped cut, then slice and roll back the turf.

**2** Loosen the compacted ground with a fork, incorporating bone meal or a slow-release fertilizer at the same time.

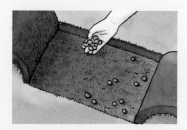

**3** Scatter the bulbs randomly so that they look more natural, then plant individually where they have fallen. Do not bury deeply as they will be covered by the turf.

**4** Level and compress the loosened soil, then roll the grass back down and firm flat. Remove or add soil if necessary to reinstate the former level. Water thoroughly.

## Ornithogalum nutans
*Drooping star of Bethlehem*

Charming and easy to grow, this plant produces its white and pale green nodding-bell flowers in early and mid spring.

Height: 1¼ ft. (38cm).

### Other species to look for
*Ornithogalum umbellatum* (star of Bethlehem) flowers in late spring, and is useful for following earlier blooms. It has shiny white, upward-facing star-like flowers, and is excellent for naturalizing.

### • TRY THE CHINCHERINCHEE
*Ornithogalum thyrsoides* is the South African chincherinchee, an exceptional cut flower, lasting up to three weeks in water. The spikes are densely packed with white flowers. Although not very frost-hardy (Zone 9), in areas of borderline hardiness it can still be grown and flowered in the garden if the bulbs are lifted and stored in a frost-free place for winter.

### Soil and site
Well-drained soil, in full sun or partial shade. Zone 6 (*O. umbellatum* zone 5).

### Propagation
Remove bulb offsets when the foliage dies down. Seed also germinates readily.

## Puschkinia scilloides var. libanotica
*Striped squill*

Curious and strangely beautiful, this small spring-flowering plant has pale silver-blue petals with deep blue lines down the center of each petal. It needs to be planted in a bold drift.

Height: 4 in. (10cm).

### Varieties to look for
"Alba" is white, and lacks the blue stripe.

### Soil and site
Well-drained but moisture-retentive soil, in full sun or partial shade. Zone 5.

### Propagation
Remove bulb offsets when the foliage dies down.

Below left: *Ornithogalum umbellatum.*
Bottom left: *Puschkinia scilloides*
Below: *Ranunculus "Accolade Mixed."*
Bottom right: *Scilla siberica.*

## Ranunculus asiaticus hybrids

Tuberous-rooted perennial with wonderfully bright flowers in colors that range from red to yellow and white, especially beautiful in their fully double form. Flowering period is usually late spring and early summer or early and mid summer, according to sowing or planting time.

Although widely sold as tubers, there are excellent seed-raised varieties that can be in flower five months after sowing.

In areas of borderline hardiness, plant by a warm, sunny wall, or lift the tubers in the autumn and replant in spring.

Height: 1 ft. (30cm).

### Varieties to look for
Tubers are usually sold as double mixtures. Many of the seed-raised varieties have been bred for use as potted plants, but they can still be planted for a summer garden display. "Accolade" and "Bloomingdale Mixed" are outstanding varieties.

### Soil and site
Well-drained, fertile soil with a high organic content, in full sun or partial shade. Zone 9.

### Propagation
Separate the new tubers that have been formed when the foliage dies down. Sow seed-raised varieties in warmth under glass, following the advice on the packet regarding sowing times.

## Scilla siberica
*Siberian squill*

An unassuming but easy and accommodating plant to cheer up a drab spot or provide a pocket of bright blue in the rock garden in early spring. Although small, the vibrant blue flowers command attention.

Height: 6 in. (15cm).

Left: *Sternbergia lutea.*
Bottom: A parrot tulip.
Below right: *Tigridia pavonia.*

## Varieties to look for

"Spring Beauty" is a bright China blue with a touch of ultramarine, and an improved form with larger flowers. "Alba" is white.

## Soil and site

Well-drained but moisture-retentive soil in full sun or partial shade. Zones 5–9.

## Propagation

Remove bulb offsets when the foliage dies down.

# Sternbergia lutea

From a distance this looks like a yellow spring-flowering crocus, except that it blooms in early and mid autumn! The leaves emerge with the flowers, but do not reach their full length until spring so there is little to detract from the bright yellow flowers.

Leave undisturbed to form large clumps.

Height: 6 in. (15cm).

## Varieties to look for

Normally only the species is grown, though specialty suppliers do sell varieties with slight variations.

## Soil and site

Well-drained soil, in full sun. Zone 7.

## Propagation

Divide established clumps when the foliage dies down.

# Tigridia pavonia
*Peacock flower, tiger flower*

An extraordinary flower, producing a succession of short-lived blooms with three large petals and three small spotted petals between them, all spread out almost flat. The colors are mainly reds, oranges, and yellows, often with contrasting spots. They will attract attention in mid and late summer.

## Varieties to look for

Named varieties exist but they are usually sold as mixtures.

## Soil and site

Well-drained soil, in full sun, in a warm and sheltered position. Zone 7.

## Propagation

Remove bulb offsets when the leaves die down.

# Tulipa
*Tulip*

Tulips require no description, but there are many kinds. Examples of the main types are described on pages 152–153.

Tulips should not be planted too early (unless especially prepared for forcing indoors).

## Varieties and species to look for

See pages 152–153 for examples of the main types.

## Soil and site

Well-drained soil, in full sun or partial shade. Typically zone 5 or 6, but it depends on the species.

In warm climates where winters are frost-free they may not flower well unless the bulbs are chilled (in the crisper or salad section of the refrigerator, for example) for about six to eight weeks just prior to planting.

## Propagation

Remove bulb offsets when the foliage has died down.

# Super Shrubs

Shrubs are the backbone plants of the garden – they give it the structure that is always there, summer or winter. They also add an element of height that is needed in every garden, especially where there are no trees.

Like trees, it is important to choose shrubs carefully and plant them with thought. They take years to become well established and look mature, by which time they are difficult to move or discard if the wrong choice has been made.

Dedicated shrub borders can be difficult to accommodate in a small garden, but shrubs can be used creatively with border plants in a mixed border, or as specimen plants to be viewed in splendid isolation. Some make excellent tub plants. It is also among the shrubby plants that you will find some of the best year-round ground covers.

## Features

SUPER SHRUBS

## Azalea
*See Rhododendron*

## Berberis darwinii
*Darwin's barberry*

One of the best-known evergreen barberries, with small holly-shaped leaves, most attractive in early and mid spring when covered with clusters of small orange-yellow flowers. Blue-black fruits hang in clusters in autumn.
　Height: 8 ft. (2.4m).

### Other species to look for
There are several useful dwarf evergreen species useful for ground cover or the front of a border. These include *B. buxifolia* "Nana" at 1½ ft. (45cm), bright yellow flowers and *B. verruculosa* at 3 ft. (90cm) with yellow flowers.

### Soil and site
Undemanding regarding soil, best in full sun or partial shade; will tolerate full shade. Zone 7 (*B. buxifolia, B. verruculosa* 5).

### Propagation
Take softwood cuttings in summer.

## Berberis thunbergii
*Japanese barberry*

Versatile and widely planted, it comes in many forms. The species has yellow flowers in spring, green leaves in summer, and bright red autumn leaves and berries. Purple-leaved forms are popular, both as freestanding shrubs and as hedges.
　Height: 5 ft. (1.5m).

### Varieties to look for
The reddish-purple *B. t. atropurpurea* is popular for hedges. For a dwarf hedge, *B. t.* "Atropurpurea Nana" is widely used. "Rose Glow" is a full-sized plant but the dark purple leaves are splashed pink. "Harlequin" is another impressive variegated variety. "Aurea" grows to 3 ft. (90cm) and has lime to pale green leaves in spring, aging to a deep yellow. Finally there are red shades as the autumn color begins to show.
　Where space is limited, consider "Bagatelle" which makes a dwarf, compact mound of red-purple foliage or "Helmond Pillar" with red-purple foliage and narrow, upright growth.
　*Berberis dictyophylla* is worth growing for the white bloom on the young stems and on the red berries.

### Soil and site
Undemanding regarding soil, best in full sun or partial shade. Zone 4.

### Propagation
Take semi-ripe cuttings in summer.

## Brachyglottis "Sunshine" (formerly Senecio "Sunshine")

A gray-leaved plant grown mainly for foliage effect, but the bright yellow daisy flowers in summer are a worthwhile bonus.
　Height: 5 ft. (1.5m).

### Other species to look for
Similar is *B. greyi* (formerly. *Senecio greyi*).

### Soil and site
Well-drained soil, in full sun. Zone 8.

### Propagation
Take semi-ripe cuttings in mid summer.

# Buddleja davidii
*Butterfly bush*

An extremely popular plant with butterflies, and widely planted in gardens. The long racemes of flowers at the end of arching stems are usually shades of blue or purple, but sometimes white. Unless pruned annually in the early spring, the bushes become tall and lanky.

   Height: 10 ft. (3m), but more compact if pruned annually.

## Varieties to look for
"Black Knight" is very dark purple, "Empire Blue" is violet-blue, "Royal Red" is purple-red. "Harlequin" with purple flowers is variegated.

## Soil and site
Undemanding regarding soil, in full sun. Zone 5.

## Propagation
Take softwood cuttings in summer, or hardwood cuttings in winter.

# Calluna vulgaris
*Heather*

This is the heather of late summer and early autumn, usually purple-pink or white. Unlike the winter-flowering ericas, the callunas are more demanding to grow and will not thrive on alkaline soils. Like most heathers, they are best grown in bold drifts rather than as isolated plants.

   Height: 9–24 in. (23–60cm).

## Varieties to look for
Although there is only one species, there are hundreds of varieties. For flowers, good ones include "County Wicklow" with double, pink flowers and "Darkness" with bright crimson flowers.

   For colored foliage as well as flowers, try "Gold Haze," golden foliage, white flowers; "Robert Chapman," golden foliage in spring, turning to orange, then almost red in winter, and pale purple flowers; "Silver Queen," with silver-gray foliage and pale mauve flowers; and "Sister Anne" with gray foliage, pink flowers.

## Soil and site
Must have acid soil, preferably in full sun though some shade is tolerated. Zone 4.

## Propagation
Take cuttings in early or mid summer.

## ● TIPS TO TRY
Callunas make good ground cover plants if given appropriate treatment and planted in bold groups. To be sure of a good show:

   Only plant in acidic soil – if it is not naturally acidic (with a low pH), work a generous quantity of peat and decomposed leaves into the planting area until it is suitably acid.

   Plant in groups of at least five plants, and if growing different varieties bear in mind that a large number of one or two varieties usually look more pleasing than a large collection of just a few plants in each group.

   Keep the plants neat and compact by trimming them with shears when flowering has finished. If you fail to do this, they often become straggly and flower more sparsely.

## ● NOW YOU KNOW!
If you've wondered why the familiar *Buddleja* is now often spelled *Buddleja*, it has to do with the rules of botanical nomenclature. The first name validly published is the one that counts. It was intended to be *Buddleja*; botanists tell us that the *i* was wrongly written as a *j* when it was first published!

SUPER SHRUBS

Below left: *Ceanothus arboreus*
"Trewithen Blue."
Below right: *Chaenomeles* x *superba*
"Crimson and Gold."

Left: *Camellia japonica* "Elegans"
(foreground) and *Camellia* "Donation"
(background).

## Camellia hybrids

Among the finest flowering evergreens for growing on acid soil, camellias are especially valued because they flower from early spring – some even bloom in winter. Their large single, semi-double or double blooms, in shades of pink or red, as well as white, are often 3 in. (8cm) or more across.

These are not delicate plants, but cold winds and frosts can damage the flowers. Grow them in the shelter of other shrubs, or by a wall if there is no more suitable position. They also make attractive shrubs in tubs provided an ericaceous (acid) potting soil is used.
Height: 8 ft. (2.4m).

### Varieties to look for

These are just of few examples from hundreds of varieties: "Adolphe Audusson" has red, semi-double flowers; "Donation," pink, semi-double; "J. C. Williams," pale pink, single; and "Lavinia Maggi" (syn.

"Contessa Lavinia Maggi") has flowers with pale pink and cerise stripes, double.

### Soil and site

Acid soil, preferably peaty or with plenty of leaf mold, ideally in partial shade, though can be grown in full sun. Zone 7 or 8, depending on parentage.

### Propagation

Take cuttings in early or mid summer.

## Ceanothus "Autumnal Blue"
*California lilac*

This is a contender for the title of one of the best blue flowering shrubs. There are both deciduous and evergreen ceanothus; this one is evergreen and flowers in late summer and early autumn. Ceanothus often benefit from the protection of a wall, but this variety is tougher than most.
Height: 6 ft. (1.8m).

### Varieties to look for

Other pleasing evergreen varieties are "Burkwoodii" and "Cascade," which flower in spring.

"Gloire de Versailles," flowering in mid and late summer, is one of the best deciduous varieties.

### Soil and site

Well-drained soil, preferably in full sun but tolerates some shade.

Ceanothus "Autumnal Blue" is best in a sheltered position. Zone 6 ("Cascade" and "Gloire de Versailles" 7, "Burkwoodii" 8).

### Propagation

Take softwood cuttings in summer or hardwood cuttings of deciduous kinds in late autumn or winter, semi-ripe cuttings of evergreens in mid summer.

## Chaenomeles japonica
*Japonica, Japanese quince*

These spring-flowering shrubs, grown mainly for their red, pink, or white flowers, sometimes have decorative quince fruits later that ripen to yellow. Japonica can be grown as a free-standing shrub in a border or trained against a wall or fence.

Height: 10 ft. (3m), but can be kept smaller, as a trained plant, by regular pruning.

### Species and varieties to look for

Some of the most prolific flowerers are varieties of C. *speciosa*, such as "Moerloosei" (syn. "Apple Blossom") with pink flowers or "Nivalis," white, and C. x *superba*, for example "Knap Hill Scarlet" and "Rowallane" with crimson flowers.

### Soil and site

Undemanding regarding soil, in full sun or shade. Zone 5.

### Propagation

Take semi-ripe cuttings in mid summer.

# Long-season shrubs

*Below left: Shrubby potentillas are not the most eye-catching of shrubs, but they are utterly reliable and remain in flower for many months.*

*Shrubs with a long period of changing interest are especially useful for small gardens where every plant has to earn its space. The shrubs suggested here will enhance any border, whatever its size.*

Evergreens are invaluable for providing a backdrop of foliage throughout the year, but too many of them can begin to look predictable and even boring. Non-evergreen shrubs, with a succession of features, also have a long period of interest, but a changing one.

## Two-timers
These shrubs have attractive flowers in spring and colorful berries and/or foliage in autumn.

*Amelanchier canadensis*
White flowers in spring, colorful autumn leaves.

*Amelanchier lamarckii*
White flowers in spring, colorful autumn leaves.

*Berberis thunbergii*
Yellow flowers in spring, colorful autumn leaves. "Aurea" has golden leaves becoming greener later.

*Left: The versatile* Cotoneaster horizontalis *will hug the ground or grow upward against a support such as a wall, fence, or rock.*

*B. t. atropurpurea* Purple leaves all summer.
*Calluna vulgaris* "Blazeaway"
An example of a heather with colorful foliage. Lilac-mauve flowers in late summer and early autumn, red foliage in winter.
*Cornus alba* "Sibirica"
Autumn foliage color, red winter stems.
*Cotoneaster horizontalis*
White flowers in early summer, vivid autumn leaf color, bright red berries into winter.
*Enkianthus campanulatus*
Red-veined cream flowers in spring, colorful autumn leaves. Needs acid soil.
*Fothergilla major*
White "bottlebrush" flowers in spring, golden autumn leaves (*F. monticola* has red autumn leaves).
*Hamamelis mollis*
Yellow flowers in mid winter, yellow leaf coloring in autumn.
*Pyracantha*
White flowers in summer, red, orange, or yellow berries in autumn and winter.
*Rosa rugosa*
Large single, fragrant flowers in summer, large orange-red hips in autumn.

## Long flowering
A few shrubs flower almost the whole summer, and sometimes a bit beyond. Some of the best for a long flowering period are abelias and shrubby potentillas.

The abelias are festooned with small pinkish-white or rosy-lilac flowers on arching stems. The many varieties of *Potentilla fruticosa* are seldom without at least a few flowers from early summer to early autumn. Colors are mainly yellows, but there are pinks, oranges and whites.

163

# Know your clematis

*There are clematis in flower from spring to autumn ... some even flower in winter if the climate is not too harsh.*

Understanding the different types of clematis will help you to appreciate the different pruning requirements, and provide inspiration for a collection of clematis that will provide interest for most of the year.

### Early-flowering species
These flower on shoots produced the previous season, so pruning is always modest and never done before they flower in spring. The most popular species include the ubiquitous *C. montana*, and treasures like *C. alpina* and *C. macropetala*. Do not grow these through shrubs that require regular pruning; otherwise there will be a conflict of requirements.

### Early large-flowered varieties
The large-flowered hybrids are grown for their size and beauty of flower. They bloom mainly in early and mid summer. "Nelly Moser," "The President," and "Lasurstern" are

examples. They flower on shoots produced the previous year so are pruned only when necessary and not severely in spring.

### Late species and varieties
Late-flowering clematis like *C. viticella* and its varieties, and *C.* "Jackmanii" and related varieties, bloom in late summer and into autumn on shoots produced in the current year. These are pruned to within about 1 ft. (30cm) of the ground in spring to encourage flowers on new stems that are not too tall.

### Evergreen too
The evergreen clematis *C. cirrhosa*, with fern-like leaves, has white bell-shaped flowers between mid winter and early spring. Plant *C. armandii*, with clusters of fragrant white flowers, to follow in early and mid spring. These species are not as hardy as the others described, and are best by a sheltered wall.

**Above: The Viticella clematis flower in late summer and into autumn so extend the flowering period. Typical of this group is *Clematis* "Viticella Rubra."**

**Top right: "Nelly Moser" is one of the best known of the early-flowering large-flowered hybrids. It typically flowers in early and mid summer.**

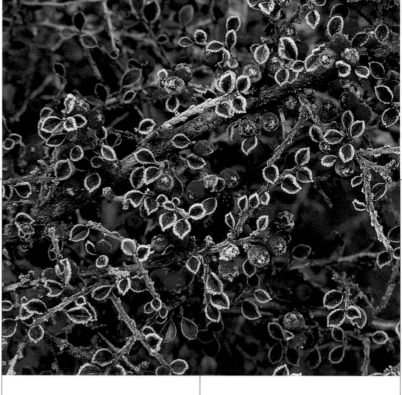

Below: *Choisya ternata* "Sundance."
Bottom: *Cornus alba* "Elegantissima."
Right: *Cotoneaster horizontalis*.

## Choisya ternata

*Mexican orange blossom*

An outstanding aromatic evergreen with white starry orange-scented flowers in mid and late spring, and glossy foliage that is aromatic when crushed. In areas of borderline hardiness the leaves may be damaged by frosts and cold winds, but the plant usually recovers with the new growth.
Height: 6 ft. (1.8m).

### Varieties to look for

"Sundance" is an outstanding golden form that looks pleasing throughout the year, especially viewed against darker shrubs behind.

### Soil and site

Undemanding regarding soil, in full sun or partial shade. Best in a sheltered position. Zone 7.

### Propagation

Take softwood cuttings in summer.

## Cornus alba "Sibirica"

*Red-barked dogwood*

Easy to grow and outstanding for winter interest, this is one of several dogwoods grown for their colored stems that are seen to advantage once the leaves have fallen. When they have been established for a couple of years, severe pruning to a framework of stumps close to the ground every spring, or every second spring, will ensure plenty of young shoots. These have the best color. There is sometimes a super bonus of rich autumn foliage color before the leaves drop. They are best planted in a large group rather than as individual plants.
Height: 8 ft. (2.4m).

### Varieties and other species to look for

"Elegantissima" has white-edged leaves, "Spaethii" gold and green. For greenish-yellow winter stems, try *C. stolonifera* "Flaviramea."

### Soil and site

Undemanding regarding soil, and tolerates wet ground well, in sun or shade. Zone 3 (*C. stolonifera* zone 2).

### Propagation

Take hardwood cuttings in autumn or winter, or layer the plants.

## Cotoneaster horizontalis

*Fishbone cotoneaster*

One of several first-rate prostrate cotoneasters suitable for ground cover. This one can also be trained up a fence or wall, and can be pleasing cascading over the edge of a pond or the rocks by a waterfall. The leaves turn red before they fall, and this makes a spectacular sight when the plant is already covered with red berries.
Height: 1 ft. (30cm) as a ground cover, 6 ft. (1.8m) up a wall or fence.

### Other species to look for

Other outstanding ground-cover cotoneasters are *C. conspicuus* "Decorus" with orange-red berries, and *C. dammeri* with bright red berries and a wide-spreading habit. Both of these are evergreen.

### Soil and site

Undemanding regarding soil, in full sun or partial shade. Zone 4 (*C. dammeri* 5, *C. conspicuus* zone 6).

### Propagation

Take semi-ripe cuttings in mid summer.

### ● TIP TO TRY

If you already have the normal *Cotoneaster horizontalis*, try planting the variegated form for added interest. "Variegatus" (now considered by botanists to be more correctly *C. atropurpureus* "Variegatus") has leaves edged creamy-white.

# Winter wonderland

*A well-designed garden has pockets of interest and color every month of the year ... and shrubs play a vital role in helping to achieve that vital winter color.*

Winter-interest shrubs should be planted with the winter in mind, and not simply as part of a mixed planting. Position them for maximum impact.

The most spectacular winter shrubs can be used as focal points to take the eye to various parts of the garden, but those with small stature or small flowers are best grouped

together, perhaps with winter-flowering border plants like *Helleborus niger* and *Iris unguicularis*, and maybe underplanted with snowdrops and winter aconites.

## For a focal point

Choose a few large or particularly bold plants that look good in winter, and position them in an otherwise uninteresting area. This will reduce the number of "low" spots in the garden at this time, and take the eye to a particular view across the winter garden.

Most winter flowers are small — some can only be described as insignificant — so rely on foliage to provide color from a distance. A large *Elaeagnus pungens* "Maculata," with its gold-splashed leaves, will look magnificent as the winter sun catches the gold ... an effect highlighted if the surrounding plantings are drab or uninteresting.

A number of mahonias flower in winter, but one of the tall, upright kinds that rises almost aggressively to make a narrow column of growth with big spiky leaves, will make a bold statement. According to where you place it, a plant like *Mahonia lomariifolia* or *M.* x *media* "Charity" will bring interest to the back of a border or a group of winter-

Above: Although eventually large, *Hamamelis mollis* is one of the brightest and most dependable winter-flowering shrubs, and is always appreciated.

flowering plants, or it can stand alone to be a focal point when viewed across the garden. The fragrant yellow flowers bloom even during the gloomiest days.

The witch hazel (*Hamamelis mollis*) takes few years to look its best, but it will bring light and life to an apparently dormant area of open woodland or a lightly shaded part of the garden. It often looks its best in a sunny position in a lawn where it can be viewed against a dark background, such as a hedge. The fragrant yellow flowers are borne on leafless branches in mid winter, often packed so tightly that its beauty can be appreciated even from a distance.

Far left: The red stems of *Cornus alba* "Sibirica" are colorful all winter long, and light up the garden when winter sunshine falls on them.

Left: *Hamamelis mollis* is like a ray of sunshine on a cold winter's day, but it takes a few years to become established and make a really super show.

Grow the silk tassel bush (*Garrya elliptica*) where you can see the long and long-lasting catkins to advantage. On an established plant it will look as though they are dripping from the branches. In cold areas the protection of a wall is necessary, but it makes a pleasing wall shrub where it will benefit from the protection provided. "James Roof" is a variety with spectacular catkins … often more than 1 ft. (30cm) long. Although this is not a colorful plant, it makes a wonderful specimen shrub or focal point.

## Twigging the solution

Twigs and stems may not sound stimulating, but anyone who has grown trees with attractive bark, or shrubs with colorful winter stems, will know that they are more colorful and longer lasting than almost all the winter flowers. In a large garden, a group of them — some with red stems, some with green or yellow stems — makes a superb feature in winter sunshine, but even a single shrub is worth having in the border.

The dogwoods, widely grown for winter color, are best pruned back to just above ground level every spring (or every second spring) to maintain a supply of young shoots, which have the most intense color. Two of the brightest are *Cornus alba* "Sibirica" (bright red), and *Cornus stolonifera* "Flaviramea" (greenish-yellow). The scarlet willow (*Salix alba vitellina* "Britzensis," syn. *S.* "Chermesina"), can be pruned severely every second year and grown as a shrub with brilliant orange-scarlet winter shoots.

If there is space for its long, arching stems and vigorous growth, grow the whitewash bramble (*Rubus cockburnianus*). Cut it down

Above: It's clear to see why *Rubus cockburnianus* is sometimes called the whitewash bramble!

literally to the ground every spring: the new arching canes that arise from the ground have a white bloom which make them a real feature whether or not the sun is shining.

## Winter flowers

Any garden planted for winter interest must surely include a winter jasmine (*Jasminum nudiflorum*); its bright yellow flowers start to appear in late autumn and continue through till early spring. It is usually grown against a wall (see page 173).

Winter-flowering heathers — varieties of *Erica carnea* and *E. x darleyensis* — look best in bold drifts, especially around the base of a deciduous tree with attractive bark, such as a white-barked birch.

Not all winter flowers are colorful or fragrant. *Viburnum tinus* is an unassuming evergreen that grows to about 8 ft. (2.4m), with clusters of white or pink-tinged flowers, but it starts to bloom in mid autumn and is usually still flowering in early spring.

## Getting scent

Quite a high proportion of winter flowers is fragrant (to attract what few insects are around). The plants most widely grown are perhaps *Viburnum x bodnantense* and *V. farreri* (syn. *fragrans*). These produce rather insignif-

Above: Several desirable mahonias flower in winter, and *Mahonia lomariifolia* is one of them.

icant pink or white flowers on bare stems, but fragrance is a useful bonus.

Winter sweet (*Chimonanthus praecox*) makes a large shrub, and the waxy-looking yellow flowers with purple centers are not particularly attractive from a distance. They are, however, deliciously fragrant.

Sarcococcas (sometimes called Christmas or sweet box) win no prizes for beauty, but you will appreciate their fragrance … often before you can even spot the plant. The white flowers are insignificant, and the foliage uninspiring, but they don't take up much space. *Sarcococca hookeriana* var. *digyna* and var. *humilis* are the ones usually grown. Try planting one close to a path that you use regularly in winter.

## Daphne mezereum

*Mezereon*

An ever-popular shrub for early purplish-red flowers clustered along the bare stems in late winter and early spring. It is one of the most fragrant of all spring-flowering shrubs. Plant it close to a path.

   Height: 3 ft. (90cm).

### Varieties to look for

There is a white variety, *D. m. alba*, but it lacks the impact of the species, and is slightly less vigorous. *D. m.* var. *rubra* has larger flowers and a stronger color.

### Soil and site

Deeply cultivated, humus-rich soil, moist but not waterlogged, in full sun or partial shade. Zone 4.

### Propagation

Layer in summer, or sow seed (the plants may be variable and this method is slower).

## Elaeagnus pungens "Maculata"

An outstanding foliage shrub that looks especially pleasing in winter sunshine. The evergreen leaves are boldly splashed with bright yellow. Small but fragrant flowers are produced in mid or late autumn.

   Height: 8 ft. (2.4m).

### Other species and varieties to look for

There are variegated varieties of the similar *E.* x *ebbingei*, such as "Gilt Edge" which has a wide gold margin and green center.

### Soil and site

Undemanding, but avoid very alkaline (chalky) soils, in full sun or partial shade. Zone 7 (*E.* x *ebbingei* zone 6).

### Propagation

Take semi-ripe cuttings in early summer.

## Erica carnea (syn. E. herbacea)

*Winter heather, heath*

An invaluable dwarf evergreen shrub, blooming between mid winter and mid spring, depending on variety. Best used in bold drifts or as ground cover rather than as individual plants.

   Height: 9–18 in. (23–45cm).

### Varieties to look for

There is a huge range of varieties from which to choose, and these are just a few of the best ones: "Ann Sparkes" has orange-yellow foliage, tipped bronze-red, and purple-red flowers from late winter; "Foxhollow" has golden summer foliage turning pinkish-red in winter and a few lavender flowers from mid winter; "Myretoun Ruby" has ruby-red flowers from mid winter; "Springwood White" has white flowers from mid winter; and "Vivellii" has vivid carmine flowers from mid winter.

### Soil and site

Well-drained soil, in full sun. Although many heathers require an acid soil, this one is much more tolerant. It is best to avoid alkaline (chalky) soils, but the plants will thrive on neutral soils. Zone 5.

### Propagation

Take softwood cuttings in early or mid summer.

# Pick of the bunch

*Most shrubs are uninspiring out of flower, so they should justify their place with either attractive foliage or breathtaking blooms. Emphasize the showy ones or those with a long flowering season.*

## Big, bold blooms

The following plants have big showy flowers that will be a focal point in the border, and possibly across the garden.

**Camellia**
Large, rose-like blooms, mainly pinks and reds, also white, in spring. Evergreen.

**Carpentaria californica**
Large white flowers with golden anthers in early and mid summer.

**Hibiscus syriacus**
Large flowers, in shades of blue, pink, and white, in late summer and early autumn.

**Hydrangea macrophylla**
There are two main types: mopheads (rounded head packed with flowers) and lacecaps (flat, lacy-looking flower heads).

**Paeonia suffruticosa**
Flowers like herbaceous peonies in late spring, but on shrubby plants.

**Rhododendrons (some)**
Mainly spring-flowering, the hybrids have large heads of funnel-shaped flowers in a wide range of colors. Evergreen. Require an acid soil.

**Romneya coulteri**
Flowers like large white poppies in mid and late summer.

**Rosa, shrub**
See pages 188–197.

**Yucca, various**
Large rosettes of spiky, sword-like leaves and bold spikes of white bell-like flowers in summer.

## Covered with flowers

The individual blooms on the plants below may be small in size, but they make up for this by the sheer amount they produce.

Often the whole shrub is covered in flower.

**Amelanchier canadensis**
White, spring.

**Amelanchier lamarckii**
White, spring.

**Berberis darwinii**
Yellow, spring. Evergreen.

**Berberis x stenophylla**
Yellow, spring.

**Caryopteris x clandonensis**
Blue, late summer and early autumn.

**Ceanothus (deciduous and evergreen)**
Blue, spring or late summer and early autumn (depends on type).

**Forsythia x intermedia**
Yellow, spring.

**Kolkwitzia amabilis**
Pink, late spring and early summer.

**Philadelphus hybrids**
White, summer.

**Rhododendrons and azaleas (some)**
Wide range of colors, spring. Require acid soil.

**Spiraea japonica "Bumalda" (often sold as Spiraea x bumalda)**
Pink or red, summer.

## Staying power

The following shrubs flower over a long period. Usually there is a main flush of flowers followed by intermittent flowering for the rest of the season.

**Abelia x grandiflora**
**Abelia schumannii**
**Fuchsia magellanica**
**Hypericum "Hidcote"**
**Potentilla fruticosa**

# Bright and beautiful

*Use foliage shrubs lavishly to keep your borders bright from spring to autumn.*

Foliage shrubs will ensure a cheerful border long before and after most flowering plants have had their fling. Don't overlook shrubs with gold or silver foliage as well as variegated plants. Use yellow or golden leaves against a dark background such as a hedge or other dark-leaved shrubs, and silver-leaved plants next to blue or red flowers if possible.

**Above: Varieties of *Berberis thunbergii* have flowers in spring, attractive summer foliage, and autumn tints.**

**Above right: The multi-colored *Berberis thunbergii* "Rose Glow" remains a focal point all summer.**

Variegated plants should not be penned in by flowering plants – place them where you can see the whole plant, perhaps toward the front of the border. Avoid using a number of variegated plants close together. Space them out, or use those with colored but unvariegated leaves as companions.

## Gold and green
*Shrubs with gold and green variegation*
Aucuba japonica "Crotonifolia," "Variegata"
Cornus alba "Spaethii"
Elaeagnus pungens "Maculata"
Euonymus fortunei "Emerald 'n' Gold"
Ilex x altaclarensis "Golden King"
Ilex aquifolium "Golden Queen"
Salvia officinalis "Icterina"

## Silver and green
*Shrubs with silver or cream and green variegation*
Cornus alba "Elegantissima"
Euonymus fortunei "Emerald Gaiety"
Euonymus fortunei "Silver Queen"
Ilex aquifolium "Argentea Marginata"
Ilex aquifolium "Handsworth New Silver"
Ligustrum ovalifolium "Argenteum"
Weigela "Florida Variegata"

## Yellows and golds
*Shrubs with yellow or golden leaves*
Acer japonicum "Aureum"
Berberis thunbergii "Aurea"
Calluna vulgaris "Gold Haze"
Choisya ternata "Sundance"
Erica carnea "Foxhollow"
Fuchsia magellanica "Aurea"
Ligustrum ovalifolium "Aureum"
Lonicera nitida "Baggesen's Gold"
Philadelphus coronarius "Aureus"
Ribes sanguineum "Brocklebankii"
Sambucus racemosa "Plumosa Aurea"

## Purples and reds
*Shrubs with purple or red foliage*
Acer palmatum "Atropurpureum"
Berberis thunbergii atropurpurea & "Red Chief"
Cordyline australis "Purpurea"
Corylus maxima "Purpurea"
Cotinus coggygria "Royal Purple"
Phormium tenax "Purpureum"
Prunus x cistena "Crimson Dwarf"
Salvia officinalis "Purpurascens"

## Silvers and grays
*Shrubs with silver or gray foliage*
Artemisia arborescens
Brachyglottis (formerly Senecio) "Sunshine"
Caryopteris x clandondensis
Convolvulus cneorum
Hebe pinguifoia "Pagei"
Perovskia atriplicifolia
Santolina chamaecyparissus

Left: *Euonymus fortunei* "Emerald 'n' Gold," with *Loncicera nitida* "Baggensen's Gold" behind.
Bottom: *Fuchsia magellanica*.
Right: *Forsythia x intermedia* "Lynwood."

# Euonymus fortunei

There are several widely planted varieties of this useful low-growing evergreen. Use it as ground cover or plant it against a wall and let it slowly grow vertically.

Height: 2 ft. (60cm), when grown as ground cover.

## Varieties to look for

"Emerald 'n' Gold" has green and gold leaves, "Emerald Gaiety" white and gray-green. "Silver Queen" starts creamy-yellow, then becomes green and creamy white.

## Soil and site

Undemanding regarding soil, in full sun or partial shade. Zone 5.

## Propagation

Take softwood cuttings in early summer. The leaves of "Coloratus" turn almost purple in winter, but turn green again in spring.

# Forsythia x intermedia
*Golden bells*

Almost certainly one of the best-known spring-flowering shrubs, with the bright yellow bell flowers clustered along bare branches, creating a really bright splash of color.
Height: 10 ft. (3m).

## Varieties to look for

There are several varieties, differing mainly in the size of the flower, but "Lynwood" is outstanding, with large flowers and strong color. Other spectacular varieties with large flowers are "Beatrix Farrand" and "Karl Sax," both deep canary yellow in color.

## Soil and site

Undemanding regarding soil, in full sun or partial shade. Zone 5.

## Propagation

Take semi-ripe cuttings in mid summer or hardwood cuttings in autumn or winter. Can also be layered.

# Fuchsia magellanica
*Hardy fuchsia*

The flowers lack the size of the hybrids so loved by fuchsia enthusiasts, but this species makes up for that by producing them prolifically all summer and well into autumn if there are no frosts. Although often

described as hardy in Zones 7, 8, and 9, for example, the top growth will be killed by moderate frosts. Fortunately the roots usually survive, especially if protected with a winter mulch in cold parts of these zones, and new growth arises from the base in spring. Where winter frosts do not cut them back, the height can be double that suggested here.
Height: 5 ft. (1.5m).

## Varieties to look for

"Riccartonii" (which is now considered a hybrid and not a variety of this species) has a deeper colored calyx and broader sepals.

There are some delightful variegated forms: *F. m.* var. *gracilis*, "Variegata," and "Versicolor."

## Soil and site

Well-drained but moisture-retentive and fertile soil, in full sun or partial shade. Zone 6.

## Propagation

Take softwood cuttings in summer.

## ● TIP TO TRY

Leave the old stems on Fuchsia magellanica until spring, then cut them back to the ground. The new shoots that grow from the base produce an abundance of blooms.

Leaving on the old shoots helps to protect the plant in a cold winter, but if you find them unattractive you can shorten them to about 1 ft. (30cm). Cut them right back as new growth emerges.

Below left: *Garrya elliptica*.
Bottom: *Hamamelis* x *intermedia*
"Sunburst."
Right: *Hebe* "Midsummer Beauty."

## Garrya elliptica
*Silk tassel bush*

Distinctive and decidedly imposing, the evergreen garrya manages to create more impact with its long, slender grayish catkins than many plants with brighter flowers. It's at its best in mid and late winter, just when something is needed to create a strong focal point.

In mild areas it is grown as a free-standing shrub in the border, but in colder regions it is better planted close to a wall for protection. Try planting one where it will become a focal point.

Height: 12 ft. (3.5m).

### Varieties to look for
"James Roof" is outstanding – the catkins can be more than 1 ft. (30cm) long.

### Soil and site
Undemanding and does well on chalky soils, in full sun or partial shade. Zone 8.

### Propagation
Take semi-ripe cuttings in mid summer. Can also be layered.

## Hamamelis mollis
*Witch hazel*

Invaluable winter-flowering shrub where there is space for it. The bare branches are covered with sweet-smelling spidery-looking yellow flowers in winter. The leaves also have pleasant autumn tints before they fall.

Height: 12 ft. (3.5m).

### Varieties to look for
There are varieties with flowers in various shades of yellow or orange, but an outstanding one is "Pallida" with large sulphur-yellow flowers, now considered as a variety of *H*. x *intermedia*.

### Soil and site
Neutral to acid, well-drained but humus-rich soil, in full sun or partial shade. Will not tolerate very alkaline (chalky) soil. Zone 6.

### Propagation
Layering is the best method for amateurs, though commercially they are grafted.

## Hebe x franciscana

This is a representative species of many excellent evergreen dwarf hebes, some grown primarily for foliage effect, others for flowers. It has purple flowers tinged pink, in late summer and into autumn. The different species and hybrids vary in hardiness, so in areas of borderline hardiness for hebes, check with a local supplier that a particular hebe is likely to survive.

Height: 1½–5 ft. (45–150m), depending on species or variety.

### Varieties and other species to look for
It is usually the variegated varieties of *H*. x *franciscana* that are grown, such as "Variegata," but "Blue Gem" is a particularly desirable plant with bright blue flowers. *H. pinguifolia* "Pagei" is a carpeter with gray-green foliage and white flowers. "Red Edge" is an outstanding foliage hybrid, with gray leaves edged red.

Some hebes have foliage resembling that of a conifer such as a cupressus, *H. armstrongii* being typical of this group.

Among those grown mainly for their conspicuous flowers are "Autumn Glory," with violet flowers in late summer and early autumn, and "Midsummer Beauty" with purple-blue flowers produced over a long period.

### Soil and site
Well-drained soil, in full sun or partial shade. Plant in a sheltered position if possible. Zone 7 (*H. pinguifolia* 6, *H. armstrongii* 8).

### Propagation
Take softwood cuttings in early summer or semi-ripe cuttings in mid summer.

# Up the wall

*Walls present wonderful opportunities. For a minimal amount of ground it is possible to clothe otherwise wasted vertical space with flowers or foliage.*

The shrubs listed here are simply plants that can conveniently be grown against a wall or fence. Some are true climbers, like the self-clinging ivy and wisteria; others are ordinary shrubs that can be trained against a wall, such as pyracanthas. A few shrubs, such as winter jasmine, support themselves in the wild by growing through other plants as a support; these could be provided with a trellis. It is best to use plants that fulfill a purpose rather than confining the choice to strictly climbing plants. Many wall shrubs grow particularly well against a wall or fence because of the extra warmth and protection provided. Plants of borderline hardiness that will not survive a severe winter in the open garden may pull through against a wall, especially if a little extra protection is provided.

## How high?

The likely height of any shrub is difficult to forecast with accuracy – much depends on climate and conditions. Height of climbers should be treated with even more caution. A vigorous climber such as *Clematis montana* will grow to 30 ft. (10m) with a tree as support, but confine itself to a 4 ft. (1.2m) fence by growing horizontally. An ivy that will reach the top of a house will also grow horizontally as a ground cover, or simply as high as its support will allow.

## For a shady wall

*Berberidopsis corallina*
*Hedera helix*, green varieties
*Hydrangea petiolaris*
*Parthenocissus tricuspidata, P. quinquefolia, P. henryana*

## For a sunny wall

*Actinidia kolomikta*
*Campsis radicans*
*Clematis*
*Fallopia baldschuanica* (formerly *Polygonum baldschuanicum*)
*Hedera helix*, variegated
*Hydrangea petiolaris*
*Jasminum officinale*
*Lonicera periclymenum*
*Lonicera brownii*
*Parthenocissus tricuspidata, P. quinquefolia, P. henryana*
*Passiflora caerulea*
*Polygonum baldschuanicum, see Fallopia*
*Solanum crispum*
*Vitis coignetiae*
*Wisteria floribunda, W. sinensis*

## For foliage

*Actinidia kolomikta*
*Hedera helix*
*Parthenocissus tricuspidata, P. quinquefolia, P. henryana*
*Vitis coignetiae*

Above: No garden is complete without *Jasminum nudiflorum* to provide winter color – it starts flowering in late autumn, and goes through until spring.

## For flowers

*Campsis radicans*
*Clematis*
*Fallopia baldschuanica* (formerly *Polygonum baldschuanicum*)
*Hydrangea petiolaris*
*Jasminum officinale*
*Lonicera periclymenum*
*Lonicera brownii*
*Passiflora caerulea*
*Polygonum baldschuanicum, see Fallopia*
*Solanum crispum*
*Wisteria floribunda, W. sinensis*

## Wall shrubs for flowers

*Ceanothus*, evergreen types
*Chaenomeles*
*Fremontodendron californicum*
*Garrya elliptica*
*Jasminum nudiflorum*
*Magnolia grandiflora*

## Wall shrubs for foliage

*Euonymus fortunei*

## Wall shrubs for berries

*Cotoneaster horizontalis*
*Pyracantha*

# Hibiscus syriacus
*Tree hollyhock*

One of the best shrubs for late summer, with large flowers the shape of individual hollyhock blooms, continuing into autumn. Colors are mainly shades of blue and pink, but there are whites.

　Height: 8 ft. (2.4m).

### Varieties to look for
"Blue Bird" ("Oiseau Blue") is an outstanding variety; "Woodbridge" has rose-pink flowers with a dark eye and is another justifiably popular one.

### Soil and site
Well-drained soil, in full sun or partial shade. Best in a sheltered position. Zone 5.

### Propagation
Layering or semi-ripe cuttings in mid summer is the easiest method for amateurs, though commercially they are often grafted.

# Hydrangea macrocarpa

Outstanding shrubs, always eye-catching in flower though often unpredictable in coloring. There are two main groups: the Mopheads or Hortensias have almost globular heads packed with florets all over; Lacecap varieties have the ordinary florets around the edge of the head but small flowers without the usual petals in the center. Late summer is the peak flowering time.

　The exact color depends partly on variety and partly on the pH of the soil (how acid or alkaline it is). Some varieties are pink on alkaline soil, red on neutral soil, and blue on acid soil. Varieties that respond to acid soil can be made blue by using a proprietary product that alters the soil chemistry.

　Height: 7 ft. (2.1m).

### Varieties to look for
Examples of Hortentia varieties are "Altona," a pink that blues well; "Europa" with deep pink flowers; "Generale Vicomtesse de Vibraye," a vivid rose that blues well; and "Goliath," deep pink or purplish-blue. Outstanding Lacecaps include "Blue Wave," "Lanarth White," and "White Wave."

### Soil and site
Deeply cultivated, moisture-retentive soil, in partial shade. Zone 5.

### Propagation
Take softwood cuttings in early summer.

# Lavandula angustifolia
*Lavender*

This popular aromatic herb requires no introduction, but the versatility of lavenders is not always exploited. They make charming dwarf hedges, perhaps as internal dividers within the garden, or in a herb garden, can be interplanted

with roses, and make desirable border plants if set in small groups rather than as isolated plants.

　Height: 3 ft. (90cm), but lavender clips well and can be kept more compact.

### Varieties and species to look for
There are many varieties, white as well as shades of blue, purple and lavender. Two outstanding varieties are "Hidcote," violet-blue, and "Twickel Purple."

　For a different kind of lavender, but still very attractive, consider *L. stoechas,* which has dark purple fragrant flowers in mid and late summer.

### Soil and site
Well-drained soil, in full sun or partial shade. Does well on alkaline (chalky) soils. Zone 5.

### Propagation
Take semi-ripe cuttings in early or mid summer.

# "Architectural" shrubs

*Every garden benefits from a least one focal-point shrub with a distinctive or interesting shape — one of the so-called "architectural" plants.*

"Architectural" plants are used by garden designers rather as an interior designer might use an ornament. Such plants have a distinctive shape or profile. Avoid using too many in close proximity, as the impact is lessened.

### Catalpa bignonioides "Aurea" (Indian bean tree)

This golden version of the Indian bean tree is not as vigorous as the green form usually seen as a tree, and it can be grown as a bushy foliage plant. Buy a multi-stemmed plant, or buy a young one and cut the main shoot back to about 1 ft. (30cm) to encourage low branching. Hard pruning every spring or every second spring is necessary.

### Cordyline australis

A palm-like evergreen. It forms a thick trunk crowned with gray-green sword-like leaves. Mature plants may bear scented creamy-white flowers.

**Shaped box (*Buxus sempervirens*) make superb focal points. These have been trained into a "lollipop" shape, but pyramids and spirals are also popular.**

### Fatsia japonica

The evergreen leaves are large, exotic-looking and hand-shaped. Variegated variety. Mature plants produce ball-like white flower clusters in mid or late autumn.

### X Fatshedera lizei

This is a bigeneric hybrid between *Fatsia japonica* and an ivy. Growth starts off upright, then flops and become less of a neat focal point. The lobed leaves resemble a fatsia, but are not as large. There is a variegated form.

### Juniperus scopulorum "Skyrocket"

A blue-gray conifer with very narrow, columnar growth. Despite earlier advice not to plant too many architectural plants in close proximity, a group of about three of these looks good.

### Mahonia "Charity"

This is just one of several good hybrid winter-flowering mahonias with narrow, upright growth and very large evergreen leaves. It looks good on its own in a lawn or in a shrub border.

### Paulownia tomentosa (Foxglove tree)

Left unpruned this makes a very large tree. Grow it as a shrubby plant by pruning back hard each spring to stimulate the growth of new shoots, which have enormous leaves.

### Rhus typhina (Stag's-horn sumac)

A truly sculptural plant, that looks half tree, half large shrub. It is usually grown in isolation in a lawn as a specimen plant, but it makes a good back-of-border shrub. The large pinnate leaves hang from tiered branches, turning magnificent reds and yellows in autumn. Cones of small red flowers appear in early and mid summer, followed by crimson fruits. An outstanding plant.

### Viburnum rhytidophyllum

A fast-growing evergreen with long, corrugated leaves, grayish on the underside.

### Yucca

All have sword-like leaves, arising from a basal rosette with some species, from a short trunk with others. Stiff spikes of white bell-shaped flowers are produced in summer.

# Dwarf conifers

*Don't dismiss conifers as drab or uncolorful. They come in an amazing variety of greens, "blues," and golds, and vary in shape from small globes and cones to ground-hugging horizontal spreaders and pencil-like thin columns.*

Dwarf conifers are useful for the rock garden or special conifer beds, and associate well with heathers.

Be cautious about the term "dwarf." All conifers described as dwarf are likely to be small in comparison with their normal full-sized equivalents, but after about 15 years some so-called dwarfs may be 8 ft. (2.4m) or more tall, and a few could have a spread of about 15 ft. (4.5m). Any with the word "pygmy" in their description are likely to remain small.

Many are slow-growing so it will take many years before they outgrow their space.

**Some conifers have attractive horizontal growth, like this *Juniperus horizontalis* "Aurea."**

Dwarf conifers are difficult to place among other shrubs. They don't look right, and their slower growth rate means they don't keep up as shrubs planted at the same time mature. They are best used to add height to a heather garden, or in a special conifer bed, the appeal of which is derived from the many contrasting shapes and colors.

There are hundreds of readily available dwarf and slow-growing conifers, and those mentioned here are just a few of the popular kinds. Garden centers will offer many more, and specialty conifer nurseries can offer an exciting choice of less common ones. There are even variegated kinds.

### For the rock garden

These are slow-growing and will remain dwarf, taking years to reach about 2 ft. (60cm).

***Chamaecyparis obtusa* "Nana Gracilis"** Distinctive, shell-like whorls of dark green foliage.

***Chamaecyparis obtusa* "Tetragona Aurea"** Rather angular with gracefully curved branches and moss-like golden-yellow foliage.

***Cryptomeria japonica* "Vilmoriniana"** Globular, compact shape, with deep green "mossy" foliage that turns more bronze in autumn.

*Juniperus communis* "Compressa"

One of the most popular choices for a rock garden, and dwarf enough to be used in a sink garden! It makes a narrow column of gray-green foliage.

*Picea abies* "Nidiformis"

Densely crowded branches, forming a flat-topped bush. Dark green foliage.

## Tall and thin

*Juniperus scopulorum* "Skyrocket"

Upright branches form a narrow column. Will eventually grow tall, but will provide height where space is limited.

*Juniperus virginiana* "Glauca"

Makes a narrow column with gray-green foliage, though there are varieties with blue-green leaves.

## Low and spreading

These can cover a large area of ground and are more suitable for ground cover than in a small bed of mixed conifers, though they can be included in a large conifer bed.

Left: There are conifers dwarf enough for a rock garden or even a sink garden, and *Juniperus communis* "Compressa" is one of the most suitable.

*Juniperus horizontalis*

Prostrate growth with dense foliage. There are several admirable varieties, such as "Bar Harbor," which has steel-blue foliage. 1 x 6 ft. (30 x 180cm).

*Juniperus sabina* "Tamariscifolia"

Prostrate growth and dense foliage, the branches being built up in layers. 1 x 4 ft. (30 x 170cm).

## Blues and golds

*Chamaecyparis obtusa* "Crippsii"

Frond-like sprays of golden-yellow foliage on branches that droop at the tips. 6 x 2½ ft. (180 x 75cm).

*Chamaecyparis pisifera* "Boulevard"

Intense silvery-blue color in summer. 6 x 4 ft. (1.8 x 1.2m).

*Juniperus communis* "Depressa Aurea"

Spreading shape. The leaves start the season butter-yellow, turn gold, then become almost bronze in winter. 1½ x 4 ft. (45 x 120cm).

*Juniperus squamata* "Blue Star"

Compact and bushy, with steel-blue foliage. 1½ ft. x 2 ft. (45 x 60cm).

*Taxus baccata* "Standishii"

An upright, columnar golden yew. Looks especially good in winter.

*Thuja orientalis* "Aurea Nana"

An oval-shaped plant with golden-yellow summer foliage turning bronzy-green in winter. 2½ x 1½ ft. (75 x 45cm).

Left: Conifers won't look boring if you contrast shapes and colors. Here *Juniperus squamata* "Blue Carpet" associates happily with *Juniperus horizontalis*.

Above: The foliage of *Juniperus communis* "Depressa Aurea" start the season a bright yellow, then turns gold, and in winter becomes almost bronze.

## For the larger conifer bed

*Chamaecyparis lawsoniana* "Ellwoodii"

Compact, pyramidal habit, gray-green but more bluish in winter. 6 x 3 ft. (1.8 x 1m). "Ellwood's Gold" is slower and smaller, but it's not really gold – the tips of the shoots are tinged yellow in summer.

*Chamaecyparis lawsoniana* "Minima Aurea"

This makes a rounded pyramid with ascending shoots that twist to reveal golden foliage. 2 x 1½ ft. (60 x 45cm).

*Juniperus media* "Pfitzeriana Aurea"

A spreading plant with branches tending to grow out at an angle of up to 45°. The tips of the shoots are golden in spring and early summer, but the foliage is yellowish-green for the rest of the year. 4 x 8 ft. (1.2 x 2.4m).

*Picea glauca* var. *albertiana* "Conica"

Cone-shaped. Bright green tips to the shoots in spring. 2½ ft. x 1½ ft. (75 x 45cm).

## Lavatera "Rosea"
*Tree mallow*

One of several excellent hybrids where a large and long-flowering shrub is required. The large, single, saucer-shaped pink flowers are produced from early summer through to autumn. The shrubby lavateras are eye-catching plants that can dominate a shrub border, and make splendid focal points.
   Height: 10 ft. (3m).

### Varieties to look for
"Rosea" is often listed as a variety of *L. arborea*. "Barnsley" is one of several other good hybrids, all in shades of pink.

### Soil and site
Well-drained fertile soil, in full sun. Zone 8.

### Propagation
Take semi-ripe cuttings in early summer or hardwood cuttings in winter.

## Mahonia x media

The mahonias listed here are all winter-blooming evergreens with large heads of fragrant yellow flowers. Their tall, upright early growth gives them an "architectural" appearance, ideal for a winter focal point.
   Height: 12 ft. (3.5m).

### Varieties to look for
"Buckland," "Charity," "Lionel Fortescue," and "Winter Sun" are all first-rate shrubs.

### Soil and site
Tolerates a wide range of soils, but best in moisture-retaining soil with high humus content, in full sun or partial shade. Zone 7.

### Propagation
Take semi-ripe cuttings in early or midsummer.

## Perovskia atriplicifolia
*Russian sage*

Particularly useful for a mixed border, as it has the appearance and stature typical of many herbaceous plants. The spikes of lavender-blue flowers appear in late summer and early autumn. The gray-green leaves smell of sage when crushed. Cut all the stems back to about 6–9 in. (15–23cm) above the ground in spring.
   Height: 4 ft. (1.2m).

Varieties to look for
"Blue Spire" has slightly larger and bolder flowers than the species.

### Soil and site
Well-drained soil, in full sun. Zone 6.

### Propagation
Take semi-ripe cuttings in early summer.

## Philadelphus "Beauclerk"
*Mock orange*

Particularly fragrant white flowers, borne in profusion in mid summer.
   Height: 10 ft. (3m).

### Varieties to look for
There are many species and varieties, all similar from a distance, the differences being mainly in height and whether the flowers are single or double. "Belle Etoile," "Sybille" and "Virginal" are all recommended hybrids to grow for their flowers. *P. coronarius* "Aureus" is grown mainly for its golden

foliage, though it also has fragrant white flowers. The leaf coloring is strongest in spring and early summer, becoming green later.

**Soil and site**
Undemanding regarding soil, in full sun or partial shade. Zone 5.

**Propagation**
Take semi-ripe cuttings in early summer, or hardwood cuttings in winter.

## Potentilla fruticosa
*Shrubby potentilla, shrubby cinquefoil*

Best regarded as a workhorse shrub, it will never be the most spectacular plant in the border but it produces its yellow, orange, white, occasionally red, small single flowers from early summer to early autumn, though the best display is in mid summer.
Height: 4 ft. (1.2m).

**Varieties to look for**
There are about a hundred varieties that you could buy, many of them with similar characteristics and some with only slight variations in color. If there is space for only a couple of plants, this is a useful short list: "Abbotswood," white; "Daydawn," pinkish cream; "Elizabeth," yellow; "Goldfinger," golden yellow; "Katherine Dykes," primrose yellow; "Longacre Variety," sulphur yellow; "Primrose Beauty," primrose yellow; "Red Ace," red; "Tangerine," yellow shaded orange, with the color best in light shade. Some of these may sometimes be listed as varieties of *P. dahurica*.

**Soil and site**
Undemanding, but best in well-drained soil, in full sun or partial shade. Zone 7.

**Propagation**
Take softwood cuttings in spring or semi-ripe cuttings in summer.

## Pyracantha
*Firethorn*

Widely planted for autumn berries, which are normally red or orange, sometimes yellow. Clusters of white flowers in early summer, much loved by bees and other insects, are a bonus. The evergreen foliage is helpful in softening a wall if the plant is wall-trained. Pyracantha can be grown very successfully as a free-standing shrub, but they are more often trained against a wall for a more decorative effect.
Height: 12 ft. (3.5m), but can be trained to fit available space.

**Varieties to look for**
Most of the varieties grown are hybrids. Look for "Orange Glow" with orange-red, long-lasting berries, "Soleil d'Or" with yellow berries, "Watereri" with red berries. *Pyracantha coccinea* makes a large shrub with clusters of red berries; orange-red in its variety "Lalandei."

**Soil and site**
Undemanding regarding soil, in full sun or partial shade. Zone 6.

**Propagation**
Take semi-ripe cuttings in early summer.

179

# Scented shrubs

*When fragrance combines with the beauty of a flower like a rose or a lilac, all the senses are heightened and gardening really does seem a magical pastime. But don't overlook those scented shrubs with less spectacular flowers.*

Position fragrant shrubs with thought. Spread them throughout the border: if you concentrate them in one place the scents may conflict and confuse rather than being intensified. Plant several of the same kind together to concentrate the scent. Don't place them too far back in the border, especially if the scents are not especially strong. Place those with fragrant foliage, such as *Choisya ternata* and rosemary, where you can easily crush a leaf to release the scent as you pass.

**Right: Lavender is almost synonymous with scent, and it's a super shrub to grow for color. There are many kinds – this one is *Lavandula angustifolia* "Hidcote."**

## Summer borders

Elaeagnus are important foliage shrubs, with a bonus of fragrant flowers once the plants are mature enough to flower well. The flowers are insignificant, however, and you will probably smell the fragrance long before you spot a flower. *Elaeagnus commutata* flowers in late spring, *E. angustifolia*, the oleaster, in early summer, and *E. x ebbingei* in autumn, so you can spread the benefits of the fragrance by planting all three species.

The mock oranges (philadelphus) are famed for their scent. The single or double white flowers are produced in profusion in early and mid summer. Some of them grow large, but whenever possible allow them to overhang the edge of the border a little.

Lavenders make pretty front-of-border plants as well as aromatic dwarf hedges. There are many kinds; a whole collection of them dotted about a border is very pleasing.

A little further back in the border try *Romneya coulteri* or *R. hybrida*, which have fragrant flowers that resemble large white poppies.

No summer shrub border would be complete without at least one wonderfully fragrant shrub rose, and there are many of them to choose from (see pages 188–197).

Left: Sarcococcas are not the most beautiful winter-flowering shrubs, but they are among the most fragrant. This one is *Sarcococca hookeriana* "Purple Stem."

Although spring-flowering, it's worth including the clove-scented buffalo currant (*Ribes odoratum*, syn. *R. aureum*) in any planting of fragrant shrubs. The bright yellow flowers are followed by black "currants," and the autumn leaf color is pleasing. Osmanthus are also spring-flowering, with masses of small white flowers, but include them in the summer border for early scent. *O.* x *burkwoodii* and *O. delavayi* are both exquisitely fragrant.

Lilacs (*Syringa vulgaris*) span late spring and early summer, and are almost indispensable for any collection of fragrant shrubs.

The Carolina allspice (*Calycanthus floridus*) has unusual star-shaped fragrant reddish-purple flowers in mid and late summer, but it lacks impact in a border and is more likely to be appreciated as a specimen in a lawn.

The sweet pepper bush (*Clethra alnifolia* "Paniculata") is worth including for its late summer flowers, which continue into early autumn. The white upright flower spikes, about 6 in. (15cm) long, are not especially beautiful, but they are sweetly scented.

## Pineapple and honey brooms

The pineapple-scented Moroccan broom (*Cytisus battandieri*) seldom fails to attract favorable attention in early summer. The cone-shaped clusters of yellow flowers, on tall gray-leaved stems, have a delicious pineapple scent. It grows fast and tall – often to 3m (10 ft.) or more, and needs a sheltered position at the back of a wide border. It is often grown against a tall wall, where the plant benefits from the protection.

The Spanish broom (*Spartium junceum*) has honey-scented pea-shaped yellow flowers all summer. The fragrance is strong enough to be appreciated from a distance, but it's not a good plant for a small border: at 8 ft. (2.4m) or more it needs plenty of space.

## Winter scent

There are many fragrant shrubs, such as winter sweet (*Chimonanthus praecox*) and sweet box (*Sarcococca hookeriana*). These are described on pages 166–167. Honeysuckles are usually thought of as summer-flowering climbers, but there are winter-flowering shrubby non-climbing types with unexciting small white flowers but a super scent. *Lonicera fragrantissima*, *L.* x *purpusii*, and *L. standishii* all flower from early winter to early spring.

## Woodland scents

Some azaleas (especially the Ghent and Occidentalis groups) have a wonderful, heady fragrance. These are not always successful in a mixed shrub border, however, as some grow large, and they require an acid soil. Check that the varieties you buy are fragrant – some types lack scent.

Below: Some scents are fascinating and provide a talking point among visitors. *Cytisus battandieri* has flowers that smell deliciously of pineapple.

# Living carpets

*Carpeting shrubs make ideal permanent ground cover that looks better than bare soil and suppresses weeds too.*

Ground cover plants are used to improve the appearance of an otherwise bare area of ground, suppressing weeds and making it look more attractive. Evergreens are ideal because the ground is permanently covered, but even deciduous shrubs can be satisfactory as the soil is only exposed during the period when weeds are least likely to germinate. Weed seedlings that do germinate usually perish as they are deprived of light when the ground cover comes into leaf in spring.

Ground cover shrubs are especially useful for clothing banks and other areas that are not easily planted with grass and mown, or cultivated as beds or borders.

**Above: Although a rather plain plant, *Pachysandra terminals* is ideal for covering the ground in a shady spot. There is a brighter variegated form.**

**Above: Ivies will grow along the ground as happily as up a wall or a tree. Variegated varieties look more interesting – this one is *Hedera helix* "Sulphurea."**

## Flowering plants for sunny sites

Heaths and heathers (ericas and callunas) make perhaps the finest flowering ground cover. Those with colored foliage tend to lack quality and quantity of flowers compared with the best of the ordinary varieties, but they make a more interesting ground cover taking the year as a whole. They do best in full sun but will tolerate partial shade.

Sun or rock roses (*Helianthemum nummularium*) are great for carpeting a sunny bank, and they are happy growing in chalky ground. They come in shades of pink, red, and yellow, as well as white, with the main flush of flowers in late spring and early summer. They are semi-evergreen, but winter cover is not good.

One for an inaccessible bank, but not for a position where its invasive growth can be a problem, is the rose of Sharon (*Hypericum calycinum*). It grows to about 1 ft. (30cm) and spreads freely by underground shoots. It's evergreen except in severe winters, but shear it down to just above ground level in spring before growth starts, to stimulate fresh shrub.

Periwinkles (*Vinca minor* and *V. major*) will grow almost anywhere, but choose a variegated variety; otherwise they look drab for those months of the year when the blue, purple, or white flowers are absent.

Above: *Helianthemum nummularium* needs a sunny spot, and is ideal for a sunny bank. There are many varieties, in shades of red, pink, yellow and white.

Right: *Hypericum calcyinum* is a rather aggressive plant that spreads readily, but it's ideal for clothing a bank that is difficult to cultivate.

## Bright berries

There are several excellent ground-hugging evergreen cotoneasters, such as *C. dammeri*, *C. conspicuous* "Decorus," and *C. microphyllus*. The deciduous fishbone cotoneaster *C. horizontalis* is sometimes used for ground cover, and this has the bonus of bright autumn tints before the leaves fall. Expect bright red autumn berries from all of them. They are happy in full sun or partial shade.

For an acid soil in partial shade, *Gaultheria procumbens* makes a pretty carpet of small evergreen leaves, studded with red berries in autumn and into winter.

## Foliage effect

The ubiquitous *Euonymus fortunei* makes a very attractive evergreen ground cover, and there are varieties with gold or white variegation (the leaves may also be tinged pink or red in winter). They all grow well in sun or shade.

Some dwarf hebes are suitable for a sunny position, or partial shade. One of the best for carpeting is the silvery *H. pinguifolia* "Pagei." The small white flowers in late spring and early summer are a bonus, but it looks good for most of the year.

*Pachysandra terminalis* is regarded by some

as a dull and uninspiring plant, but it's excellent as a ground cover for dry and shady spots where many plants would not thrive. Grow "Variegata," however, as the white variegation helps to lighten a dull spot.

## Creeping climbers

Ivies will grow along the ground as well as up a support, and in time make a dense ground cover in shady places where few other plants thrive. For a large area, try *Hedera colchica* "Dentata Variegata" instead of the smaller leaved *H. helix* varieties, though these are worth considering for a small area.

183

# Shrubs for shade

*Whether you have a woodland area in your garden or simply suffer shade cast by your house or your neighbor's, shade-tolerant shrubs can be invaluable.*

The majority of shrubs will tolerate shade for part of the day, but if the area is shady for most of the day shade-tolerant shrubs are best. Areas that are permanently shady need plants naturally adapted to these conditions: they will probably have large leaves and uninspiring flowers, but these plants have their own calm beauty and texture.

Shade shrubs need special care at planting time and until they become established. Permanent or dense shade also means dry soil, at least for most of the year; whatever casts the light shadow also creates a rain shadow, and although some rain reaches the ground it will be far less than on open soil.

An established plant that has sent its roots well into the surrounding soil will be able to survive, but a young plant with the roots still in its root-ball will suffer severely if it dries out. Always enrich the planting area with moisture-holding material such as garden compost, or rotted leaves, or manure, and tease a few roots out from the root-ball when the plant has been removed from its pot.

Water thoroughly after planting, and for the first few months.

Some shade plants are woodlanders and, when planted in their natural environment, receive recycled nutrients from decaying leaves. Shrubs planted by a building or within the shadow of a wall or fence lack this naturally nutritious soil: incorporate a slow-release fertilizer at planting time.

## Dry shade

### Aucuba japonica (spotted laurel)
There are several good varieties, with spots and splashes of gold on their glossy green leaves. Red berries are a bonus, if both male and female plants are present. Evergreen. Lime-tolerant.

### Berberis (barberry)
There are both evergreen and deciduous species, with yellow or orange flowers in spring and small fruits in autumn. Unfortunately those with the best flowers tend to have the least attractive fruits. Evergreen (some). Lime-tolerant.

### Buxus sempervirens (box)
One of the few shrubs that will even grow in the dense shade of beech trees. There are many forms, some with variegated leaves. Evergreen. Lime-tolerant.

### Cotoneaster
There are many species and varieties, from ground-hugging carpeters to tall shrubs. Most are grown for their berries; a few of the deciduous ones also have autumn leaf color. Evergreen (some). Lime-tolerant.

### Danae racemosa
Arching stems with narrow, shiny leaves. Not especially attractive, but useful for difficult shady places. Evergreen. Lime-tolerant.

### Euonymus fortunei
Popular low-growing or ground-cover shrub, usually sold in its many variegated varieties. Evergreen. Lime-tolerant.

### Hedera helix (ivy)
Ivies need no introduction. Although usually grown as climbers, they make excellent ground-cover plants for shade between trees and shrubs. Evergreen. Lime-tolerant.

### Ilex (holly)
All the varieties of *I.* x *altaclerensis* and *I. aquifolium* do well in shade, and make good woodland shrubs. Depending on variety, they are grown for foliage effect or berries (female varieties only). Evergreen. Lime-tolerant.

### Lonicera pileata
A non-climbing honeysuckle, but the almost hidden flowers are fragrant. Purple berries in autumn. Semi-evergreen. Lime-tolerant.

### Mahonia aquifolium (Oregon grape)
Although not the best mahonia for a small garden, it has attractive yellow flowers in spring and grape-bloomed fruit in autumn. Evergreen. Lime-tolerant.

## Pachysandra terminalis

A creeping sub-shrub that forms a level carpet about 1 ft. (30cm) tall. The tiny flowers in spring go almost unnoticed, but "Variegata," with white-edged leaves, is quite decorative.

### Prunus laurocerasus (cherry laurel)

Large, glossy green leaves, and white flowers in spring. The species itself grows too large except in a woodland area, but there are dwarf, varieties such as "Otto Luykens," suitable for a shrub border.

### Ruscus aculeatus (butcher's broom)

A clump-forming spiny plant with insignificant flowers, but it's useful for difficult shady areas and there are marble-sized bright red berries in autumn (plants of both sexes are required). Evergreen.

### Symphoricarpos albus (snowberry)

Makes a thicket of twiggy shoots; the flowers are unexciting. Long-lasting white berries in autumn are the main attraction.

### Vinca (periwinkle)

Invaluable ground cover for shade. Although the leaves are not large they cover the ground densely, and there are attractive blue, purple, or white flowers over a long period. Evergreen.

## Moist shade

### Camellia

A must for a shady position and acid soil. There are many varieties, mainly in shades of

*Below: Kalmia latifolia is a beautiful evergreen flowering shrub, but requires a moist, acidic soil.*

pink and red, single and double. The plants are tough but the early flowers may require protection in harsh areas. Flowers late winter to late spring. Evergreen. Lime-hating.

### Clethra alnifolia "Paniculata" (sweet pepper bush)

Small spikes of scented white flowers in late summer and early autumn. Lime-hating.

### Cornus florida (American dogwood)

White or pink flowers in early summer. Susceptible to spring frosts. Lime-hating.

### Fatsia japonica (false castor oil plant)

A very "architectural" plant, with huge, hand-shaped glossy leaves. Evergreen. Lime-tolerant.

### Gaultheria mucronata

Still widely sold under its older name of *Pernettya mucronata*. Uninspiring white flowers in late spring or early summer, but wonderful red, lilac, purple, or white berries in autumn. Lime-hater.

### Gaultheria procumbens (partridge berry, checkerberry, wintergreen)

A carpeter making a mat of dark green foliage useful as a ground cover. Small white flowers in spring, scarlet fruits in autumn. Evergreen. Lime-hating.

### Hamamelis mollis (witch hazel)

Scented yellow flowers in winter. Good autumn color. Lime-hating.

*Left: Pieris, rhododendrons, and azaleas do well in shady woodland areas, but need acid soil to grow well.*

*Below: Hollies grow well in sun or shade, and tolerate most soils. This is Ilex x altaclerensis "Silver Sentinel."*

### Hydrangea

The hydrangeas usually grown are the popular *H. macrophylla* varieties, but *H. paniculata*, with its big flower heads like giant buddlejas, should be considered where there is space.

### Kalmia latifolia (calico bush)

Quaintly crimped pink flowers in early summer. Excellent shrub but needs plenty of moisture. Evergreen. Lime-hating.

### Pernettya mucronata

See *Gaultheria mucronata*.

### Pieris

There are several good species and varieties to choose from, but all have clusters of white or pink flowers resembling lily-of-the-valley (convallaria), and brilliantly colored young leaves, which are red and usually more conspicuous than the flowers. Evergreen. Lime-hater.

### Rhododendron

The rhododendrons (including azaleas) are natural woodland plants so thrive in shade. Many excellent species and varieties, from dwarfs to tall ones suitable only for the largest gardens. Evergreen. Lime-hater.

Right: *Rhododendron.*
Bottom left: *Rhododendron* "King George."
Bottom right: *Rosmarinus officinalis*
"McConnell's Blue."

## Rhododendron (includes Azalea)

Much-admired shrubs, only suitable for gardens with an acid soil – though many can be grown in containers filled with an ericaceous (acid) potting soil. Azaleas are kinds of rhododendrons, and there are both evergreen and deciduous kinds, some very fragrant. Rhododendrons are evergreen, and often bigger and more robust plants – though not always as there are dwarf rhododendrons small enough for the rock garden. With thousands of species and varieties, this is an important group of plants for anyone with suitable soil and sufficient space.

Height: depends on the species or variety.

### Varieties and species to look for

Any selection from among so many excellent plants must be arbitrary. These are only examples from the main types: "Pink Pearl" is a widely planted large-flowered hybrid – it will remain compact in a large container or grow very large in the ground if conditions suit. "Blue Diamond" is a dwarf hybrid with lavender-blue flowers. *R. yakushimanum* is a pleasing compact shrub that grows to about 3 ft. (90cm) with pink buds opening to almost white flowers, but outstanding for the small garden are the Yakushimanum hybrids, such as "Dusty Miller," peachy-yellow, and "Dopey," red. "Vuyk's Scarlet" is an impressive example of an evergreen azalea suitable for a small garden.

### Soil and site

An acid soil is essential for good results, though they will grow in neutral soil, in partial shade. Zone depends on the species or hybrid, but usually in the range 6–8.

### Propagation

Layer or take semi-ripe cuttings in summer.

## Rosmarinus officinalis
*Rosemary*

Popular herb with aromatic gray-green foliage and small, usually blue flowers in spring. Widely used in herb gardens, but makes an attractive informal hedge; a large specimen makes a good border shrub.

Height: 4 ft. (1.2m).

### Varieties to look for

"Seven Seas" is a dwarf form with brilliant blue flowers, "Miss Jessopp's Upright" (syn. "Fastigiatus") has narrow, upright growth which makes it a good choice for a hedge or where space is limited.

### Soil and site

Well-drained soil, in full sun. Zone 6.

### Propagation

Take semi-ripe cuttings in late spring or early summer.

## Salvia officinalis
*Sage*

Low-growing aromatic herb that is also very ornamental in its variegated forms. Attractive toward the front of a shrub or mixed border as well as in a herb garden.

Height: 3 ft. (90cm).

### Varieties to look for

Choose the variegated varieties for the ornamental garden:

Below: *Salvia officinalis* "Purpurascens."
**Right:** *Yucca filamentosa.*
**Bottom:** *Viburnum tinus.*

## Varieties to look for

The following varieties add a little more color than the white of the species: "Eve Price" has carmine buds opening white shaded pink, "Gwenllian" has pink buds opening white tinged pink.

## Soil and site

Undemanding regarding soil, in sun or partial shade. Zone 7.

## Propagation

Take semi-ripe cuttings in early summer.

## Yucca

There are both trunk-forming species (*Yucca gloriosa*) and those that just make a large clump of foliage (such as *Y. filamentosa*), but all are imposing foliage plants with large strap-like or spear-like leaves and show-stopper flowers: spikes of large white bells.

Yuccas have a reputation for being slow to flower, and you may have to wait for about five years for *Y. gloriosa* to bloom, but *Y. filamentosa* and *Y. flaccida* may flower within a season or two of planting.

Height: up to 10 ft. (3m) in flower, depending on species or variety.

## Varieties to look for

For the biggest flower spikes and most imposing plants out of flower, *Y. gloriosa* is difficult to beat, but *Y. filamentosa* is more suitable for a small garden and easier to place among other shrubs. *Y. flaccida* is also a desirable species of modest size, and "Ivory" is a good performer.

## Soil and site

Well-drained soil, in full sun. Zone 7.

## Propagation

Remove rooted suckers in early or mid spring, or cut off the "toes" (ends of rhizomes with buds) to plant in a nursery bed until they produce leaves.

"Icterina" has green and gold leaves; "Purpurascens" has the stems and young foliage suffused purple; "Tricolor" has gray-green leaves splashed creamy-white, suffused pink and purple.

## Soil and site

Well-drained fertile soil, in full sun. Best in a sheltered position. Zone 5.

## Propagation

Take softwood cuttings in early summer.

## ● TIP TO TRY

Take a few cuttings of these sages every year to maintain a supply of young replacement plants. They are sometimes lost or damaged in a severe winter, and old plants tend to become straggly and unattractive after a few years.

## Senecio "Sunshine"

*see Brachyglottis*

## Viburnum tinus

*Laurustinus*

A subdued shrub, never bright or brash, but absolutely dependable for winter flowers. The first flowers usually appear by mid autumn and are usually there until spring. Although white (pinkish in some varieties) they show up well against the dark evergreen leaves.

Height: 10 ft. (3m).

187

# Romantic Roses

Roses are perhaps the world's best-known flower, with a huge following and specialty societies devoted to them. Even people with no love of gardening know the rose and have an affection for it.

The rose is a more versatile plant than many realize, and breeders are constantly striving to give us an even greater array of these wonderful plants to choose from. Modern ground-cover varieties really do cover the ground with a mass of flowers for months; dwarf floribundas are ideal for containers and beds on patios (the term *patio rose* is often used to described them), and there are even varieties suitable for use in hanging baskets.

Breeders have improved the disease resistance of many modern roses, and they have also strived to achieve a long flowering season.

Despite all the exciting developments with modern roses, the old-fashioned shrub roses still have pride of place in many gardens: their flowering season may be shorter but they often have big, showy blooms and an exquisite scent.

With climbers and ramblers, not to mention standards and miniatures, there are roses to be used all around the garden.

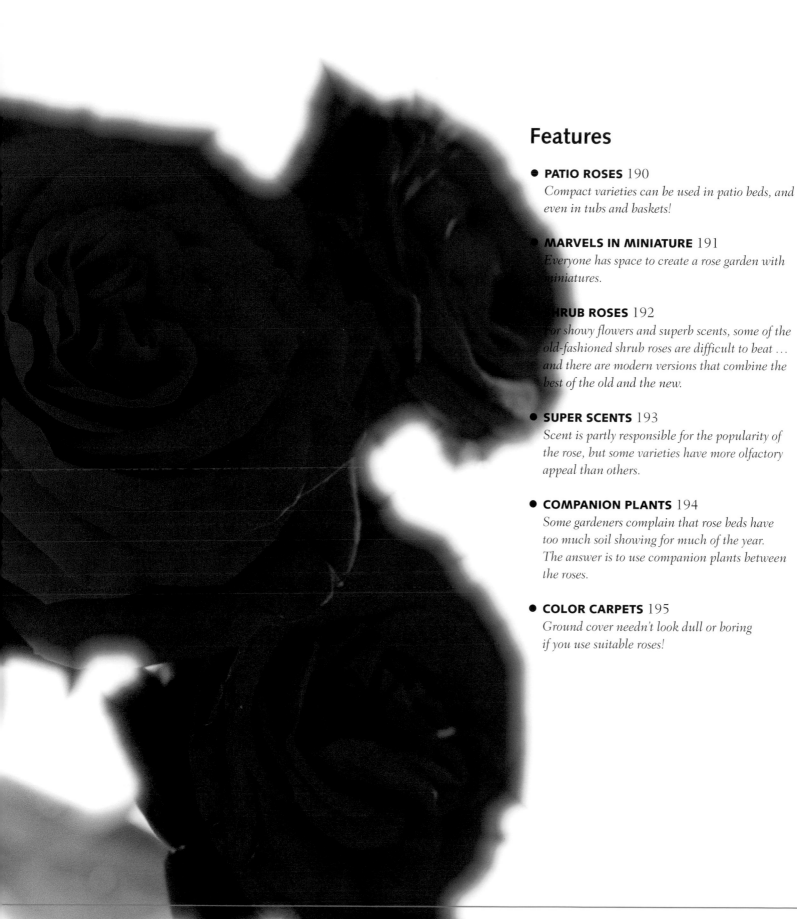

# Features

ROMANTIC ROSES

# Patio roses

*Patio roses are generally compact floribunda (cluster-flowered) roses suitable for growing in containers or in patio beds.*

Although small in stature, most of them create just as much color as their larger relatives and most have a profusion of flowers for many months. Most patio roses are really dwarf varieties of ordinary cluster flowered roses (floribundas), and some catalogs may simply describe them as dwarf varieties. The boundary line between roses of different types can be blurred, however: some varieties grown as patio roses are also sold as ground-cover roses, and the largest of the miniatures can be almost as tall as the smallest of the patio roses. Most patio roses grow about 1½ ft. (45cm) tall, some perhaps 6 in. (15cm) shorter or taller.

### In containers

Patio roses can be grown successfully in containers provided the following guidelines are followed:
• The container must be at least 10 in. (25cm) wide and deep.
• There must be drainage holes.
• Plant in a good proprietary potting soil. A loam-based type is better than one based on peat or a peat substitute, as it will contain a better natural reserve of nutrients.
• Re-pot after two years. To keep in the same-sized container, shake off some of the old soil and replenish with new.

Above: The varieties sometimes described as patio roses are useful for small beds and some are suitable for containers. This variety is "Sweet Dream."

• Water regularly to ensure the potting soil does not dry out.
• Feed during the growing season.

### Bedding and edging

Plant in a single row about 1½ ft. (45cm) apart to produce a ribbon of color as an edging. Or try planting in rectangular blocks of color using the same spacing between plants. Used like this they have a similar effect to traditional summer bedding but without the need for annual replanting.

## PLANTING AND PROPAGATING

Although the different kinds of roses described here vary considerably in appearance, they have similar soil requirements.

It is a myth that a heavy clay soil is essential for good roses – superb results can be achieved on light soils as well as heavy ones, and there is no reason why roses cannot be enjoyed on chalky soils. The key lies in careful preparation and cultivation of the soil.

Deep digging, preferably double digging, will pay dividends. It will also improve drainage, which is beneficial as roses will not thrive in waterlogged soil. Incorporate plenty of humus-forming material, such as garden compost and well-rotted manure, when preparing the ground.

Only add lime to adjust the pH (and then not at the same time as applying manure) if a test shows it is less than pH6. Roses will thrive in the range pH6–6.5. If the soil is very alkaline, perhaps because it overlies chalk, add more humus-forming material, and if the soil is shallow, add lime-free topsoil to raise the bed. Regular mulching thereafter will help. Once established, regular feeding and mulching will do much to ensure your roses remain healthy.

All roses do best in full sun, but most will tolerate partial shade – climbers and ramblers trained against a wall become used to living in the shade.

### Propagation

Commercially, roses are usually budded onto a rootstock. Some enthusiastic amateurs try this too, but it is not always easy to obtain a suitable rootstock and budding is a skill that has to be acquired. For just a few plants, cuttings are probably preferable.

Cuttings do not have the advantages that some rootstocks confer, such as a tolerance of particular soil types, but roses on their own roots are perfectly adequate for most gardens. Some large-flowered roses (hybrid teas) do not do well on their own roots, but most other roses should be successful.

Take hardwood cuttings in early autumn, and plant in a piece of spare ground. Miniature roses are best rooted in pots and wintered in a greenhouse or indoors.

Layering is suitable for roses with long and flexible stems, such as ramblers, though it can also be done with some shrub roses. Mid and late summer is a good time to layer roses.

# Marvels in miniature

*Miniature roses need to be used in ways that will allow their diminutive blooms to be appreciated.*

There's nothing new about miniature roses. In the 1800s, many were used as flowering potted plants – they were thought to be too delicate to grow outdoors and in need of special care. Nowadays miniature roses are used as garden plants, though there is a big market in miniature roses as short-term house plants.

### Indoors

Miniature roses are sold in large numbers as potted plants, usually as they are coming into bloom. If you regard them as short-term plants for the home you won't be disappointed. They do not, however, make good long-term house plants. The best way to grow them is in a small group in a larger container: you can keep them in their pots and pack moss between and over the pots if you plan to plant them outdoors later.

### Outdoors

Better still, grow your miniatures in raised beds or a miniature rose garden, perhaps on the patio. Plants bought for indoors are best planted in the garden once the main flush of flowers is over. Miniatures are not ideal for normal tubs and troughs – the proportions look wrong. A collection of them in a window box can be attractive, but they are best on their own rather than in a mixed group.

### Standards and climbers

Miniature standards look best as part of a miniature rose garden. Some miniature climbers, however, tend to look out of proportion in a miniature garden and are best against a patio wall, perhaps behind a bed of miniatures.

## CHOOSING A ROSE

There are thousands of rose varieties and species, so choosing one is always difficult. The illustrations here are just examples to show the diversity of what is available.

Specialty rose growers have catalogs which usually offer a far greater range than a garden center can stock, and there may be varieties – old or new – unique to that supplier. The best catalogs also offer useful advice about the merits of the various varieties.

The very best way to choose roses, however, is to see them growing. Do not be tempted by cut blooms at a show…see what the bushes look like in the ground.

That will give an indication of how floriferous they are and you will have a good idea of likely height and spread.

Scent may be an important part of choosing a rose, and no matter how detailed a written description is it is no guide to whether it will appeal to you personally.

Most countries have rose gardens where a wide range of varieties can be viewed (and sniffed), and many public parks and gardens grow a wide range of roses. Most rose growers will allow you to look around their nursery when the roses are in bloom.

## Gallica roses

*Rosa gallica* itself is rarely grown, but some of its varieties are among the best-known of all roses. Typically they have showy flowers about 2–3 in. (5–7.5cm) across in early summer, followed by large red tips in late summer and autumn, on plants about 3 ft. (1m) tall. *R. g.* "Versicolor," historically known as "Rosa Mundi," dates from about the 12th century. The semi-double red, white, and pink striped blooms are strikingly distinctive, but the fragrance is only moderate. *R. g.* var. *officinalis* is historically known as the apothecary's

rose or in England as the red rose of Lancaster. Its flat, semi-double flowers are pinkish-red.

Gallica roses are suitable for a shrub or mixed border as well as a dedicated rose bed, but be prepared for mildew.

191

Left: *Rosa rugosa*.
Right: *Rosa moyesii*.

## Rugosa roses

Rugosa roses are very distinctive, with large, wrinkled leaves and fragrant, cup-shaped single flowers about 3 in. (8cm) across in early summer and intermittently until autumn, followed by large orange-red tomato-shaped hips. The basic color is deep pink, but "Alba" is white and *R. r. rubra* a rose-magenta.

There are many excellent hybrids derived from *R. rugosa*, such as "Frau Dagmar Hastrup" and "Scabrosa," which make excellent flowering hedges, and are almost as decorative when the large and long-lasting hips appear.

Rugosa roses are bushy, growing about 5 ft. (1.5m) tall and 4 ft. (1.2m) across. Single specimens are suitable for a shrub or mixed border, but they also make pleasing hedges.

The distinctive rugosa foliage is usually disease-free and always looks healthy until it turns gold in autumn.

## Rosa moyesii

This large rose is grown primarily for its beautiful red flowers in late spring and early summer and its attractive hips in autumn. It is typical of many of the species roses in being too large and spreading for a normal rose garden, sometimes reaching 12 x 10 ft. (4 x 3m).

The hybrid "Geranium" (which is more correctly called simply *Rosa* "Geranium," but is often sold as a variety of *R. moyesii*) is a better choice for most gardens. It is more compact at about 8 ft. x 6 ft. (2.4 x 1.8m), and the 2 in. (5cm) orange-red flagon-shaped hips are even more decorative in the autumn than those of the species.

There are other very pleasing hybrids such as "Highdownensis" and "Sealing Wax."

Tall and spreading species like this rose are best placed toward the back of a large shrub border.

# Shrub roses

*Shrub roses are generally large, and the flowering season short, so plant them in a shrub or mixed border rather than in a rose bed.*

### Space-filling

Use a shrub rose to fill a gap in an existing border, but check the size first. Try to plant a fragrant rose near the front of the border.

### Mass color

Where there is space to plant for large pools of color, grow three or five of the same kind together, rather than dotting them around.

### Specimen plants

Shrub roses can make attractive plants in a lawn, but avoid very tall and spreading varieties such as Bourbon and Alba roses. Rugosa roses are a better choice because they have superb summer flowers, with some repeat flowering, and bright tips in autumn. The so-called English shrub roses, such as "Constance Spry" and "Graham Thomas," make good specimen roses and combine repeat flowering with the charm of the old roses.

"Constance Spry" is one of the English roses, bred by crossing modern roses with old shrub roses.

### Flowering hedges

Many shrub roses, and especially the Rugosa varieties, make superb flowering hedges. Plant a row of the same variety for maximum impact from a distance, or mix different varieties within the row for a less formal effect with a more random appearance.

# Super scents

The best way to select a rose for fragrance is to sniff it yourself. Sense of smell can vary enormously from one individual to another: what smells strong to one person may not to another. Whether a particular smell is attractive or not also depends on personal taste.

Compilers of catalogs and garden writers may also suffer shortcomings in their ability to describe scents. Good rose catalogs give an indication of how fragrant each variety is, from no fragrance to very fragrant. These are probably a more useful guide than descriptions that of their fragrances in words.

*A rose without some scent appears to lack an essential attribute, no matter how beautiful the color or perfect the shape of the bloom. For massed effect from a distance, scent doesn't matter so much, but if you have just a few roses it makes sense to select those with the best fragrance.*

**Above left:** "Fragrant Cloud" is an old hybrid tea with some shortcomings, but it's still well worth growing for its wonderfully powerful fragrance.
**Above:** "Paul Shirville" is fragrant as well as beautiful.
**Above right:** Among the fragrant floribundas, "Korresia" is an outstanding all-round variety that's bright, compact, and has a wonderfully spicy scent.

## Making the most of scent

In a large garden, a whole bed of one very fragrant variety will almost take your breath away with its intensity. In a small garden it's seldom possible to devote a whole bed to one variety: you will have to accept the overall blending of scents that results from a mixed bed.

A bed of mixed roses can be planted for beauty as well as fragrance. It may be preferable to space out the very fragrant varieties a little, the better to appreciate individual scents. Plant a bed with the most fragrant roses around the edge so that each one can be savored, and even then it's a good idea to alternate very fragrant plants with those that have particularly beautiful blooms but aren't outstandingly fragrant.

The scent will be more intense if the bed is in a sheltered part of the garden rather than an exposed or windy position.

# Companion plants

*Rose enthusiasts may consider it heresy to underplant roses with other flowers. But if you are looking for a general garden display, consider some of these companions for your roses.*

The arguments against underplanting roses are that the companion plants take nutrients from the roses, makes mulching and other soil treatments impractical or more difficult, and the feeding necessary for a top-rate display may be unsuitable for the other plants. On a subjective level, some rose enthusiasts consider that other flowers detract from the roses. If you have a bed devoted to roses and they are closely planted, it may not be practical to grow other plants with them: in summer the growth will be too dense. It may be necessary to allow extra space between the roses when planting.

### Try these partners

Red roses and blue flowers go well together. Try blue catmint (nepeta) or lavender between red floribunda roses. The fragrant lavender and scented roses can make a very powerful combination! Single-color beds can be difficult, but stunning when they work. Yellow roses with compact yellow day lilies, and even yellow achilleas, sounds unlikely but can work if the roses are large and vigorous.

"Neutral" colors are easier to work with, especially in a bed of mixed roses. Some grasses can be surprisingly effective, but the top of the grass should be lower than the height of the rose flowers. A good grass to start with is the foxtail barley or squirreltail grass (*Hordeum jubatum*). This grows to 1–2 ft. (30–60cm) and is easily raised as an annual. If you don't like the effect, try

**Blue catmint is a happy companion for roses of many kinds. Here it has been used with a shrub rose in a border with alliums and osteospermums.**

something different the following year: it will only have cost you the price of a packet of seeds. The grass has arching feathery plume-like flower spikes and looks pleasing over a long period in summer.

If you just want to cover the ground and have a little color when the roses are out of bloom, underplant with pansies. Winter-flowering pansies will provide color when the rose bed otherwise looks boring.

## Rosa sericea omeiensis pteracantha

Do not be put off by the name – it is an exceptionally beautiful shrub with decorative thorns as its main feature! These are especially attractive on young wood, being about 1 in. (2.5cm) long, almost triangular in shape, and a glowing red that seems to light up in sunlight. Regular pruning is important to stimulate plenty of new wood with the attractive thorns. Without pruning it will also grow to 8 x 6 ft. (2.4 x 1.8m).

The small white flowers in early summer are not especially impressive, but the ferny foliage is a pleasing backdrop for the red thorns.

This kind of vigorous rose is best in a large shrub border, but in this case positioned where the young stems and spectacular thorns can be appreciated, perhaps illuminated by shafts of sunlight.

## Rosa xanthina "Canary Bird"

This is one of the shrub roses grown primarily for their beautiful flowers. It is also one of the first to bloom, in late spring. It makes a large shrub about 6 x 6 ft. (1.8 x 1.8m) tall. The single yellow blooms are borne in profusion along arching stems, and flowering lasts for about a month. It is sometimes available as a standard, and its cascading stems studded with large yellow flowers can make a spectacular feature.

"Hugonis" is a similar rose, but the flowers to do not open as reliably as "Canary Bird." "Canary Bird" is usually listed simply as a hybrid, and "Hugonis" may be found described as *Rosa hugonis.*

These are plants for a shrub border or large rose bed, or perhaps the back of a mixed border. "Canary Bird" makes a superb specimen plant in a lawn when grown as a standard.

# Color carpets

*Roses are good ground-cover plants. They will suppress weeds in summer and clothe the ground with color that other shrubs can't match.*

### Planting and training

Ground-cover roses vary considerably in their growth and height, depending on their parentage. Some of the older types are best if their long shoots are pegged down (you can make suitable pegs by cutting up and bending wire coat hangers), but the modern compact growers are simply planted at the appropriate spacing.

### Some of the best

Older ground-cover roses tend to be large and vigorous: "Grouse" carries its pink flowers on plants up to 10 ft. (3m) across, despite being little more than 1 ft. (30cm) tall. "Partridge" is similar, but with white flowers.

"Pheasant," with clusters of pink flowers, is a little taller but has a similar spread, and is useful for banks.

Typical of the more compact ground-cover roses are "Nozomi" with pink to white flowers, which grows to about 1 ft. (30cm) but can spread to 4 ft. (1.2m), and the white "Snow Carpet," which is a little less vigorous.

The more recent ground-cover roses, like "Suffolk," "Surrey," and "Sussex," with flowers in scarlet, pink, and apricot-buff respectively, are bushier and more compact.

195

Right: Climbing rose "Compassion."
Bottom left: Rambling rose "Albertine."
Bottom right: Floribunda rose "Iceberg."

## Ramblers

Unlike climbing roses, these generally produce new shoots freely from the base, and therefore have many spreading shoots. Also unlike some climbers, which may have repeat flowering, ramblers tend to have one short but spectacular display in early summer. The flowers are sometimes small, but in large clusters. Many are exquisitely fragrant.

"Albertine" has coppery buds opening pink, and is very fragrant, and "Dorothy Perkins" has coral pink flowers, but prone to mildew. Both are old varieties but are no less desirable for that.

Some ramblers are very rampant and will cover a pergola or grow into a tree: "Seagull" is pure white with a golden center and "Wedding Day" has huge clusters of creamy-yellow to white flowers. Both are examples of spectacular ramblers that unfortunately need a lot of space.

Most ramblers can be trained against a rustic trellis, up a pillar, or over a pergola. The very vigorous ones are best allowed to grow through a natural support such as a tree. Try to match the tree to your rose.

## Climbing roses

Climbing roses generally have larger flowers than ramblers, though in smaller clusters, and they may bloom intermittently throughout the summer. Flowering performance depends very much on variety: modern climbers are generally shorter-growing but with a long flowering season.

Climbers come in many flower forms, some with full but loose flowers, others with pointed flowers like large-flowered hybrid tea roses (some are climbing variations of bush varieties). Most of them grow tall, but can be constrained by pruning.

Examples of popular climbers are: "Compassion," apricot-pink, very fragrant; "Dublin Bay," deep red; "Handel," creamy blush; "Maigold," golden yellow; and "New Dawn," pink. "Zéphirine Drouhin," also known as the Thornless Rose, is still a popular choice despite being a very old variety prone to mildew and black spot. Its very fragrant carmine-pink flowers, and vigorous but not rampant growth, make it an attention-grabbing variety.

Among the climbing sports (variations) of large-flowered hybrid tea and cluster-flowered floribunda roses, "Climbing Iceberg" with white floribunda type flowers and "Climbing Etoile de Hollande" with dark crimson hybrid tea flowers are still popular despite their age.

There are now patio climbers that grow to about 6–8 ft. (1.8–2.4m). Examples are "Laura Ford," yellow, and "Warm Welcome," orange.

Climbing roses usually look their best growing against a wall or over a pergola. Patio climbers make good pillar roses, but can also be grown in a large patio pot if given a suitable support.

## Cluster-flowered (floribunda) roses

Cluster-flowered floribunda roses are perhaps the best for general garden display, blooming prolifically over a long period and with a huge range of varieties from which to choose. Dwarf varieties are sometimes

classed as patio roses (see page 190). The varieties below grow to 2–3 ft. (60–90cm).

Popular varieties include: "Eyepaint," scarlet with white center; "Flair," orange with yellow centers; "Korresia," yellow; "Margaret Merril," blush white; "Schneewittchen" (syn. "Iceberg"), white; "Sexy Rexy," pink; "Sheila's Perfume," red and yellow; and "The Times," red.

## Large flowered (hybrid tea) roses

These usually have large flowers with a pointed center. Although there may be many flowers on a stem they do not form large clusters. The emphasis is on the perfection of individual flowers rather than overall effect.

Most large-flowered hybrid tea roses grow to 2½–3 ft. (75–90cm), and are best in dedicated rose beds. They can be grown in mixed borders, but their beauty and fragrance can become lost among the other

flowers of summer. The main flush of flowers is in early or mid summer, but they continue to produce until autumn.

Good all-round varieties include: "Freedom," yellow, with good disease resistance; "Ingrid Bergman," deep red; "Paul Shirville," pink; "Peace," an old but famous rose, yellow edged with pink; "Peaudouce," primrose; "Silver Jubilee," peach and silver; and "Tequila Sunrise," yellow and red.

## Patio roses

Dwarf cluster-flowered roses that grow to about 1½–2 ft. (45–60cm) are sometimes called patio roses. They are ideal for planting in narrow borders, in spaces between paving, or in large tubs and troughs.

Examples of patio roses include: "Cider Cup," deep apricot; "Peek a Boo," apricot to pink; "Sweet Dream," peach to apricot; and "Top Marks," a vibrant vermilion.

## Miniature roses

The borderline between the largest miniatures and smallest patio roses becomes blurred and some varieties are classified in one group by some growers, and in the other group by others. Generally, however, a miniature is not more than 1 ft. (30cm) tall, and is often much smaller.

There are many varieties in all the usual colors, but popular ones include: "Baby Masquerade" with flowers that change from yellow to pink and then rosy-red; "Lavender Lace," mauve-lavender; "Orange

Sunblaze," orange-scarlet; and "Pour Toi," creamy white.

In a garden setting, miniature roses are best displayed in raised beds, densely planted for maximum effect.

## Ground-cover roses

There are many kinds of ground-cover roses, varying in vigor and height as well as in flower type and color.

"Nozomi" is a versatile variety that is sometimes seen as a cascading standard, or as a miniature climber, as well as a ground-cover rose. Its trailing stems have small pinkish-white flowers. Pegging the stems down improves its ground-covering powers.

"Grouse," with pale pink flowers on sprawling, prostrate stems, is typical of another group of ground-cover roses, at their best in mid and late summer.

A more recent group of ground-cover roses, named after English counties, has widened the scope still further. These flower prolifically, usually on compact plants. "Surrey" is one example, with double pink flowers that bloom over a long period through the summer months.

Do not expect ground-cover roses to suppress weeds in heavily infested ground – make sure the bed is weed-free first.

# Top Trees

Trees give a garden height and impart a sense of permanence and maturity. They give it structure and form a backdrop against which the garden is viewed.

No garden is too small for a tree or two. There are fastigiate (narrow, columnar) trees for confined spaces, dwarf weeping trees, and slow-growers that should not outgrow their welcome. You can even grow trees in tubs!

The trees included here are all small or moderately large trees suitable for gardens. Forest and very large trees – though beautiful in their own right where there's space – have not been included in this book.

Trees require very careful positioning, taking into consideration their eventual height (heights given here are after about 20 years in good growing conditions). Tall ones will cast shade and take nutrients and moisture from the soil, so positioning should be part of the overall garden design. Bear in mind that trees that could be a hazard to drains or buildings should be planted a sufficient distance away not to cause damage.

# Features

TOP TREES

199

Below left: *Acer griseum.*
Bottom: *Betula pendula.*
Right: *Betula papyrifera.*

## Acer griseum
*Paperbark maple*

One to grow in splendid isolation, perhaps in a lawn, where it can be viewed as a specimen tree and admired in all its many moods.

In spring this beautiful tree has small sulphur-yellow flowers; in summer it makes an attractive small tree with its brown peeling bark a feature in sunshine; in autumn there is super leaf color before they drop, and in winter the decorative bark becomes a focal point again.

Height: 4.5m (15 ft.).

### Other species to look for
Other acers to grow for bark effect are the snake-bark maples, which have a striated pattern that resembles a snake's skin. These include *A. capillipes* with good autumn color, *A. davidii*, also good autumn color, and *A. pensylvanicum* with bright yellow autumn color. *A. grosseri* var. *hersii* also combines an attractive bark with good autumn color.

### Soil and site
Undemanding but avoid very alkaline soils, in full sun or partial shade. Zone 5 (*A. pensylvanicum* 3, *A. davidii* 6).

### Propagation
Sow seed in autumn, but most amateurs buy plants.

## Betula pendula
*Silver birch*

Sometimes dismissed as too commonplace, this birch has much to offer. It's fast-growing, undemanding, has a light and graceful canopy that makes it possible to grow plants such as spring-flowering bulbs beneath it, and the silvery bark is especially attractive in winter. It will grow tall but the weeping form "Youngii" is a slow growing compact variety more suitable for small gardens.

Height: 30 ft. (9m).

### Varieties to look for
Among the varieties are three particularly interesting variations: "Fastigiata" is narrower and more columnar; "Golden Cloud" has golden foliage; and "Youngii" makes a small weeping tree that does not make great demands on space.

### Soil and site
Well-drained soil, in full sun or partial shade. Zone 1.

### Propagation
Sow seed for the species, graft named forms, but most amateurs buy plants.

## Betula utilis var. jacquemontii
*Paper birch*

One of several magnificent birches grown primarily for their white, peeling bark. This is an attractive feature year round, but is especially pleasing in winter when it can be seen to best effect. Like most birches, it can grow large.

Height: 30 ft. (9m).

### Varieties and other species to look for
*B. papyrifera* is another super tree with bark that peels in large sheets to reveal shining white beneath. For a different kind of peeling bark, try *B. nigra*, the black birch, also called river birch, which has dark shaggy bark.

### Soil and site
Well-drained soil, except for

# Arbors, Arches & Pergolas

# Arbors, Arches, & Pergolas

Raise your sights by using vertical space and creating stunning features with arbors, arches, and pergolas. All of them make pleasing features in their own right, but also provide an excellent reason for planting lots of stunning climbers!

In a large garden you can indulge in large arches, even a tunnel of arches, and pergolas with brick or stone pillars, but a simple arbor or rustic pergola can usually be accommodated even in a small town garden – often with great impact.

Rustic arches and pergolas are simple do-it-yourself jobs, but elegant metal arches can be bought if you want something large or especially elegant.

Always allow sufficient height for foliage to hang well clear of head level – especially important if growing a thorny plant such as a rose.

**Above:** Roses are a popular choice for growing over rustic pergolas, and "American Pillar" is ideal for the job.

**Left:** Imagine sitting beneath an arbor of fragrant roses on a hot summer day ... what better way to contemplate the appeal of gardening?

**Left:** You can create a stunning arch like this in a season! Gourds are annuals, so you won't have to wait for several years for this kind of impact, as you would with woody plants.

**Overleaf:** Even in a wild part of the garden, a simple arbour can be created by training rambler roses such as 'Albertine' over a framework to meet in the centre. Add a seat, for you'll want to linger long.

Left: *Catalpa bignonioides.*
Bottom: *Cercis siliquastrum* "Bodnant."
Right: *Cornus kousa.*

B. *nigra* which likes moist but not permanently waterlogged ground, in full sun or partial shade. Zone 7 (*B. papyrifera* 1, *B. nigra* 4).

## Propagation

Sow seed in autumn, but most amateurs buy plants.

## DID YOU KNOW?

*Betula papyrifera* is also called the canoe birch, because the bark was used in the construction of canoes.

# Catalpa bignonioides
*Indian bean tree*

Sure to attract comment when the tree is festooned with long seed pods that hang like long cylindrical beans. The old pods hang on into winter, creating interest even after the large leaves have fallen. The white flowers are also attractive, but they are generally produced well above eye level.

Height: 25 ft. (7.5m), but the golden form is more compact.

## Varieties to look for

"Aurea" is a choice tree, with large yellow leaves, but it tends to be less hardy.

## Soil and site

Deeply cultivated, fertile soil, in full sun or partial shade. Does not do well on very alkaline soils, and the coloring of "Aurea" is better in full sun. Zone 5.

## Propagation

Sow seed or layer for the species, graft or layer "Aurea," but most amateurs buy plants.

## SHRINK IT TO A SHRUB

*Catalpa bignonioides* "Aurea" is grown mainly for its wonderful foliage. If there is insufficient space to grow it as a normal tree with a trunk, buy one trained as a multi-stemmed tree, when it will be more like a large shrub.

# Cercis siliquastrum
*Judas tree*

A fascinating tree with an interesting story (see box), grown mainly for its rose-purple pea-type flowers in late spring and early summer. They appear on

both new and old wood, and will sometimes grow out of the trunk! The broad, kidney-shaped leaves are also attractive.

Height: 20 ft. (6m).

## Varieties to look for

There is a white variety, and even a variegated one, but these lack the impact of the species.

## Soil and site

Well-drained soil, preferably neutral to acid, in full sun or partial shade. Zone 6.

## Propagation

Sow seed or layer, but most amateurs buy plants.

## DID YOU KNOW?

*Cercis siliquastrum* is popularly called the Judas tree because legend has it that it was on one of these trees that Judas hanged himself.

# Cornus controversa "Variegata"
*Wedding cake tree*

Eye-catching in a quiet sort of way, this tree has a distinctive shape and form. The branches are produced almost in whorls, and spread horizontally to give a tiered effect. Good light is needed to ensure a pleasing shape. The creamy-white variegated leaves are light enough to

show up against a background of green trees, helping to make it stand out. Creamy-white flowers crowd the upper side of the branches to make it an even more beautiful sight in early and mid summer. These are sometimes followed by a bonus of blue-black berries in autumn.

Height: 15 ft. (4.5m).

## Other species to look for

*Cornus alternifolia* "Argentea" (syn. "Variegata"), the pagoda dogwood or pagoda tree, also has variegated cream and white leaves on tiered branches.

## Soil and site

Deeply cultivated, fertile soil, in full sun or partial shade. *C. controversa* does not do well on very alkaline soils, *C. alternifolia* is more tolerant.

## Propagation

These variegated forms are grafted, and most amateurs buy plants.

# Multi-merit trees

*Unless you have a large garden, the number of trees you can plant will be limited, so it makes sense to choose multi-merit trees whenever possible.*

### Shrubby trees

The snowy mespilus (*Amelanchier larmarckii* and the very similar *A. canadensis*) is often listed as a shrub. But it can be regarded as a multi-stemmed tree, and is sometimes sold in proper tree form, with a head on a single trunk. It will remain small enough for most gardens, and it stays looking good from first leaf in spring to last leaf in autumn. Masses of white flowers appear about the same time as the leaves open, creating a cloud of bloom. In early summer there may be a

bonus of edible black fruits, and it says good-bye to autumn in a blaze of red foliage.

The Indian bean tree (*Catalpa bignonioides*) is only suitable for a large garden, where its big leaves, white flowers in mid and late summer, and slender "bean pods" in winter, provide a succession of interest. More suitable for a smaller garden is the yellow-leaved "Aurea." It's one of the best yellow trees, and it can be grown as a multi-stemmed plant that makes it more like a large shrub.

**Left:** In spring *Malus* "Golden Hornet" can be relied upon to produce a magnificent show of flowers, and it can be a useful pollinator for eating apples.

**Right:** By autumn *Malus* "Golden Hornet" will be festooned with small deep yellow fruits. These usually remain decorative for several months.

**Left:** *Acer griseum* is a choice small tree that has superb autumn color in most years. After the leaves fall, you can enjoy the wonderful bark.

### Flowers, fruit and foliage

*Cornus kousa* deserves to be more widely grown. It's a slow-growing tree and not suitable for dry, shallow, or chalky soil, but well worth waiting for if you can plant it in moist but well-drained soil in sun or partial shade.

The spreading branches are covered with star-like flowers (the "petals" are actually bracts surrounding the true flowers), in late spring and early summer. If conditions suit, these are followed later by edible (but seedy and insipid) fruit that resemble strawberries in appearance. In autumn the leaves take on shades of crimson and bronze.

Hawthorns are useful small-garden trees, with flowers in late spring or early summer and red or orange fruits in autumn, which

often persist into winter. Two of the most popular for showy flowers are *Crataegus laevigata* (syn. *C. oxyacantha*) "Paul's Scarlet" and "Rosea Flore Pleno," but for all-round performance choose *C. prunifolia*, which has white flowers in early summer, is a blaze of orange and red leaves in autumn, and produces bunches of rich red long-lasting fruits.

*Crataegus monogyna* is not so good for autumn tints, but flowers prolifically in late spring and the branches are usually laden with red fruits in autumn.

The ornamental crab apples (*Malus*) are invaluable multi-merit small garden trees. They are covered with blossom in mid or late spring (white, pink, red, or purple according to variety); the purple-leaved ones like "Profusion" are colorful all summer, and most have very attractive, long-lasting red or yellow fruits in autumn. Some also have good autumn color: *M. tschonoskii* turns yellow,

Right: Amelanchiers have superb autumn tints in most years, like the *A. lamarckii* shown here. This show can be as brilliant as the blossom of spring.

Left: The amelanchiers, such as *A. canadensis* and *A. lamarckii*, which are very similar, are a mass of white flowers in spring as the leaves begin to unfurl.

orange, purple, and scarlet before the leaves fall, which is why it is sometimes called the bonfire tree.

Sorbus are neat, small or medium-sized trees, and those grown for their berries are at their best in autumn and early winter. The flattened heads of creamy-white flowers in late spring and early summer are unspectacular but a useful bonus. It's the autumn berries that bring these trees to life, and they come in shades of red, orange, pink, and white, according to species and variety. Many have brilliant foliage color to light up those autumn days. "Joseph Rock" is particularly useful for autumn color, the leaves turning a fiery combination of orange, red, copper, and purple ... at the same time as the berries deepen from creamy-yellow to amber-gold.

## Add an acer
This is a huge family of trees, some dwarf enough for a large rock garden, others more

Above: *Acer griseum* has very appealing bark the year round, but is often appreciated most after leaf-fall. At any time looks superb lit by shafts of sunlight.

suitable for a forest. A couple of them are good small-garden trees with multiple merits.

*Acer griseum* is grown mainly for its cinnamon-colored peeling bark, which is a feature at all seasons, but the tree looks especially good in autumn sunshine. The foliage turns vivid scarlet and flame and the tree can glow like a fire. It has the considerable advantage of remaining small.

*Acer pseudoplatanus* "Brilliantissimum" is a kind of sycamore, but don't be put off. This tree remains small in comparison and it looks spectacular in spring when the foliage opens shrimp pink. It later changes to yellow-green and finally to green.

## Cherries to cherish
Flowering cherries and other *Prunus* species generally have beautiful blossom ... some also have purple summer foliage or intense autumn tints before the leaves fall. These are described in more detail on page 215.

203

# Space savers

Below: *Pyrus salicifolia* "Pendula" is a charming gray-leaved small tree that's even amenable to being trained over a decorative arch.

*Space-saving trees are great for small gardens, as well as useful for cramped corners in a large garden.*

Where you need the height and sense of permanence that a tree provides, but where space or spread is restricted, try some of these trees – look for trees described as "fastigiate" (narrow and columnar). These trees are also useful even where there is ample space for a normal spread but you wish to limit the shadow cast on beds and borders. Many weeping trees are ideal for a small garden where height has to be restricted but spread is less important. Although weeping trees can be grown in a border, they look best as specimen plants set in a lawn, or perhaps near the edge of a pond.

### Tall and narrow

*Acer rubrum* "Scanlon" is a tall, columnar tree that turns into a pillar of red as the foliage colors in autumn.

Among the birches, *Betula pendula* "Fastigiata" makes a medium to large tree, but lacks the grace of the more popular pendulous birches.

*Carpinus betulus* "Fastigiata" is a hornbeam grown for the texture created by the dense foliage. Although narrow when young, it broadens at the base with age and grows too large for a really small space.

*Crataegus monogyna* "Stricta" is a small hawthorn with white flowers.

For a fastigiate beech, try *Fagus sylvatica* "Dawyck," a tall, slender tree when young but broadening with age.

The magnificent *Liriodendron tulipifera* "Fastigiata" is a medium-sized tree that's narrow when young but broadens with age.

*Malus tschonoskii* is a small to medium-sized ornamental crab apple with superb autumn foliage colors.

Often seen as a windbreak, the Lombardy poplar (*Populus nigra* "Italica") stands like a tall sentinel. Strictly for a large garden.

*Prunus* "Spire" (which may be sold as *P.* x *hillieri* "Spire") is one of the best small flowering trees. *Prunus* "Amanogawa," columnar Japanese cherry, is justifiably popular too, forming a column of pink flowers in spring.

*Sorbus aucuparia* "Fastigiata" makes a small, stiff-looking tree, with red berries an attraction at the end of summer.

*Ulmus minor* "Dampieri Aurea" is much more likely to be found under its other name:

*U.* x *hollandica* "Wredei." It's a good, compact tree with conical growth and golden leaves.

### Low and weeping

Young's weeping birch (*Betula pendula* "Youngii") is a small, mushroom-headed tree with branches that cascade to the ground.

Suitable for even a tiny garden, *Cotoneaster salicifolius* "Pendulus" is a very small weeping tree with long cascading shoots studded with red berries in autumn.

*Crataegus monogyna* "Pendula Rosea" is a small hawthorn with pink flowers.

The weeping beech is surprisingly small: *Fagus sylvatica* "Purpurea Pendula" makes a small or very small tree with a mushroom-shaped head of dark purple leaves.

Among the hollies, *Ilex aquifolium* "Pendula" makes a broad mound of weeping stems studded with red berries in autumn and winter.

*Morus alba* "Pendula" is a small or very small tree with close-packed branches that form a curtain of foliage to the ground.

There are some delightful weeping cherries. *Prunus* "Kiku-shidare-zakura" is one of the best for a small garden, with double pink flowers in mid spring. *Prunus pendula* "Pendula Rosea" forms a mushroom-headed tree with long weeping branches, on which pink buds open to white in early/mid spring.

*Pyrus salicifolia* "Pendula," the weeping willow-leaved pear, makes a mound of silvery-gray and remains small. The white flowers in mid spring may go unnoticed.

*Ulmus glabra* "Camperdownii," the Camperdown elm, remains a small tree with densely packed branches clothed to the ground with dark green leaves.

Left: *Crataegus laevigata* (syn.
*C. oxyacantha*).
Below: *Eucalyptus pauciflora niphophila*.
Right: *Gleditisia triancanthos "Sunburst."*

## Crataegus laevigata (syn. C. oxyacantha)

*Hawthorn*

Often under-rated, the hawthorns are good small-garden trees. Although some excel in autumn when the leaves color and branches are laden with berries, the best-known one are grown primarily for their flowers in late spring and early summer. They are slow-growing and often remain compact.

Height: 15 ft. (4.5m).

### Varieties and other species to look for

Two of the best for flowers are Paul's Scarlet" (syn. "Coccinea Plena"), with pinkish-red, double flowers, and "Rosea Flore Pleno" with pink, double flowers. One of the best to grow for autumn tints and bright berries is *C. persimilis* "Prunifolia" (syn. *C. prunifolia*), which also has white flowers in early summer.

### Soil and site

Undemanding regarding soil, in full sun to partial shade. Zone 5.

### Propagation

Bud or graft, but most amateurs buy plants.

## Eucalyptus pauciflora niphophila

*Snow gum*

Magnificent in their stature and beautiful in bark, the euca-lypts are always worth growing where there is space and the climate is favorable. This one has a patchwork trunk of green, gray, and cream, and gray-green aromatic foliage. Eucalypts have the potential to be tall and typically grow to 65 ft. (20m) or more, so they are not a good choice for a small garden. All are evergreen.

In areas of borderline hardi-ness they may survive most winters but be cut back or even killed by a cold one. Do not fell the tree until it has had chance

to regrow if damage has not been terminal. Choose a sheltered position whenever possible.

Height: 30 ft. (9m).

### Other species to look for

*E. gunnii*, the cider gum, is another tough species, with rounded juvenile foliage and lance-shaped adult leaves.

*E. dalrympleana* is a vigorous species with creamy-white young bark that becomes pink-ish-gray with age, peeling attractively. *E. perriniana* has a spreading shape and is fast-growing. The gray-blue leaves are long and pendulous on mature trees.

There are many other superb eucalypts, but check their hardiness and suitability before buying.

### Soil and site

Well-drained soil, in full sun or partial shade. Zone 7 (*E. dal-rympleana*, *E. gunnii* and *E. perriniana* 8).

### Propagation

Sow seed in late winter or early spring.

### GROWING UP

The juvenile (young) foliage on eucalypts often looks very different from the leaves on mature branches. Juvenile leaves are often rounder, the adult foliage more elongated.

## Gleditsia triacanthos "Sunburst"

*Honey locust*

One of the best golden trees, though the pinnate foliage does become greener as the season progresses. Autumn brings a boost of color when the leaves turn yellow before dropping.

Height: 20 ft. (6m).

### Varieties to look for

*Gleditsia* "Rubylace" has purple-tinged foliage in spring, becoming bronze-green, but it lacks the impact of "Sunburst."

The true species is less attractive but has interesting thorny trunks.

### Soil and site

Deeply cultivated, fertile, well-drained soil, in full sun or light shade. Zone 3.

### Propagation

Graft new plants, but most ama-teurs buy plants.

Left: *Crataegus laevigata* (syn.
*C. oxyacantha*).
Below: *Eucalyptus pauciflora niphophila*.
Right: *Gleditisia triancanthos "Sunburst."*

## Crataegus laevigata (syn. C. oxyacantha)

*Hawthorn*

Often under-rated, the hawthorns are good small-garden trees. Although some excel in autumn when the leaves color and branches are laden with berries, the best-known one are grown primarily for their flowers in late spring and early summer. They are slow-growing and often remain compact.

Height: 15 ft. (4.5m).

### Varieties and other species to look for

Two of the best for flowers are Paul's Scarlet" (syn. "Coccinea Plena"), with pinkish-red, double flowers, and "Rosea Flore Pleno" with pink, double flowers. One of the best to grow for autumn tints and bright berries is *C. persimilis* "Prunifolia" (syn. *C. prunifolia*), which also has white flowers in early summer.

### Soil and site

Undemanding regarding soil, in full sun to partial shade. Zone 5.

### Propagation

Bud or graft, but most amateurs buy plants.

## Eucalyptus pauciflora niphophila

*Snow gum*

Magnificent in their stature and beautiful in bark, the eucalypts are always worth growing where there is space and the climate is favorable. This one has a patchwork trunk of green, gray, and cream, and gray-green aromatic foliage. Eucalypts have the potential to be tall and typically grow to 65 ft. (20m) or more, so they are not a good choice for a small garden. All are evergreen.

In areas of borderline hardiness they may survive most winters but be cut back or even killed by a cold one. Do not fell the tree until it has had chance

to regrow if damage has not been terminal. Choose a sheltered position whenever possible.

Height: 30 ft. (9m).

### Other species to look for

*E. gunnii*, the cider gum, is another tough species, with rounded juvenile foliage and lance-shaped adult leaves.

*E. dalrympleana* is a vigorous species with creamy-white young bark that becomes pinkish-gray with age, peeling attractively. *E. perriniana* has a spreading shape and is fast-growing. The gray-blue leaves are long and pendulous on mature trees.

There are many other superb eucalypts, but check their hardiness and suitability before buying.

### Soil and site

Well-drained soil, in full sun or partial shade. Zone 7 (*E. dalrympleana*, *E. gunnii* and *E. perriniana* 8).

### Propagation

Sow seed in late winter or early spring.

## GROWING UP

The juvenile (young) foliage on eucalypts often looks very different from the leaves on mature branches. Juvenile leaves are often rounder, the adult foliage more elongated.

## Gleditsia triacanthos "Sunburst"

*Honey locust*

One of the best golden trees, though the pinnate foliage does become greener as the season progresses. Autumn brings a boost of color when the leaves turn yellow before dropping.

Height: 20 ft. (6m).

### Varieties to look for

*Gleditsia* "Rubylace" has purple-tinged foliage in spring, becoming bronze-green, but it lacks the impact of "Sunburst."

The true species is less attractive but has interesting thorny trunks.

### Soil and site

Deeply cultivated, fertile, well-drained soil, in full sun or light shade. Zone 3.

### Propagation

Graft new plants, but most amateurs buy plants.

# Kaleidoscope of conifers

*Use medium-sized conifers lavishly if you have the space. Your garden will never look drab or boring if you mix colors and shapes, and they make an excellent backdrop throughout the year for the rest of the garden.*

The conifers included here are the medium-sized ones suitable for most gardens. Dwarf conifers are included with shrubs (see pages 158–187), and very tall conifers more suitable for parks and plantations are not discussed here: despite their magnificent stature and appearance, they are inappropriate except for the largest gardens.

## Classic cedars

The cedars are sometimes grown in small gardens, but they are best given plenty of space, set into a large lawn. They are ideal conifers where a specimen tree is required as a focal point, but best planted for the next generation to enjoy at maturity. A very respectable specimen can be grown within 10–20 years, however, and these younger specimens are more attractive trees because they are often still well clothed with foliage to the base.

The blue Atlas cedar (*Cedrus libani atlantica* "Glauca") is silver-blue, with statuesque ascending branches when young, spreading with age. The deodar (*Cedrus deodara*) has a more graceful appearance, drooping growth and tiered branches making it a "light" and unoppressive tree despite its size.

**Left:** This very unusual treatment of a *Ginkgo biloba* shows how versatile some conifers can be. This one has been trained against a wall.

**Left:** The monkey puzzle tree (*Araucaria araucana*) is great as a focal point and usually stimulates conversation among visitors.

## Talking-point trees

The maidenhair tree (*Ginkgo biloba*) does not even look like a conifer. Its leaves are fan-shaped and not needle-like, and it sheds them in winter. It does not produce cones; instead it has small, yellow, plum-like fruits (though these are seldom formed on garden trees).

It's the last survivor of an ancient family, the ancestors of which were growing in many parts of the world about 160 million years ago. It is regarded as a sacred tree in parts of the East, and planted near Buddhist temples.

It's a medium to large tree, not suitable for a small garden, but excellent as a specimen tree in a lawn. The foliage turns a butter yellow before falling.

The monkey puzzle tree (*Araucaria araucana*) is a stiff-looking tree with branches that look like thick, curved ropes as the triangular

**Below:** The cedars make superb specimen trees to plant in a prominent position in a large lawn. This one is *Cedrus deodara*.

Above: *Ginkgo biloba* does not even look like a conifer – its leaves are fan-shaped rather than needle-like, and it sheds them in winter.

and pointed leaves clasp the stems. The common name is said to have originated when someone at a ceremonial planting remarked that it would puzzle a monkey to climb such a tree. It's too often planted in small gardens – it will grow to 20 ft. (6m) in about 20 years, much taller in time.

The dawn redwood (*Metasequoia glyptostroboides*) grows too tall for any but a very large garden, but it makes a magnificent conifer where you have the space and moist ground in which to grow it. At one time this tree was known only from fossils; then one was discovered in the grounds of a Chinese temple in 1841. Unusually for a conifer, it sheds its leaves in autumn.

## Go for gold

There are golden forms of the cedars mentioned above (*Cedrus libani atlantica* "Aurea" and *C. deodara* "Aurea"), which look stunning and are not quite so tall.

The popular Lawson's cypress (*Chamaecyparis lawsoniana*) has spawned a whole collection of golden varieties. Don't be misled by the name "Ellwood's Gold," however, because it's only the tips of the shoots that are gold at certain times of the year.

Right: Conifers vary greatly in size, shape and color. Here *Cedrus deodara* "Nana" contrasts with the "blue" *Abies procera* "Glauca" behind.

"Lane," "Lutea," and "Stewartii" are three medium-sized golden varieties that won't disappoint, "Lane" being the brightest.

"Goldcrest" is an outstanding variety of the Monterey cypress (*Cupressus macrocarpa*), but you should plant it in a sunny position for the best color.

## Blue-grays

Perhaps the lightest silvery-blue conifer is *Picea pungens* "Hoopsii." It is pyramidal to conical in outline with broad, silver-blue needles, silvery gray in winter.

*Picea pungens* "Koster" is another popular choice for silver-blue foliage.

Left: Cedars can grow large, when cones are often a bonus feature. This one is a majestic *Cedrus libani atlantica* "Glauca."

Among the false cypresses, *Cupressus lawsoniana* "Pembury Blue" is a striking silvery-blue.

## Conifers for autumn color

Not all conifers are evergreen, and some have a change of leaf color even though the needles are retained.

*Cryptomeria japonica* "Elegans" has green summer leaves that turn reddish-bronze in

Above: A few conifers shed their leaves in winter, and *Larix decidua* is one that can be relied upon for a final fling of autumn color before they fall.

winter. *Cunninghamia lanceolata* leaves turn from green to brown in autumn.

The larch (*Larix decidua*) sheds its leaves in autumn … but not before they turn gold. The dawn redwood (*Metasequoia glyptostroboides*) also sheds its leaves in autumn, after they have changed to gold.

*Taxodium distichum*, the swamp cypress, is also deciduous, the leaves turning bronzy-yellow before falling.

Left: *Laburnum* x *watereri* "Vossii."
Below left: *Koelreuteria paniculata* with its bladder-like fruits.
Below right: *Magnolia* x *soulangeana*.
Right: *Liquidambar styraciflua* "Worplesdon."

# Koelreuteria paniculata
*Golden-rain tree*

Large pinnate leaves make this an attractive foliage tree, but where summers are warm enough the loose sprays of bright yellow flowers in mid or late summer become a focal point. These are followed by bladder-like fruits. In areas where the summers are poor, flowering can be disappointing. Ensure it has a sheltered position in full sun.
   Height: 20 ft. (6m).

**Varieties to look for**
"Fastigiata" has narrower, more upright, growth.

**Soil and site**
Deeply cultivated, fertile soil, in full sun. Does not do well on thin, alkaline soils. Zone 6.

**Propagation**
Sow seed in early spring or mid autumn. Graft "Fastigiata," but most amateurs buy plants.

# Laburnum x watereri
*Golden-chain tree*

Laburnums are one of the most popular spring-flowering trees, with their long tassels of golden flowers festooned from the branches in late spring. The plants can also be trained over a frame to make a spectacular laburnum arch.
   Height: 15 ft. (4.5m).

**Varieties to look for**
"Vossii" is the variety of choice, with long racemes and many of them.

**Soil and site**
Undemanding regarding soil, and will grow in partial shade, but best in full sun. Zone 6.

**Propagation**
Sow seed in mid autumn, but graft "Vossii." Most amateurs buy plants.

## WATCH THOSE SEEDS!
Laburnum seeds are poisonous and unfortunately can be tempting to young children. Beware of planting a laburnum where small children have access to the garden, although "Vossii" produces fewer of the seeds.

# Liquidambar styraciflua
*Sweet gum*

An aristocrat among trees for autumn color, but conspicuous at all times. The lobed, maple-like leaves have gorgeous crimson coloring in autumn. It can grow large – to over 50 ft. (15m) in time.
   Height: 25 ft. (7.5m).

**Varieties to look for**
"Lane Roberts" is outstanding for autumn color.

**Soil and site**
Well-drained, fertile soil, preferably in full sun though partial shade is tolerated. Unsuitable for shallow or alkaline soils. Zone 5.

**Propagation**
Sow seed in mid autumn, layer or graft named varieties, but most amateurs buy plants.

# Magnolia x soulangeana
*Tulip magnolia*

Stars among the flowering trees, the magnolias are magnificent…but some are also very tall. This one is small enough for most gardens, but sacrifices nothing when it comes to flowering. The white flowers, stained rose-purple at the base, are about 6 in. (15cm) across,

and borne profusely in mid spring before the leaves open. Although the tree can grow large, it will probably be many years before it outgrows its space.
   Height: 15 ft. (4.5m).

**Varieties and other species to look for**
Some of the most impressive varieties are "Alexandrina" with large white flowers, flushed purple at the base, free-flowering; "Lennei" with large flowers, rose-purple outside, creamy-white but stained purple inside; and "Rustica Rubra" with cup-shape rosy-red flowers. "Lennei

Alba" is a good ivory-white.

M. grandiflora is one of the most magnificent evergreens, growing larger than M. x soulangeana, with fragrant creamy-white flowers that can be 10 in. (25cm) across and produced throughout summer and into autumn, though not in large numbers. It is often grown as a large wall shrub in areas of borderline hardiness, and even in Zone 8 or 9 if the position is otherwise exposed.

### Soil and site
Tolerates a wide range of soils, including heavy clay, but it does not do well on alkaline soils.

If possible, plant M. x soulangeana in a light position but where it does not receive early morning sun in spring – if frosted flowers thaw too quickly they turn brown. Zone 5 (M. grandiflora 6).

### Propagation
Take semi-ripe cuttings in early summer.

## Malus floribunda
*Flowering crab*

Ornamental malus are multi-merit trees with colorful spring blossom and, in many cases attractive fruit in autumn. Some also have good autumn color. M. floribunda, with pink and white blossom, is one of the best for flowers.

Height: 15 ft. (4.5m).

### Hybrids to look for
Many of the purple-leaved crab apples also have beautiful blossom. These include "Profusion" and "Royalty," both with wine-red flowers. Some of those

grown primarily for their fruit, such as "John Downie" also blossom well.

### Soil and site
Well-drained soil, in full sun or partial shade.

### Propagation
Bud or graft, but most amateurs buy plants.

### • TIP TO TRY
*Malus* make neat and desirable trees to plant in a lawn. But don't plant in the center of the lawn – it will probably look more pleasing if the tree is planted to one side, perhaps near a border.

## Malus "John Downie"
*Ornamental crab apple*

One of the best to grow for fruit, which are conical and about 1 in. (2.5cm) long in shades of orange, scarlet, and yellow. The spring blossom is also an attractive feature.

### Other varieties to look for
*Malus* x *zumi* "Golden Hornet" (usually sold simply as *M.* "Golden Hornet") has long-lasting yellow fruits.

### Soil and site
Well-drained soil, in full sun or partial shade. Zone 4.

### Propagation
Bud or graft. Most amateurs buy plants.

### NOW YOU KNOW!
The large fruits of "John Downie" can make a mess on lawns and create a slippery hazard on paths once they start to fall. Before this happens, think about using them to make crab apple jelly.

The fruits on many other ornamental crabs remain on the tree for longer, and being smaller do not make such a mess when they fall.

209

# Good weepers

*Weeping trees make good focal points, but plant them in a lawn or in a bed with low carpeting plants rather than a border, so their shape can be appreciated.*

### Small weeping trees

*Betula pendula* "Youngii," Young's weeping birch, grows into small dome-shaped or mushroom-shaped tree. Even smaller is the uncommon *Caragana arborescens* "Pendula," which has yellow pea-type flowers in early summer. It's tough and suitable for even a small garden.

Do not be put off by the prospect of planting the weeping purple beech (*Fagus sylvatica* "Pendula"), which makes a compact mushroom-headed tree suitable for a small garden despite being a beech.

*Prunus* "Kiku-shidare-zakura" (syn. "Kiku-shidare Sakura") is a charming small weeping cherry with arching branches covered with deep pink double flowers in spring. *Prunus pendula* (formerly *P.* x *subhirtella*) "Pendula Rosea" is another kind of cherry, but larger. It has pink flowers in early and mid spring. "Pendula Rubra" has deep rose flowers.

The willow-leaved pear (*Pyrus salicifolia* "Pendula"), with its silvery-gray foliage on weeping branches, is very suitable for a small garden. So it *Salix caprea* "Kilmarnock" (syn. *S. c. pendula*), a small, umbrella-like tree with

**Left:** *Fagus sylvatica* "Pendula."

**Right:** *Salix caprea pendula,* **now more correctly called** *S. caprea* **"Kilmarnock."**

**Left:** *Pyrus salicifolia* "Pendula."

attractive catkins in spring. Try it where space is very limited.

### Large weeping trees

Grow *Chamaecyparis nootkatensis* "Pendula" as a superb specimen conifer with branches hanging almost vertically like streamers. Brewer's weeping spruce (*Picea breweriana*) is also a beautiful weeping conifer, with streamer-like shoots that hang from the slightly spreading branches like a green curtain.

*Salix* x *sepulcralis* "Chrysocoma" (formerly *S.* "Chrysocoma") is a medium-sized weeping tree with golden-yellow slender branchlets. It is a superb waterside tree, but is too large for a small garden. *S. purpurea* "Pendula," with its long, pendulous branches, and purplish shoots, grows to only about 10 ft. (3m), so it is more easily accommodated.

Left: *Populus* x *candicans* "Aurora."
Below: *Prunus* "Kiku-shidare-zakura."
Right: *Prunus cerasifera* "Nigra."

## Populus x candicans "Aurora"

Always an eye-catcher in spring or early summer, when the leaves are splashed creamy-white and often tinged pink. As the season progresses they turn green. The foliage is balsam-scented when young. Although it will eventually grow to 65 ft. (20m) or more, the best way to treat this tree is to keep it pruned hard (see box).

Height: 30 ft. (9m).

### Varieties to look for
This is the only one. The ordinary species is green and not a particularly desirable garden tree.

### Soil and site
Undemanding regarding soil, and will tolerate wet ground. Best in full sun, but tolerates partial shade. Zone 2.

### Propagation
Take hardwood cuttings between mid autumn and early winter.

### BE CRUEL TO BE KIND
The best foliage effect is created by cutting back new growth every third or fourth year to simulate plenty of young growth, which will have larger leaves. It can even be pollarded by cutting back to a stump annually in early spring, but this will create a shrubby plant rather than a typical tree shape.

## Prunus, flowering cherries

Some of the most spectacular flowering trees for spring. According to variety, they flower between early and late spring, usually with pink or white blossom. Shapes vary considerably, and include narrow upright pillars such as "Amanogawa" and weeping trees like "Kiku-shidare-zakura." See page 215 for more about these and other Prunus species.

Height: typically 20–30 ft. (6–9m).

### Varieties and species to look for
See page 215 for a short list of some popular choices.

### Soil and site
Deeply cultivated, fertile soil, in full sun if possible, otherwise partial shade. Zone typically 6.

### Propagation
Bud or graft, but most amateurs buy plants.

## Prunus cerasifera "Nigra"
*Purple-leaved plum*

A useful multi-merit tree, with pink flowers in early spring before the leaves, followed by dark purple leaves that retain their color all summer.

This attractive tree can also be used as a hedging plant or tall screen if clipped from an early age.

Height: 20 ft. (6m).

### Varieties to look for
"Pissardii" is similar, with dark red foliage turning to deep purple with age. The pink buds open to white flowers in early to mid spring.

### Soil and site
Fertile soil, in full sun. In partial shade the leaf color is less intense. Zone 4.

### Propagation
Take hardwood cuttings in winter.

# Final fling

*Make sure the growing season goes out with some fireworks. Although the intensity of color and the length of the display will depend on the season, these trees are sure to put on a good show.*

It's gloriously colored red and scarlet when the leaves turn.

## Acers

There are probably more trees to choose among the acers than any other genus. As they vary in size from some of the compact Japanese maples to tall trees, there are sure to be some that are suitable.

Among the medium to tall trees, *Acer cappadocicum* is a fast-growing tree with leaves that turn butter yellow. The variety "Rubrum" first turns red and green, then gold. Although only suitable for a large garden, the Norway maple (*A. platanoides*) can be depended on for a display of yellow and red. The red maple (*A. rubrum*) is one of the most reliable acers for autumn color, especially the variety "Schlesingeri." It's one of the first to turn, and creates a splash of deep red while many other trees are still green. For a small garden, *A. griseum*, one of the paperbark maples, is an excellent choice.

*Acer japonicum* varieties make small trees, sometimes more like large shrubs when grown with multiple stems. Two particularly fine varieties for autumn color are "Aconitifolium" (ruby-red and crimson in autumn) and "Vitifolium" (brilliant red).

## Color classics

A few (unfortunately large) trees are almost synonymous with autumn color.

The leaf shape of the sweet gum (*Liquidambar styraciflua*) resembles that of a maple, and it's an attractive tree during the summer with shining green foliage. Attractive autumn coloring.

The tupelo (*Nyssa sylvatica*) is grown mainly for its autumn dress, but only where there is space for a large tree. When the dark, glossy leaves are drained of summer green they go through shades of yellow, orange, and scarlet, and the whole tree erupts into a blaze of color.

The red oak (*Quercus rubra*) is a large tree to be avoided in a small or even medium-sized garden. It eventually makes a magnificent specimen tree, at its best in autumn when the leaves turn rich red or yellow, though the coloring can be variable.

The tulip tree (*Liriodendron tulipifera*) makes a magnificent tree where there's plenty of space, with quaint tulip-like yellowish-green flowers in summer and butter-yellow autumn leaves.

## Small trees to make a big splash

*Amelanchier lamarckii* and *A. canadensis* have white flowers in spring and orange and red autumn leaves. They are more often grown as large shrubs.

The columnar crab apple *Malus tschonoskii*, with pink-flushed white flowers in spring, has small fruits in autumn and brilliant foliage colors that include shades of yellow, orange, purple, and scarlet.

*Parrotia persica* is an uninspiring tree for most of the year but in autumn it comes alight as the deep green leaves change to fiery scarlet and gold.

*Prunus sargentii* is an ornamental cherry with pink flowers in early and mid spring, and a rich display of orange and crimson autumn color.

The stag's-horn sumac (*Rhus typhina*) is grown for its very large pinnate leaves, which are one of the spectacles of autumn when they turn red, scarlet, orange, and yellow.

Many sorbus have superb autumn color, including *S. commixta*, *S. c.* "Embley," *S.* "Joseph Rock," and *S. vilmorinii*.

# Bark up the right tree

*Ornamental bark is a year-round feature, but it's appreciated most in winter, especially when the trunk of a deciduous tree can be seen in all its glory.*

Trees with decorative bark are best planted in a lawn, or toward the front of a border, so the full beauty of the coloring and textures can be appreciated.

Use compact ground-cover shrubs around the trees if you want to plant the area in front. A bold drift of winter-flowering heathers looks superb around the base of a white-barked birch. The green and white foliage of *Pachysandra terminalis* "Variegata" makes an attractive base around the cinnamon-colored bark of *Acer griseum*.

The coloring and markings may change as the tree ages, so don't judge them by a young tree in a garden center – view a mature specimen. With snake-bark maples, however, the effect can be more pleasing on trees that are not too old.

The trees suggested below are only a few of those with beautiful barks. Don't dismiss the common silver birch (*Betula pendula*), for example. And if you have a large garden there are delights to be discovered like *Arbutus* x *andrachnoides*, with its remarkably beautiful cinnamon-red trunk and branches.

## Snake-bark maples

These have reticulated or striated bark that resembles a snake's skin.

### *Acer capillipes*
Small tree, striated bark, new growth coral-red, autumn leaf color.

### *Acer davidii*
Green and white striated bark, autumn leaf color.

### *Acer grosseri* var. *hersii*
Marbled bark, autumn leaf color.

### *Acer pensylvanicum*
Young stems are beautifully striped white and pale green. "Erythrocladum" has pink young shoots with pale striations in winter.

Left: The polished mahogany finish of the *Prunus serrula* bark make this a tree that most people feel compelled to touch as well as admire.

## Flaking and peeling

### *Acer griseum*
A paperbark maple with orange-brown old bark that peels to expose cinnamon-colored new bark beneath. Autumn leaf color.

### *Betula albo-sinensis* var. *septentrionalis*
Sometimes called the Chinese red-barked birch. The flaking bark is marbled fawn or orange-brown and pinkish-red, with a gray "bloom."

### *Betula jacquemontii*
See *B. utilis*

### *Betula nigra*
The river birch has blackish shaggy bark, which is more attractive than it sounds. Needs moist but not waterlogged ground.

### *Betula papyrifera*
The paper-bark birch has a smooth white bark that peels like sheets of paper.

### *Betula utilis*
The Himalayan birch has brown bark that peels. *B. u.* var. *jacquemontii* (often sold as *B. jacquemontii*) is the white-barked Himalayan birch and has dazzling white peeling bark.

## Mahogany finish

### *Prunus serrula*
Small but vigorous tree grown for its red-brown bark that looks like polished mahogany when new, peeling in bands.

### *Prunus maackii*
The Manchurian cherry has golden flaking bark that also looks like polished wood on young trees.

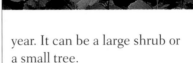

Left: *Pyrus salicifolia* "Pendula" Silver Pear.
Below left: *Pyrus salicifolia* "Pendula."
Below right: *Robinia pseudoacacia* "Frisia."
Right: *Rhus typhina*.

## Prunus x subhirtella "Autumnalis"
*Winter-flowering cherry*

Any tree that promises to flower throughout the winter deserves a place in the garden. The flowers are small and white, and will be affected by severe weather, but they emerge on bare branches during mild spells between late autumn and early spring.
   Height: 25 ft. (7.5m).

### Varieties to look for
"Autumnalis Rosea" has rosy-pink flowers. Two pretty weeping winter-flowering trees are *P. pendula* "Pendula Rosea" and "Pendula Rubra" with pale pink and deep rose respectively, and both flower in early spring. They are mushroom-headed trees that do not grow as tall as *P. x subhirtella*. Both may be found listed as varieties of *P. x subhirtella*.

### Soil and site
Well-drained, fertile soil, in full sun. Zone 5.

### Propagation
Bud or graft, but most amateurs buy plants.

## Pyrus salicifolia "Pendula"
*Weeping willow-leaved pear*

An ideal small-garden tree, making a dome of silver-gray foliage clothed to the ground.
   Height: 10 ft. (3m).

### Varieties to look for
None.

### Soil and site
Well-drained, fertile soil, in full sun. Zone 4.

### Propagation
Bud or graft, but most amateurs buy plants.

## Rhus typhina
*Stag's-horn sumac*

When the leaves color in autumn this small tree stands out from almost all others. The huge pinnate leaves turn rich orange, yellow, red, and purple in autumn. Dense conical clusters of crimson fruits are also decorative at the end of the

year. It can be a large shrub or a small tree.
   Height: 15 ft. (4.5m).

### Varieties to look for
"Dissecta," which is usually sold under the name "Laciniata," has more deeply cut leaves.

### Soil and site
Undemanding regarding soil, but best in full sun or partial shade. Zone 3.

### Propagation
The best way to propagate the plant is to dig up the root suckers, which are freely produced.

## Robinia pseudoacacia "Frisia"
*Golden acacia*

Perhaps the best golden tree, eye-catching even from a distance and retaining its color throughout the season. White pea-type flowers are produced on mature trees, but this is one

to grow for foliage effect alone.
   Height: 30 ft. (9m).

### Varieties to look for
"Frisia" is the only golden one, but "Inermis" (now more correctly "Umbraculifera") makes an attractive mop-headed tree.

### Soil and site
Deeply cultivated, moisture-retentive fertile soil, in full sun or partial shade. Too much shade may cause the leaves to turn green. Zone 3.

### Propagation
Graft, but most amateurs buy plants.

# Know your Prunus

Left: A pale form of *Prunus* "Kiku-shidare-zakura," sometimes called cheal's weeping cherry.

*Prunus are among the most commonly planted garden trees. There are many kinds.*

### Flowering almonds

The true almond (*P. dulcis*) is not grown as an ornamental, but a hybrid with the peach (*P. persica*) called *P.* x *amygdalopersica* "Pollardii" makes an attractive tree in early spring, with single pink flowers on bare branches.

### Flowering plums

The "plums" widely planted as ornamentals are varieties of *P. cerasifera*. "Nigra" has ruby-red leaves that change to blackish-purple, with pale pink flowers in spring. "Pissardii" has dark red young foliage changing to deep purple, with white flowers.

Below: *Prunus* "Shirotae," a beautiful Japanese cherry sometimes called "Mount Fuji."

### Bird cherries

These hold their white flowers in spikes or pendulous racemes in late spring. *P. padus* "Grandiflora" (syn. "Watereri") is a medium-sized tree and one of the best.

### Early-flowering cherries

These are hybrids of garden origin with generally small flowers, usually in late winter or early spring. Examples are "Accolade," a small tree with pink semi-double flowers in early spring, and "Kursar" with small pink flowers in profusion in early and mid spring.

### Large-flowered Japanese cherries

The showiest *Prunus*. There are many varieties with pink, white, or cream, single or double flowers, in late spring. They have Japanese names – "Kanzan" which has stiffly ascending branches with double pink flowers and "Shirotae" (syn. "Mount Fuji") with wide-spreading and slightly drooping branches with single or semi-double white flowers.

### Weeping cherries

A single weeping cherry as a specimen in a lawn, or in a conspicuous position in a border, can light up a garden in spring.

"Kiku-shidare-zakura" (syn. "Kiku-shidare Sakura") is one if the best for a small garden: masses of double pink flowers cover the stiffly arching branches. *Prunus pendula* "Pendula Rosea" is a small mushroom-headed tree with long weeping branches covered with small single pink flower in early and mid spring.

Less commonly planted, but highly desirable, is *P.* x *yedoensis* "Shidare-yoshino," with pale pink flowers in early or mid spring on branches that cascade to the ground.

### Beautiful bark

Several *Prunus* are grown for their beautiful barks as well as flowers, especially *P. serrula*. The small white flowers in spring are unspectacular, but the trunk has a mahogany-like "polished" bark.

### Lovely leaves

Many *Prunus* have good autumn leaf color. Most Japanese cherries color well, but species like *P. sargentii* can be particularly striking – this one goes out in shades of yellow, orange, and flame.

215

# Berried treasures

*Berries and fruits of all kinds give a much longer display than most flowers ... and at a time when color is scarce.*

Above: Crab apples – various *Malus* hybrids – are a feature of autumn, and the display will last much longer than the fleeting blossom of spring.

Growing trees with attractive fruits will provide patches of color right until mid winter, and even beyond. This will also attract wildlife, especially birds, to the garden.

Consider continuity: some sorbus are at their best in late summer and early autumn (by which time the birds will probably have stripped them); other species retain their fruits until mid winter and beyond.

## Sorbus spectaculars

The species of *Sorbus* grown mainly for their autumn color and fruits have many fruit colors: reds, oranges, yellows, pinks, and white. Many are excellent small-garden trees.

The first to ripen its berries is usually the mountain ash (*Sorbus aucuparia*). The fruits are typically orange-red, hanging in large bunches. Unfortunately birds find them attractive too, and they are among the first trees to be stripped of their bounty.

Some of its varieties have berries of different colors. "Fastigiata," for example, has sealing-wax red berries. "Xanthocarpa" has amber-yellow fruits.

If autumn color and bright berries are equally important, *S. commixta* is a good choice, with excellent autumn color and small bright red or orange-red berries.

A charming species for the small garden is *S. vilmorinii*, which makes a small tree or large shrubby plant with almost fern-like foliage. The loose, drooping clusters of berries gradually change color, starting rose-red, turning pink, then finally white flushed rose. That has got to be good value for money!

"Joseph Rock" is an outstanding hybrid with rich autumn tints and clusters of conspicuous berries that start creamy-yellow, deepening to amber-yellow as they mature.

Try to include *S. cashmiriana* in any selection, not only because its gleaming white marble-like berries look so distinctive, but also because they last so long. They hang long after the leaves have fallen, sometimes into early winter.

## Crab apples

There are many *Malus* to choose for their attractive crab apples. The small apple-like fruits will soon drop from some varieties while others last well into winter (birds permitting).

Far left: Crab apples like these on *Malus* x *robusta* "Red Sentinel" will often remain attractive into winter, or until birds make a meal of them.

Left: Many *Sorbus* have colorful berries, but some are quickly stripped by birds while others will hang into autumn and beyond.

"John Downie" is one of the most decorative, with large, conically-shaped yellow fruits attractively flushed red. If you want fruits to harvest for crab-apple jelly as well as a decorative garden display, this is a good choice because they are so large. Unfortunately they drop early and can make an unattractive mess on the ground and paths around the tree if not cleared up.

*Malus* x *zumi* "Golden Hornet" is one of the best all-round crab apples: its yellow fruits are bold and conspicuous, and they hang on the tree for a long time.

There are many long-lasting round, red crab apples to choose from, but *M.* x *robusta* "Red Sentinel"is a particularly good choice as the cherry-like fruits are often retained until the end of winter.

# Variegated trees

Below: Plant variegated trees where they can be seen to advantage. They make pleasing specimen trees in a lawn, like this *Acer platanoides* "Drummondii."

*Use variegated trees as specimens in a lawn, or at the back of a border between green trees, to break up the background visually. Avoid planting too many in close proximity — otherwise they lose their impact.*

### Large trees
*Acer pseudoplatanus* "Leopoldii" Splashed and speckled yellow with a hint of pink.
*Liriodendron tulipifera* "Aureomarginata" Yellow or yellowish-green and dark green.

### Medium-sized trees
*Acer negundo* "Elegans" Yellow and green.
*Acer negundo* "Variegatum" White and green.
*Acer platanoides* "Drummondii" Creamy-white and green.
*Populus candicans* "Aurora" Creamy-white and green, with pink tinges when young.

### Small trees
*Ilex* (hollies) Various combinations of gold, silver, and green.

217

# Silver and gold

Below left: The young leaves of *Sorbus aria* "Chrysophylla" are a pleasing yellow. Other varieties are grown for their silvery foliage.
Below: *Gleditsia triacanthos* "Sunburst" is another outstanding yellow-leaved tree that's widely planted.

*Too many all-green trees can look oppressive. Plant one or two with silver or gold leaves to contrast with them and act as punctuation points.*

There are relatively few trees with silver or gray foliage, but you don't need many to make an impact – a single specimen, well placed, is often sufficient.

Yellow and gold trees are always popular and they stand out superbly whether bathed in sun or in shadow. They can look particularly pleasing grouped with purple-leaved trees or shrubs.

Some yellows fade to almost green by mid summer, but others will retain their color through to the end of the season, so choose carefully if you want bright colors till the end of summer.

## Silver

*Eucalyptus*
Many kinds have silver-gray leaves. Tall. Hardiness depends on species.

*Populus alba* (white poplar)
The white undersides of the leaves are conspicuous as they blow in the wind. Tall.

*Pyrus nivalis*
White woolly leaves. Small.

*Pyrus salicifolia* "Pendula"
Small weeping tree with silver-gray leaves.

*Salix alba* var. *sericea*
Medium-sized tree with leaves that appear silvery from a distance.

*Sorbus aria* "Lutescens"
Upper surface of the leaves looks creamy-white, becoming gray-green by late summer.

*Tilia tomentosa*
A large tree with leaves that are white-felted

beneath. When ruffled in the wind the tree has a silvery appearance.

## Gold

*Acer cappadocicum* "Aureum"
A medium to large tree with bright yellow leaves (they may scorch during a very hot summer).

*Alnus incana* "Aurea"
A small to medium tree with bright yellow leaves in spring. Unfortunately they gradually turn green by late summer.

*Catalpa bignonioides* "Aurea"
One of the best, with large yellow leaves.

*Gleditsia triacanthos* "Sunburst"
An outstanding medium-sized golden tree, with the color well retained throughout the season.

*Robinia pseduoacacia* "Frisia"
Justifiably one of the most popular golden-foliaged trees. It is vigorous and will make a medium-sized or large tree, but it looks eye-catching from spring till autumn.

Left: Justifiably one of the most popular golden trees, *Robinia pseudoacacia* "Frisia" retains its color well.

Left: *Salix caprea "Kilmarnock."*
Bottom left: *Salix matsudana "Tortuosa."*
Below right: *Sorbus aucuparia "Beissneri."*
Right: *Ulmus glabra.*

## Salix caprea "Kilmarnock"

*Kilmarnock willow*

More widely sold under its older name of *S. c. pendula*, but a first-rate weeping tree for a small garden. The curtain of cascading stems almost reaches the ground, and is covered with silky "pussy willow" catkins in spring.

### Varieties to look out for

This is the most suitable weeping willow for a small garden.

### Soil and site

Deeply cultivated, moisture-retentive, fertile soil, in full sun. Zone 5.

### Propagation

Graft, but most amateurs buy plants.

## Salix babylonica pekinensis "Tortuosa"

A tortuous new name for an interesting tree! It is still usually sold under its old name of *S. matsudana* "Tortuosa." It is one of the most striking and easily recognized willows, with twisting and spiraling branches and shoots. In winter, when the branches are bare, the effect is even more dramatic, especially viewed against a blue sky.

Height: 20 ft. (6m).

### Varieties to look for

None, this is a distinctive willow.

### Soil and site

Deeply cultivated, moisture-retentive, fertile soil, full sun.

### Propagation

Take hardwood cuttings between mid autumn and late winter.

## Sorbus aucuparia

*Rowan, mountain ash*

Popular with birds as well as with people, the orange-red fruits that ripen by late summer and early autumn are also among the first to be stripped by birds. It's a spectacular display while it lasts, and there's the bonus of white flowers in late spring or early summer.

Height: 25 ft. (7.5m).

### Varieties and other species to look for

There are several readily available varieties, but particularly worth looking for are "Fructu Luteo" (syn. "Xanthocarpa"), which has amber-yellow fruits, and "Sheerwater Seedling" with its orange-red fruits on ascending branches.

There are many hybrid sorbus grown for their attractive berries. One of the best is "Joseph Rock," with yellow fruits and very good autumn color.

Other species to consider are: *S. cashmiriana*, with white, marble-like berries, usually held well into autumn; *S. commixta* "Embley," with orange-red fruits, good autumn color; and *S. hupehensis*, with white fruits, sometimes tinged pink, lasting into winter, and superb autumn foliage.

### Soil and site

Undemanding regarding soil, but best in full sun. Zone 2 (*S. cashmiriana* 5, *S. commixta* and *S. hupehensis* 6).

### Propagation

Sow seed of the species, but bud or graft named forms. Most amateurs buy plants.

## Ulmus glabra "Camperdownii"

*Camperdown elm*

Small, weeping, and easy to grow, this mushroom-headed tree is a good choice where space is limited.

It looks best when grown as an isolated specimen in a lawn, or open area.

Height: 10 ft. (3m).

### Varieties to look for

This is the best elm for a small garden. *Ulmus glabra* "Pendula" (weeping wych elm) is less popular, perhaps because it makes a much larger tree.

*U. minor* "Dampieri Aurea" (formerly *U.* x *hollandica* "Wredei") is an upright tree.

### Soil and site

Undemanding regarding soil, best in full sun or partial shade. Zone 5.

### Propagation

Bud or graft, but most amateurs buy plants.

# Hardiness Zones

*Climate, more than the soil or aspect of your garden, will determine which plants thrive and which languish or even die.*

We attempt to grow plants from many parts of the world in our gardens, so it is not surprising than we can't please them all. These hardiness zone maps will help you decide which plants are likely to survive where you live
Many factors determine the hardiness of a plant. Truly tender plants have a simple cut-off point: frost kills. Even this is not as clear-cut as it sounds, for the top growth of dahlias will turn black at the first frost, but the tubers lie protected in the soil. In areas where frosts do not penetrate deeply, they may survive without having to be lifted. Hardy fuchsias are cut to the ground by cold in many countries but grow again from the rootstock the following spring. In mild maritime climates where frosts are less common or severe, the top growth may survive and, in these areas, tall fuchsia hedges can be seen.

WESTERN EUROPE

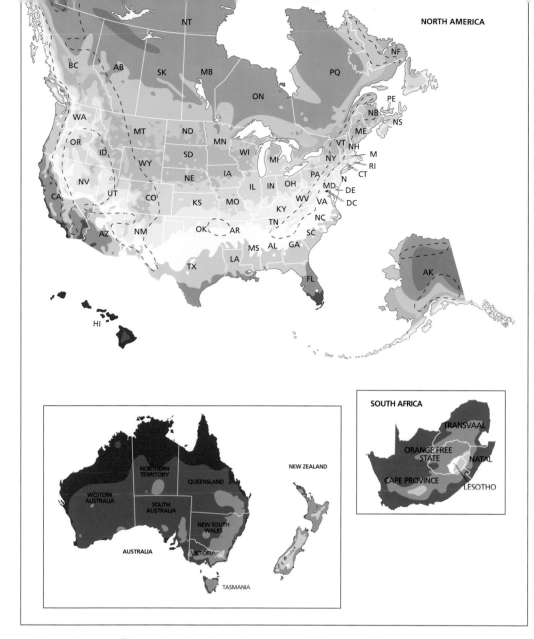

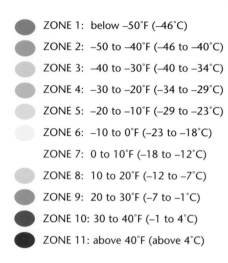

KEY TO HARDINESS ZONES

ZONE 1: below –50°F (–46°C)

ZONE 2: –50 to –40°F (–46 to –40°C)

ZONE 3: –40 to –30°F (–40 to –34°C)

ZONE 4: –30 to –20°F (–34 to –29°C)

ZONE 5: –20 to –10°F (–29 to –23°C)

ZONE 6: –10 to 0°F (–23 to –18°C)

ZONE 7: 0 to 10°F (–18 to –12°C)

ZONE 8: 10 to 20°F (–12 to –7°C)

ZONE 9: 20 to 30°F (–7 to –1°C)

ZONE 10: 30 to 40°F (–1 to 4°C)

ZONE 11: above 40°F (above 4°C)

Plants that are of borderline hardiness in a particular area may be killed by cold winds as much as cold temperatures: the wind chill factor has a devastating effect on some plants. In the same way a single night when the temperature drops very low may not be sufficient to kill a plant, yet sustained for some time, that temperature could be fatal.

Winter temperatures can vary widely even within a region: it is usually warmer in a city or by the coast, colder on exposed or high ground. Temperatures can even vary within a garden, depending on whether there are frost traps or sheltered and protected areas.

Although there can be no absolutes, these zone maps, based on average minimum temperatures, indicate which plants mentioned in this book are likely to survive outdoors. Zone numbers are given where appropriate in the plant profiles. No zones have been given for annuals and plants normally discarded at the end of the season because they are not usually kept through the winter.

There are eleven hardiness zones, defined according to lowest winter temperatures. Zone 1 represents the coldest conditions, with winter temperatures below -50°F (-46°C); zone 11 is the warmest with a minimum winter temperature of above 40°F (above 4°C). The classification of a plant into a particular hardiness zone means that the plant will normally thrive in that zone and also in any zone which is marked with a higher number.

The dividing line between one zone and the next is not rigid because the weather varies from one year to the next. Remember, too, that some plants will not thrive in climates that are too hot for them.

Use these zones as a guide, not as an absolute. The plants will usually survive a typical winter in the zone indicated, but they may not thrive – and exceptionally severe weather could be devastating for them. To be sure of a plant surviving bad winters, it is better to grow plants hardy to one zone lower than indicated for your area.

Those plants that do not thrive in hot areas are unlikely to be killed by the warmth, but they may not flourish or flower well.

# Glossary

## A

**Acid (soil)** With a pH of less than 7 (see pH).

**Alkaline (soil)** With a pH greater than 7 (see pH).

**Alpine** Technically a plant that grows above the tree line in alpine or mountainous areas, but more loosely applied to any small plant grown in a rock garden.

**Annual** A plant that completes its life cycle within a single growing season. This usually means between spring and autumn, but some of the hardier annuals may germinate in the autumn, last through winter, then die after flowering in early or mid summer.

**Aquatic** A plant that grows in water (see also bog plant, deep water aquatic, floating aquatic, marginal plant, and submerged aquatic).

**Aspect** A position in the garden facing a certain direction (for example, south-facing).

## B

**Bedding (plant)** Plants, usually annuals and biennials, used for temporary seasonal display. Spring bedding includes bulbs and biennials planted in the autumn to flower in spring; summer bedding includes half-hardy annuals and tender perennials planted out after the last frost, for a summer display.

**Biennial** A plant that completes its life cycle over two growing seasons. Hardy biennials are usually sown in late spring or early summer to bloom the following spring or summer.

**Bog plant** A plant that thrives in permanently damp soil, but does not grow in the water like an aquatic.

**Branch** A shoot from the main stem or trunk of a woody plant.

**Budding** Method of propagation in which a growth bud from one plant is grafted onto the rootstock of another.

**Bulb** Any plant with a modified stem acting as a storage organ, like an onion (see also corm, rhizome, and tuber). The term is sometimes used loosely to cover bulbs, corms, rhizomes and tubers – plants sold as dormant storage organs by bulb suppliers.

**Bulb scale** The individual segments from which a bulb is made up. These are most obvious in lilies, where they can be pulled off and used for propagation.

## C

**Carpeter/carpeting plant** A low-growing plant, usually used for ground cover (see ground cover).

**Clay** Type of soil with fine particles that is usually rich in nutrients but poorly drained.

**Climber** A plant that requires support, to which it may attach itself by twining, special aerial roots, or by means of tendrils.

**Cloche** A protective glass or transparent plastic cover, used for protecting early crops raised in the open ground, or to warm the soil before planting or sowing. May also be used to afford some protection to vulnerable wintering plants.

**Compost (garden)** Vegetable and organic matter that have been allowed to decompose.

**Compost (potting or seed)** A medium for sowing seeds or potting plants, usually based on loam or peat (or a peat-substitute), with added nutrients. Known in the U.S. as potting soil.

**Conifers** Trees and shrubs with usually needle-like leaves and seeds normally borne in cones. The vast majority are evergreen.

**Corm** A swollen stem or base, resembling a bulb and often surrounded by a papery tunic, that acts as an underground storage organ. Unlike a bulb, there are no distinct layers (like an onion) when a corm is cut through.

**Corolla** The collective name for the parts of the flower formed by the petals.

**Cultivar** A plant raised in cultivation, distinguished by one or more characteristics which are retained whether it is propagated sexually or asexually. In this book the word "variety" in its general sense has been used to cover cultivars and botanical varieties, though they are presented in a typographically correct way (see page 9 for further notes on nomenclature).

**Cutting** A leaf, shoot, root or bud that is cut off a plant for use for propagation.

# D

**Deadhead** To remove a flower head when it has died. This is sometimes done to extend the flowering season (allowing a plant to form seeds may shorten the flowering period), or to improve the visual appearance.

**Deciduous (plant)** One that loses all its leaves at the end of the growing season. Evergreen plants also shed their leaves, but over a long period so they are never leafless.

**Deep water aquatic** A plant that grows with its roots in the bottom of the pond (or in a planting basket there), rather than in the shallow water around the edge. Many deep-water aquatics will grow happily with about 1 ft. (30cm) of water over their roots.

**Deeply cultivated (soil)** Soil dug to more than the depth of a single spade blade. Usually implies double digging (worked to a depth of two spade blades).

**Division** Method of increasing plants by splitting the crown or roots up into smaller pieces, each with roots and shoots (or buds that will form shoots).

**Drainage** Free passage of water through the soil so that it is not waterlogged; a system for removing excess water from the soil.

**Drill** A shallow furrow taken out of the soil, into which seeds are sown. A drill is best taken out using a garden line or straight-edge against which the soil is removed with a stick or the corner of a hoe or rake.

# E

**Ericaceous** Refers to members of the Ericaceae (heather) family, but when referring to potting composts (potting soils) it means one with a low pH (acidic) suitable for members of the Ericaceae family.

**Evergreen** A plant that retains its leaves throughout the year.

# F

**Fastigiate** Erect, narrow, upright form, with branches growing vertically rather than horizontally.

**Floating aquatic** A plant that floats on the surface with its roots suspended in the water, from where it derives all its nutrients.

**Flower** The part of a plant containing its reproductive organs, usually surrounded by sepals and petals.

**Framework plants** The permanent plants that form the basic structure of the garden, especially trees and shrubs.

**Frost hardy** A plant that is able to withstand frost without protection, though with some plants with storage organs such as tubers and corms, the roots may survive unless the soil temperature at that level drops to freezing.

# G

**Genus** The category of plants that identifies a group of related species. *Rosa* is a genus, to which many different species belong.

**Graft** Method of propagation in which a shoot from the desired variety is joined to a specially prepared rootstock, and bound and sealed until the two unite.

**Ground cover** Plants, usually low-growing, that cover the surface of the soil and suppress weeds.

**Growing season** The period during which a plant is actively producing leaves and new growth.

# H

**Half-hardy** A plant unable to survive the winter without protection, but which does not require protection all year.

**Harden** To acclimatize plants raised in warmth to the cooler conditions in the garden. This is done by reducing the amount of warmth gradually, and using a cold frame if possible as an intermediate environment before placing in the garden.

**Hardy (plant)** A plant capable of surviving the winter in the open without protection. Not all hardy plants will tolerate cold temperatures to the same extent, however, and some are more cold-hardy than others. In this book hardiness zones have been used to give an approximate indication of how hardy particular plants are likely to be (see pages 220-221).

**Herbaceous perennial** A non-woody plant in which the upper parts die down to a rootstock at the end of the growing season.

# I

**Interplant** In the context of the ornamental garden, the planting of two or more different types of plants together. Forget-me-nots or winter pansies might be interplanted between tall tulips to cover the ground and fill in the gaps, as well as provide an improved flowering display.

# L

**Layering** Method of propagation in which a portion of stem is brought into contact with the soil and induced to root while still attached to the parent plant. Air layering is a technique in which the branch is not brought to ground level but damp material is bound around the treated wound for the roots to grow into. After rooting the branch is severed and grown on independently.

**Leaf mold** Decomposed autumn leaves, used as a soil conditioner.

**Loam** This is normally an "ideal" soil of medium texture, easily worked, that contains more or less equal parts of sand, silt, and clay, and is usually rich in humus.

# M

**Manure** Bulky organic substances of animal origin (often mixed with straw), dug into the soil or applied as a mulch.

**Marginal plant** A plant that grows partially submerged in shallow water or in moist soil at the edge of a pond.

**Mixed border** A border containing different types of plants, which can include a mixture of shrubs, herbaceous plants, bulbs, and annuals.

**Mulch** A layer of organic or other material applied to the surface of the soil to suppress weeds and conserve moisture. Organic mulches such as garden compost, chipped bark, or cocoa shells should be applied at least 2 in. (5cm) thick. Sheet mulches, such as plastics, also make efficient mulches, but in decorative parts of the garden are usually covered with a thin layer of a visually more acceptable material, such as chipped bark.

# N

**Naturalize** To establish and grow as if in the wild. Usually applied to bulbs planted informally in a lawn or in longer grass.

**Nutrient** A plant food.

# O

**Offset** A young plant that arises from around the base of the parent plant, and still attached to it initially. Bulbs also produce offsets, but this time smaller bulbs around the base of the original one: in time these become detached and grow into individual plants.

**Organic matter** Material consisting of, or derived from, living organisms. Examples are garden compost, animal manures, and leaf mold.

# P

**Peat** The remains of partially decayed vegetation such as mosses, laid down millions of years ago in waterlogged soil. It contains few nutrients but holds water well and improves soil structure. It is acid and therefore useful for acid-loving plants. Depletion of peat bogs has become an ecological threat, and nowadays many gardeners use peat substitutes wherever possible. These include seed and potting composts (potting soils) made from coir or other waste plant material.

**Perennial** A plant that lives for at least three growing seasons.

**Pergola** A trellis or framework supported on posts, usually used to support climbing plants.

**Petal** A modified leaf, forming part of the corolla, often brightly colored.

**pH** A measure of the acidity or alkalinity of the soil. pH7 is technically neutral, though pH6.5-7 is a level at which the majority of plants thrive, with higher numbers indicating alkaline soil, lower numbers acid soil. Although the whole scale runs from pH1-14, soils seldom fall outside the range pH4-8.5. Though these differences sound small, the scale is logarithmic, so pH8 is 10 times more alkaline than pH7. Simple soil test kits are available to check the pH.

**Pinching out** The removal of the growing tip from a plant to encourage the buds below to grow, so producing a bushier plant.

**Potting soil** See Compost

**Pricking out** The transplanting of a small seedling into its own pot, or into a larger tray where it is spaced out to allow more growing space.

**Propagation** The production of more plants by seed or by vegetative methods such as division, cuttings, or layers.

# R

**Raceme** A botanical term used to describe an elongated, unbranched flower cluster, in which each flower is attached to the main stem by a stalk. A laburnum has its flowers in racemes.

**Rhizome** A horizontal creeping underground stem (sometimes at the surface, as in iris) that also acts as a storage organ.

**Root-ball** The roots and soil or compost contained within them, when a plant is lifted from the ground of removed from a pot or container.

**Rooting hormone** A chemical (usually a powder but sometimes a gel or liquid formulation) which stimulates a cutting to produce roots.

**Rootstock** The crown and root system of herbaceous perennials and suckering shrubs. In propagation terms, a young plant onto which the desirable variety of certain plants is budded or grafted. The rootstock controls the vigor of the plants, sometimes making a plant more dwarf or more suitable for certain growing conditions. Rootstocks may also be used because the variety grafted or budded onto them do not root readily from cuttings or layers.

# S

**Scree** A slope with rock fragments that forms part of some mountain landscapes, and recreated as part of some rock gardens.

**Seed** A fertilized plant ovule, consisting of an embryo and its food store surrounded by a protective coat.

**Seedling** Very young plant raised from seed.

**Semi-evergreen** A plant that retains only a small portion of its leaves for more than a season. Some semi-evergreen plants may lose all their leaves in winter in cold areas.

**Sepal** One of the outermost modified leaves, behind the petals and usually green, that form part of the flower head.

**Shrub** A woody plant that branches from the base, with no obvious trunk. A few plants can be grown as shrubs or trees, depending on their initial training.

**Soft landscaping** The planted element of a garden, including beds, borders, and lawns.

**Species** A group of closely related plants within a genus.

**Specimen plant** A plant (usually a tree or shrub) grown where if can be clearly viewed. Usually this means planted within a lawn.

**Submerged aquatic** A plant that normally remains submerged beneath the surface, like *Elodea canadensis*.

**Subsoil** The layer of soil below the topsoil which is usually lacking in organic matter and nutrients. It may also look visually different, usually lighter in color.

# T

**Tap root** A strong-growing vertical root with little branching. Dandelions and carrots have tap roots.

**Tender** Plants killed by frost.

**Tilth** A fine and crumbly surface to the soil, suitable for sowing seeds.

**Topiary** The shaping of trees and shrubs into decorative shapes.

**Topsoil** The upper layer of soil that is the most fertile. It contains more organic matter and nutrients than subsoil and is usually darker in color.

**Tree** A woody plant with a head of branches supported by a single trunk (some are grown as multi-stemmed trees after early training).

**Tuber** A swollen, usually underground, organ for storing nutrients through the winter.

# U

**Underplanting** The use of low-growing plants beneath taller ones.

# V

**Variegated** Foliage marked or patterned with more than one color.

**Variety** Strictly a naturally occurring variant of a wild species, but the word is also used to describe any variant of a plant with consistently reproducible characteristics.

**Vegetative propagation** The increase of plants by asexual methods, such as cuttings or division, usually resulting in genetically identical plants.

# Index

228

230

# Photographic acknowledgments

Garden Picture Library /David Askham 69 center, 156 bottom left, 210 bottom left, /Alan Bedding 36 top left, 100 left, /Philippe Bonduel 35 top left, 45 right, 100 top right, 105 bottom, 124 right, 157 top right, 167 right, 192 top right, 211 top left, /Lynne Brotchie 66 bottom, 67 top, /Linda Burgess 37 top left, 104 bottom right, 136 center, /Chris Burrows 41 bottom, 43 top, 58 left, 73 bottom, 156 top left, Rex Butcher 25 top, /Brian Carter 22 top right, 36 top right, 43 bottom, 71 center, 84 bottom, 108 bottom, 112 bottom, 114 top left, 156 top center, 162 bottom left, 178 top left, 183 left, 183 right, 195 bottom right, 197 top, 203 top left, 205 top right, 210 top, 214 top left, 219 top left, /Bob Challinor 207 top center, /Densey Cline 59 bottom, /Henk Dijkman 38 bottom right, /David England 127 bottom, 196 top, /Robert Estall 200 top right, /Ron Evans 77 top, /John Ferro Sims 206 top, /Vaughan Fleming 63, 123 right, 215 top, /Christopher Gallagher 94 left, /John Glover 25 bottom, 26 top left, 26 top right, 38 top right, 38 bottom left, 48 top left, 62 left, 91 top, 93 top, 93 bottom right, 102 top left, 104 top right, 108 top left, 114 top right, 114 bottom, 118 top, 119 top left, 127 top, 130 top left, 139 left, 140 top, 166 top right, 167 top, 168 bottom right, 172 bottom, 174 bottom, 177 top left, 184, 185 bottom left, 186 bottom right, 201 bottom, 202 bottom left, 203 bottom, 205 bottom, 207 top left, 207 right, 208 top right, 208 bottom right, 210 bottom right, 211 right, 214 bottom left, 217 top right, 218 top, /Sunniva Harte 89 top right, /Marijke Heuff 202 bottom right, /Neil Holmes 69 top, 99 bottom, 122 top left, 136 right, 153 right, 160 top, 160 bottom left, 161 bottom, 162 bottom right, 171 top left, 174 top left, 178 top right, 181 top, 208 top left, 214 bottom right, 218 bottom left, /Michael Howes 197 bottom left, /Lamontagne 27 top, 39 top, 64 bottom, 71 bottom right, 79 center, 117 bottom, 144 bottom, 177 bottom left, 179 top left, 185 top, 201 top left, /Marianne Majerus 133 center, 175, /Mayer/Le Scanff 47, 86 top left, 195 top left, /John Miller 204 center, /John Neubauer 153 left, /Clive Nichols 133 bottom left, 156 bottom right, 168 top, /Jerry Pavia 35 top right, 82 center, 89 bottom, 182 left, 197 right, 201 right, 203 top right, /Joanne Pavia 193 top left, /Laslo Puskas 193 bottom, /Howard Rice 22 bottom right, 48 bottom, 56 left, 90 top right, 90 bottom, 103 center, 113 top, 133 top left, 157 top left, 165 top left, 166 bottom center, 173, 191 right, 202 top, 212, 217 top left, 219 bottom right, /Gary Rogers 45 left, 206 bottom left, /J S Sira 53 bottom, 84 top, 87 top center, 100 bottom center, 139 right, 147 bottom, 149 right, 152 right, 185 bottom right, 190 top, 192 top left, 206 bottom right, 208 bottom left, /Ron Sutherland 30 top, 89 top left, /Brigitte Thomas 52 bottom, 59 top, 85 top, 98 top right, 182 right, 207 bottom center, 219 top right, /Juliette Wade 79 bottom, 166 bottom left, /Mel Watson 86 bottom, /Didier Willery 83 top, 87 top right, 105 top right, 205 top left, 217 bottom, /Steven Wooster 24, 93 bottom left, 95 bottom, 96 top, 97 bottom, 194 right, 218 bottom right, /Steven Wooster/John Brookes, Denhams 82 top left; Peter McHoy 22 left, 27 bottom, 32 top, 33 top, 33 bottom, 34, 35 bottom, 36 bottom, 37 top right, 40 top, 40 bottom, 42 top, 49 top, 49 bottom, 52 top, 53 top, 56 right, 58 bottom, 61 top, 61 bottom, 64 top, 68 top, 68 bottom, 70 top, 70 bottom right, 72 top, 74 bottom, 75 top, 76 top, 76 bottom, 77 bottom, 78 bottom, 79 top, 88, 96 bottom, 110 top, 118 bottom, 119 top right, 121 bottom, 122 top right, 122 bottom, 124 left, 125 bottom left, 125 bottom right, 126, 149 left, 177 right, 187 top left, 200 bottom; Photos Horticultural 44 top, 44 bottom right, 44 bottom left, 65 bottom, 147 top right, 153 bottom, 197 bottom right, 211 bottom; Reed International Books Ltd. 103 top right, 104 bottom left, /Michael Boys 28, 65 top, 69 bottom left, 74 top, 85 bottom, 94 right, 99 right, 103 bottom left, 113 bottom, 123 bottom, 125 top left, 131 bottom, 141 top, 144 top, 152 left, 154 bottom, 162 top, 165 bottom, 170 top, 170 bottom, 172 top left, 172 top right, 174 top right, 187 top right, 196 bottom right, 209 top, 214 top right, /W.F. Davidson 115, 121 top, 160 bottom right, /Jerry Harpur 23 top right, 29 bottom, 30 bottom, 31, 37 bottom, 41 top, 42 bottom, 73 top, 82 bottom left, 83 bottom, 86 center, 87 bottom, 92 top, 92 bottom, 98 bottom, 101 left, 101 right, 102 top right, 105 top left, 105 center, 112 top, 116, 130 top right, 131 top, 142 top left, 142 bottom, 148 right, 154 top left, 161 top, 164 bottom, 168 bottom left, 178 bottom, 179 bottom, 180, 186 top, 186 bottom left, 187 bottom, /Neil Holmes 23 bottom left, 71 top right, 102 bottom, 147 top, 171 top right, /Peter Myers 6, 7, 10/11, 20/21, 24 background, 25 background, 28/29 background, 30/31 background, 34/35 background, 40/41 background, 44/45 background, 50/51, 80/81, 106/107, 112 background, 118 background, 128/129, 158/159, 188/189, 198/189, /Clive Nichols 130 bottom, 132, 134 top, 134 bottom, 135 top right, 137, 138, 140 bottom, 141 bottom, 142 top right, 143 left, 143 right, 148 left, 150 right, 151 right, 157 bottom, /Pamla Toler 193 top right, /Steve Wooster 54, 55 top, 55 bottom, 60, 191 top, 192 bottom right, /George Wright 26 bottom, 29 top, 32 bottom, 39 bottom, 48 top right, 82 top right, 90 top left, 95 top, 98 top left, 108 right, 110 bottom, 119 bottom, 135 top left, 135 bottom, 150 left, 151 left, 154 top right, 163 top, 163 bottom, 164 top, 165 top right, 169 top, 171 bottom, 176, 179 top right, 181 bottom, 195 top right, 196 bottom left, 200 top left, 209 bottom, 213, 215 bottom, 216, 219 bottom left.

### Gatefolds

Kitchen Containers: Garden Picture Library/Sunniva Harte (1 picture); Jerry Harpur/Ron Simple, Pasadena (1 picture); Andrew Lawson Photography (2 pictures); Clive Nichols Photography (1 picture), Clive Nichols Photography/Barnsley House, Gloucestershire (1 picture), /Designer: Sue Berger, Bristol (1 picture), /HMP Leyhill Garden, Hampton Court, 1995 (1 picture), /National Asthma Garden/Chelsea, 1993 (1 picture).

Ways With Water: Reed International Picture Library/George Wright (1 picture); Jerry Harpur/Malcolm Hillier, London (1 picture), /Jim Matsuo, Los Angeles (1 picture); Andrew Lawson Photography (1 picture), Andrew Lawson Photography/Kiftsgate Court (1 picture); Clive Nichols Photography /Lygon Arms Hotel, Broadway (1 picture), /Stiffkey Lamp Shop (1 picture), /Designer: Julie Toll (1 picture)

Arbors, Arches, and Pergolas: Jerry Harpur /Charles Beresford-Clark, Sussex (1 picture), /Helmingham Hall, Suffolk (2 pictures), /The Manor House, Bledlow, Bucks (1 picture), /La Roseraie, Ouigave, Morocco (1 picture); Andrew Lawson Photography (3 pictures).